Asia-Pacific Geopolitics

Asia-Pacific Geopolitics

Hegemony vs. Human Security

Edited by

Joseph A. Camilleri
Professor of International Relations, School of Social Sciences, La Trobe University, Melbourne, Australia

Larry Marshall
Associate Lecturer and Project Officer for Australian Studies, Faculty of Humanities and Social Sciences, La Trobe University

Michális S. Michael
Research Fellow, Centre for Dialogue, La Trobe University, Melbourne

Michael T. Seigel
Institute for Social Ethics, Nanzan University, Nagoya, Japan

Edward Elgar
Cheltenham, UK • Northampton, MA, USA

© Joseph A. Camilleri, Larry Marshall, Michális S. Michael and Michael T. Seigel 2007

All rights reserved. No part of this publication may be reproduced, stored in a retrieval system or transmitted in any form or by any means, electronic, mechanical or photocopying, recording, or otherwise without the prior permission of the publisher.

Published by
Edward Elgar Publishing Limited
Glensanda House
Montpellier Parade
Cheltenham
Glos GL50 1UA
UK

Edward Elgar Publishing, Inc.
William Pratt House
9 Dewey Court
Northampton
Massachusetts 01060
USA

A catalogue record for this book
is available from the British Library

Library of Congress Control Number: 2006937371

ISBN: 978 1 84720 098 3

Printed and bound in Great Britain by MPG Books Ltd, Bodmin, Cornwall

Contents

List of Tables	vii
Contributors	viii
Glossary of Acronyms	x
Preface	xiii

Introduction
1. Hegemony and Human Security: 3
   Competing Principles of Regional Order
   Michális S. Michael and Larry Marshall

Part I Hegemony and East Asia Relations
2. Hegemony, Perilous Empire and Human Security   23
   Mustapha Kamal Pasha
3. Still Anchoring an American Asia Pacific?   43
   Nick Bisley
4. Containing China: A Flawed Agenda   59
   Chandra Muzaffar

Part II Japan's Security Dilemma
5. Questioning the Rationale for Changing Japan's Peace   75
   Constitution
   Michael T. Seigel
6. Can Japan Create a Basis for its Internationality?   93
   Jiro Yamaguchi
7. Beyond the Japanese Constitutional Dilemmas   105
   Yoshikazu Sakamoto

Part III Japan and Australia: A More Constructive Role for Middle Powers
8. Japan, Australia and the UN Disarmament Agenda   123
   Michael Hamel-Green
9. Japan, Australia and Niche Diplomacy in the South Pacific   145
   Allan Patience

Part IV Global Governance and Sustainability
10. The Role of the United Nations in the Twenty-first Century 163
    Tetsuya Yamada
11. Foreign Policy in Search of a Sustainable World 175
    Shigeko Fukai

Conclusion
12. Between Alliance and Regional Engagement: 193
    Current Realities and Future Possibilities
    Joseph A. Camilleri

Select Bibliography 219
Index 231

List of Tables

1.1	Regional comparisons	4
8.1	2000 UN GA-endorsed disarmament resolutions: negative votes and abstentions by nuclear and selected non-nuclear states	126
8.2	2004 UN GA-endorsed disarmament resolutions: negative votes and abstentions by nuclear and selected non-nuclear states	128

Contributors

Nick Bisley is Senior Lecturer in the Department of Management at Monash University and a member of the Australian Committee of the Council for Security and Cooperation in Asia Pacific. He has taught and written on international trade policy, globalisation, regionalism, and international relations in Asia Pacific.

Joseph A. Camilleri is Professor of International Relations and Director of the Centre for Dialogue at La Trobe University. He has taught and written extensively on international relations, governance and international organisation, globalisation, and human rights including *Regionalism in the New Asia-Pacific Order* (2003).

Shigeko Fukai is Professor in the Department of Policy Studies at Nanzan University. Her area of specialisation is politics and international relations and the quest for a sustainable world order. She has published widely including most recently *Jizoku Kanou na Sekai Ron* [Theories on a Sustainable World] (2005).

Michael Hamel-Green is Associate Professor in the School of Social Sciences at Victoria University. He specialises in Asia-Pacific regional security, arms control, human rights and the international dimensions of community development. He has also conducted research into the history of the peace movement in Australia.

Larry Marshall is Project Officer for Australian Studies at La Trobe University. He is conducting PhD research on the peace process in Sri Lanka compared with the on-going attempts at peace in Mindanao in the Philippines. He has published on religion and culture in Asia Pacific and peace talks in Sri Lanka.

Michális S. Michael is Research Fellow in the Centre for Dialogue at La Trobe University. He has taught and written on international public policy, conflict resolution, Greece–Turkey–Cyprus, and inter-ethnic, inter-cultural and inter-religious dialogue, including co-editing *Cyprus in the Modern World* (2005).

Chandra Muzaffar is President of the International Movement for a Just World (JUST). He has written and edited more than 20 books and monographs on religion, civilisational dialogue, international politics and Malaysian society including *Global Ethic or Global Hegemony?* (2005).

Mustapha Kamal Pasha is Professor and Chair in International Relations at the University of Aberdeen. He has taught, researched and written extensively on comparative and global political economy, international relations, Islamic studies and South Asia.

Allan Patience is Professor of Political Science at Charles Darwin University. He has held Visiting Professorships in the University of Tokyo and Keio University. He has also held Political Science chairs at Victoria University and the University of Papua New Guinea.

Yoshikazu Sakamoto is Professor Emeritus at Tokyo University. He has written and published widely on international politics and peace research. He has held positions at the Asian Peace Research Association, the Stockholm International Peace Research Institute and the International Peace Research Association.

Michael T. Seigel is Research Fellow in the Institute for Social Ethics at Nanzan University. He has numerous publications in Japanese dealing with Christian faith and social issues. He was the founding director of the Japan Lay Missionary Movement, an overseas volunteer organisation.

Tetsuya Yamada is Associate Professor of International Relations at Sugiyama Women's University. He has previously worked at the Japanese embassy in the United Kingdom and the Japan Institute of International Affairs. He has published on the peacekeeping/peace-building operations of the United Nations.

Jiro Yamaguchi is Professor in the Graduate School of Law at Hokkaido University and Director of the 'Comparative Changes of Governance in the Age of Globalization' research project. He has numerous publications in Japanese on issues of governance.

Glossary of Acronyms

ABM	Anti-Ballistic Missile (Treaty)
ADB	Asian Development Bank
ADF	Australian Defence Force
ANZUS	Australia, New Zealand, United States (treaty)
APEC	Asia-Pacific Economic Cooperation
ARF	ASEAN Regional Forum
ASEAN	Association of Southeast Asian Nations
ASEAN+3	ASEAN plus China, Japan and South Korea
ASEM	Asia-Europe Meeting
ASPI	Australian Strategic Policy Institute
BCSD	Business Council for Sustainable Development (United States)
BMD	ballistic missile defence
CANWFZ	Central Asian Nuclear Weapon Free Zone
CBW	chemical and biological weapons
CCP	Chinese Communist Party
CIA	Central Intelligence Agency
CNOOC	China National Offshore Oil Corporation
CSCAP	Council for Security Cooperation in the Asia Pacific
CTBT	Comprehensive Test Ban Treaty
DFAT	Department of Foreign Affairs and Trade (Australia)
DPJ	Democratic Party of Japan
DPRK	Democratic People's Republic of Korea
EC	European Community
ECP	Enhanced Cooperation Program (Australia-PNG)
EDC	economically developed countries
EU	European Union
FDI	foreign direct investment
FMCT	Fissile Material Cut-off Treaty
G7	Group of Seven
G-77	Group of 77
G8	Group of Eight
GDP	gross domestic product
GNP	gross national product
GPG	global public good
ICISS	International Commission on Intervention and State Sovereignty

ICJ	International Court of Justice
ICZ	Islamic cultural zones
IDP	internally displaced person
IMF	International Monetary Fund
IPG	international public good
JDA	Japan Defense Agency
JSF	F-35 Joint Strike Fighter
LDC	less developed countries
LDP	Liberal Democratic Party (Japan)
LNG	liquefied natural gas
MD	missile defence
MDGs	Millennium Development Goals
MIT	Massachusetts Institute of Technology
NAC	New Agenda Coalition
NAM	Non-Aligned Movement
NATO	North Atlantic Treaty Organisation
NGO	non-governmental organisation
NPR	Nuclear Posture Review
NPT	Non-Proliferation Treaty
NWFZ	nuclear-weapon-free zone
NWS	nuclear-weapon states
OECD	Organisation for Economic Co-operation and Development
PIF	Pacific Islands Forum
PKI	Communist Party of Indonesia
PKO	UN Peacekeeping Operations
PNAC	Project for a New American Century
PNG	Papua New Guinea
PRC	People's Republic of China
PSI	Proliferation Security Initiative
RAMSI	Regional Assistance Mission to the Solomon Islands
ROK	Republic of Korea
SAS	Special Air Service
SDF	Self-Defense Force (Japan)
SEATO	Southeast Asia Treaty Organization
SHWFZ	Southern Hemisphere Nuclear Weapon Free Zone
SIPRI	Stockholm International Peace Research Institute
SORT	Strategic Offensive Reductions Treaty
SPNFZ	South Pacific Nuclear Free Zone
TAC	Treaty of Amity and Cooperation
UNCTAD	United Nations Conference on Trade and Development
UNDP	United Nations Development Program
UNGA	United Nations General Assembly

WMD	weapons of mass destruction
WTO	World Trade Organisation

Preface

Relations between Asia-Pacific countries, especially in the area of economics, have deepened enormously since the 1960s. However, despite significant cultural exchange, mutual trust and understanding remain fragile. The Asia-Pacific community faces often complex and seemingly intractable problems: violent civil conflicts, geopolitical tensions and economic uncertainties, proliferation of nuclear weapons, and flashpoints that may lead to war.

The need for common reflection and dialogue amongst actors in the region seems imperative, not only at the governmental level but also at the level of academia and civil society. The kind of dialogue envisaged here is unlikely to take place without active measures to promote it.

This book was conceived as a part of this dialogic process and sought to bring together distinguished scholars and experts on public policy, social ethics, defence, human security and sustainability to consider the future of the Asia-Pacific region. The focal point of this dialogue was an extremely useful exchange of ideas brokered by the Centre for Dialogue at La Trobe University and Nanzan University's Institute for Social Ethics. The context for these discussions, which took place at Nanzan University in September 2005, included globalisation, the 'war on terror', perceptions of vulnerability and threat, residual alliances in Asia Pacific with the world's sole superpower, opportunities for intervention by middle powers and changing definitions of human security.

Writers from Australia and Japan constitute the majority of contributors to this volume but important voices from the region and outside were also present. Scholars were invited to address the complexities of a rapidly changing landscape in Asia Pacific, which has prompted new challenges, issues and relationships. Many of the contributions in this volume focus on the ethical and policy options available to Japan and Australia, and the implications for their respective roles in the Asia-Pacific region. In reality, however, these contributors have been asked to do a great deal more. They bring to the discussion careful reflection on the wider dynamics and interplay between forces on the regional and global landscape. Conscious of the need to enlarge the perspectives offered by Japanese and Australian analysts, the book includes a powerful and controversial analysis of the rise of China by a renowned Malaysian scholar and practitioner. The geopolitical overview is further enhanced by a Pakistani academic working mainly out of Washington, who offers a penetrating analysis of the underlying currents driving US policy making and a sensibility from the South to his interpretation of the American imperial project.

A critical look at the US hegemonic role in the region directs attention to the legacy of Cold War alliances and, in particular, to a number of bilateral security relationships. The US–Japan and US–Australia alliances still play a pivotal role in US strategic and diplomatic thinking in Asia Pacific. Compliance with US wishes and priorities has, in many ways, left these two nations as outsiders looking in on important new regional developments and institutions. A detailed analysis and critique of the existing regional architecture leads a number of authors to consider a range of new policies and multilateral initiatives, including a more important role for a reformed United Nations.

The exchange of ideas that took place at Nanzan University in Nagoya in the latter part of 2005 brought home the significance of a debate that was rapidly gaining in intensity both in the Japanese Diet and in the wider Japanese community. At issue were proposed changes to Japan's peace Constitution which could not but have a profound political and psychological impact on the Asia-Pacific region. In this sense, the analysis and evaluation of regional and global arrangements nicely dovetailed with this debate. Scholars from Japan discussed the radically altered perception of threat that the proposed amendments to Article 9 might cause amongst Japan's neighbours (including China and the two Koreas) and the prospect of an ensuing (nuclear) arms race in Northeast Asia. A key section of this volume is therefore devoted to explicating the possible repercussions of such a constitutional change, precisely because it is symptomatic of powerful currents that may soon sweep the Asia-Pacific geopolitical landscape.

This book is concerned to paint as accurate a picture as possible of complex, and at times elusive, trends, but it is also intent on considering what may be appropriate responses by both states and civil society in the region. This dual objective is the thread running through most of the chapters, and is the explicit focus of the concluding chapters where the emphasis is more on the medium to longer terms. Though the book attempts to strike a fine balance between diagnosis and prescription, it is primarily aimed at stimulating a sharper debate about current trends and future possibilities.

Joseph A. Camilleri
Larry Marshall
Michális S. Michael
Michael T. Seigel
July 2006

Introduction

1. Hegemony and Human Security: Competing Principles of Regional Order

Michális S. Michael and Larry Marshall

Fifty years ago a prominent student of international relations dismissed 'Southeast Asia' as nothing more than a 'cartographic' construct, lacking homogeneity and a 'point of unity'.[1] Even in retrospect, one could be forgiven for momentarily empathising with Peffer's difficulty in imagining East Asia as a coherent, self-contained, geopolitical and geocultural regional entity. From the outset, we are confronted with a theoretical quandary in defining/re-defining the region.

Traditional theoretical notions of regionalism designate it as a sociopolitical project inspired by a common culture that forges an identity drawing on a regional consciousness that precedes the formation of nation-states by colonialism. The main feature of regionalism and region formation is its fluidity especially when trying to locate its centre and defining its outer boundaries – this is partly a cognitive problem of attempting to emulate regionalism based on a state-centric prototype. Regional narrative as regionalism is a product of historical dialectics and processes that pattern interaction in a manner that reorganises political space. In so far as they combine internal and external influences and produce new outcomes, regional formations must be seen as an evolutionary process.

From such a prism East Asia, let alone Asia Pacific, becomes a project in progress. To obtain clarity, the region under discussion may be said to operate in two partly overlapping but also conflicting theatres: Asia Pacific and Pacific Asia (or East Asia). Asia Pacific is a construct best exemplified through the Asia-Pacific Economic Cooperation (APEC). A joint Japan–Australia initiative, APEC's broad reach includes the Pacific (Papua New Guinea), Oceania (Australia and New Zealand), Pacific America (Canada, United States, Mexico, Peru and Chile) and also Russia. Pacific Asia, on the other hand, reflects varying degrees of Asia consciousness ('Asia for the Asians') – a sentiment not particularly strong in the two oddities of the region, Japan or Australia.[2]

As the comparative statistics in Table 1.1 indicate, with one-third of the world's population, exports that outstrip the combined US and EU total and boasting over forty per cent of all internet users, Asia Pacific[3] is rapidly emerging as the century's geopolitical centre. Relations between Asia-Pacific countries, especially in the economic arena, have deepened enormously since the 1960s. However, despite significant cultural exchange, mutual trust and understanding remain fragile. The Asia-Pacific community faces complex and difficult problems: civil conflicts, geopolitical tensions, economic uncertainties, proliferation of nuclear weapons, environmental and health challenges, and flashpoints that may lead to war.

The seismic shifts caused by the end of the Cold War and the further dramatic rupture of September 11 set the immediate context for our discussions of Asia-Pacific futures. The demise of the Soviet Union has transformed the traditional Cold War notion of 'strategic triangle' (Soviet Union, United States and the weaker third tier of China) as the prevalent pattern. The vacuum left by the Soviet Union has accentuated sub-regional triangular configurations that jigsaw the region (for example Australia–Indonesia–East Timor, Japan–Australia–United States, Japan–China–United States, China–Taiwan–United States, Japan–Korean peninsula–China). The diminished role of the Soviet Union in the region has had two additional consequences: it has left a significant gap which expedited the rise of China, presenting a series of questions pertaining to regional balance of power and institutional architecture. Whilst during the Cold War US protection offered itself as a 'security blanket', allowing the growth of the East Asian economies, the withdrawal of the Soviet threat sees the East Asian economic leverage posing a challenge to US hegemony.

Table 1.1 Regional comparisons

	EU	USA	Asia Pacific[3]	World
Area (000 sq km)	3,976	9,631	22,536	510,072
Population (million)	456	296	2,109	6,446
GDP (US$ trillion)	11.6	11.7	14.6	55.5
Imports (US$ billion)	1,123	1,476	2,186	8,754
Exports (US$ billion)	1,109	795	2,450	8,819
Oil consumption (million bbl/day)	14.6	19.7	18.3	77
Internet users (million)	206	159	242	604
Military expenditure (US$ billion)	210	370.7	175	900

Source: CIA World Factbook, Asia Source, Europa, SIPRI Database

The vicissitudes of the post-Cold War – to be viewed as a transient phase – have seen a region in search of certainty and stability. Two major principles compete for attention as the pathway to establishing and sustaining order and security in the Asia-Pacific region. The first pertains to a Gramscian reading of US hegemony in the post-September 11 context. The other dynamic is more elusive to define, and refers to the concept of human security. Although coming from opposite directions, at the centre of the US hegemony–human security juncture lies the notion of state sovereignty and the challenges it faces from the forces of globalisation from above and below.[4]

US HEGEMONY REVISITED

Since the end of the Second World War, the US presence in Asia Pacific has been central to the regional landscape. Unavoidably, US hegemony features prominently in any discussion of Asia-Pacific regional order and security. However, before turning to the trajectory of US hegemony in the region, a few words about our usage of 'hegemony' – which is elaborated further in Chapter 2. Hegemony is used both in its traditional definition as inter-state predominance/rule by force and in its Gramscian meaning as an organising principle. Here the use of 'hegemony' is preferable to 'imperialism' as the latter refers primarily to capitalist economic expansion driven principally by the search for resources and markets, and the complex interaction of labour and capital, supply and demand. Three factors have transformed US hegemony in the post-Cold War era: first the ideological perception of the United States as a symbol and advocate of liberal precepts (electoral democracy, natural justice, individualism, pluralism and private initiative); secondly, the accelerating pace of globalisation and the movement of ideas, images and information; and thirdly, the rise of identity politics as a major concern of international relations. With the erosion of state sovereignty and the blurring of the internal–external divide, ideas and culture underpin the nature and reorganisation of international power. Gramsci's hegemonism acquires even more currency in the post-Cold War era, which resonates with the complexity of a globalised world system and the rise of group identity politics. At a time when international dominance and influence have evolved, US leadership requires consent. Political leadership depends more than ever on intellectual and moral authority, hence on its legitimacy.[5]

US hegemony remains a contested concept and in seeking its elucidation we present four perspectives on the exercise of American power in the region. Each perspective offers contrasting readings of existing realities. Hence four sets of dualities are revealed, which we can formulate as four questions. First, is the post-Cold War period witnessing the demise or consolidation of American power? Secondly, is the exercise of this power essential for finding solutions to security issues in Asia Pacific, or is it more likely to exacerbate existing tensions? Thirdly, is America's response to September 11 appropriate and worthy of support, or can it be read as an exercise in unilateralism, and hence a threat to international law, which is itself a prerequisite of cooperative security? Finally, are the bilateral alliance systems set up during the Cold War still relevant to regional security, or are they now a hindrance to countries like Japan and Australia who seek integration into regional groupings aimed at ensuring broader human security goals?

Rise and Decline of American Power

The events of September 11 and the ensuing 'war on terror' have rekindled debate about the current state of US power; some claim that recent events have accentuated US power by consolidating gains made during the 1990s.[6] The post-September 11 period, it is argued, has seen the US presence expand across the globe with a network of forward bases stretching from Suez, across the Middle East to Central Asia and the Pacific.[7] According to this view, US dominance of international relations is increasingly globalised. US hegemony is no longer a system but as *the* system of which both Japan and China are an integral part.[8]

But there is an opposing view which maintains that US military, economic and especially political influence is in decline.[9] Since the height of the Cold War, US troops worldwide have been halved. US deployment of theatre and national missile defence systems and space weaponry are considered a poor substitute for the decline in conventional military forces. More importantly, analysts point to the decline in America's economic capacity, and in particular to the burgeoning federal budget deficit which reached US$427 billion in 2004. Compounding this trend are the twin trade and current account deficits. In 2004 the US current account deficit reached 6 per cent of GDP (almost double what it had been in the Reagan years).

Although the Iraq adventure has highlighted the military and economic costs associated with imperial overstretch, it is the political costs that are most debilitating. In line with our preferred notion of hegemony, major civilisations are judged not merely by their military prowess or the wealth of their treasuries but also by the power of their ideas. The US capacity to mobilise is now open to question. Especially striking in this context is the political resistance which the United States encountered at the UN Security Council prior to its invasion of Iraq in 2003, not least from core European allies. Although there has always been a measure of 'anti-Americanism' in the world, it is clearly on the rise in the Islamic world, in many parts of Africa and Latin America and even amongst traditional US allies. Both the Iraqi war and the 'war on terror' have severely eroded America's international credibility and legitimacy.[10]

Part of the Problem or Part of the Solution?

By the end of the 1990s the United States was confronted with an array of policy options for protecting and advancing its interests in Asia Pacific. These ranged from total withdrawal, reliance on its power-projection capacities, sustaining the status quo, entering into a strategic partnership with China, or nesting its alliances in evolving Asia-Pacific multilateral processes.[11] The Bush administration's strategic response has been to develop a unilateral pre-emptive defence posture. With its global reach US policy had come to rest on the twin principles that 'terrorism is everyone's problem' and that 'no nation can be neutral in this conflict'.[12] In this sense, September 11 has refocused attention on the nature and direction of US hegemony. Although part of a larger global equation, US hegemony in Asia Pacific poses even harder questions given the idiosyncrasies of the region and the range of environmental, financial, nuclear, military, territorial, human rights and religious crises that confront it.

The US presence in Asia Pacific, some argue, has provided stability and the 'oxygen' for East Asia's economic development in the last thirty years. However, the end of the Cold War has brought new challenges to the region. It has unleashed regional and ethnic rivalries and revived the possibility of confrontation on the Korean peninsula. Unlike NATO, the Asia-Pacific region has no collective defence organisation. This perspective sees the United States as the only credible counter to the economic and military rise of China. Through a combination of bilateral alliances, forward military deployments and diplomatic engagements, the United States has sought to bring its engagement in the Asia Pacific into line with its global security strategy of shaping the international environment, responding to crises and preparing for the future.[13]

There is, however, another perspective that considers US hegemony a liability likely to endanger regional order and security. Bilateral alliances are said to make increasingly less sense as the way to stabilise relations in a multipolar world. They work against emerging multilateral processes and negate the concept of collective security.

The situation in East Asia has become a source of rising tensions. Although China has been careful to maintain a good relationship with the United States and the West generally, the North Korean regime continues to irritate US policy makers and to challenge US hegemony by refusing to abandon the nuclear option. The US presence, it has been argued, may also encourage, wittingly or otherwise, Japanese militarisation. The 'China threat' risks becoming a self-serving prophecy.

The United States' special relationship with Japan and Australia, for example, has emboldened them to act as 'deputies' in the region. By embracing, even indirectly, the doctrine of pre-emption they risk alienating themselves from their neighbours, whilst polarising the region and weakening their potential contribution to regional integration/convergence. Furthermore, the Bush doctrine has afforded many states in the region with a convenient pretext to curtail human and civil liberties. By enacting stringent anti-terrorist legislation and empowering their intelligence and security apparatus, domestic security has been elevated at the expense of human rights as the priority item on national and regional agendas.

'War on Terror': In Search of Consent

The 'war on terror' has polarised opinion in the region between those who side with US responses and those who see these responses as aimed against their interests. The US failure to secure international consensus prior to the invasion of Iraq, the failure to find weapons of mass destruction, and the fuelling of resistance to the occupation, have projected an image of a country bent on waging a Christian 'crusade' against Islam. This is a critical factor in a region where Islam looms large. It is arguable that it is precisely because of the increasing difficulties it has encountered when attempting to impose its will (and its declining leverage) that the United States has found it necessary to consolidate the relationship with its most faithful allies in Asia Pacific, notably Japan and Australia.

Cold War Alliances

When it comes to US hegemony, we see two sets of potentially troubling trends. On the one hand, US hegemony is being supported by Japan and Australia and on the other hand, US hegemony is being challenged indirectly by China's rise and more confrontationally by North Korea – trends which may lead the United States to overplay its hand.

All of this places Japan and Australia in a difficult situation. They are both desperately trying to hang on to US coat tails, although in the case of Japan the policy represents a complex and contradictory mix of dependence on the United States and steady nationalist reassertion – which is beginning to revive regional anxieties of a resurgent militarist Japan, thereby compounding the uncertainties of the 'security dilemma'.

DEFINING HUMAN SECURITY FOR ASIA PACIFIC

In the last decade, human security has emerged as one of the most challenging attempts to redefine or at least supplement traditional notions of security. Like any neologism, human security is beset by definitional ambiguity and has been subjected to critical scrutiny with respect to such issues as scope, relevance and implementation. It points to a paradigmatic shift from a state-centric view of the world, with priority now attached to safeguarding people's lives rather than securing the apparatus of the state. At the heart of the concept of human security is its challenge to traditional notions of state sovereignty. For purposes of analytical convenience, we draw on the UNDP Human Development Report which identified two key dimensions of human security: freedom from fear and freedom from want, elaborated by the Commission on Human Security.[14] Drawing from discourses not usually associated with traditional notions of 'state' security, human security identifies the transnational nature of economic, food, health, environmental, personal, community and political security threats, whose solutions are beyond the reach of the nation-state, and offers itself as a compass for global civil society as much as for states. In this context, human security is seen as complementing rather than negating or substituting 'state' security.

By integrating such areas as peacekeeping, humanitarian and developmental aid, conflict prevention and peacemaking, human rights and foreign policy, human security presents an alternative policy focus for middle and regional powers such as Japan, Canada, Australia, South Korea and New Zealand. As a policy framework, human security is gaining prominence amongst Asian regional institutions as they discover the limitations of the state in tackling economic, social, environmental, health and political crises and the need for a collective approach.

This new understanding of the concept of security now embraces 'the protection of communities and individuals from internal violence' and it recognises the continuing dangers that weapons of mass destruction, particularly nuclear weapons, pose to humanity. Each of these security dimensions has special relevance to the Asia-Pacific region and its cultural and political environment. The non-governmental sector, in particular, is performing key functions in alleviating poverty and social marginality, empowering women, safeguarding children, dealing with problems posed by ageing populations, integrating disabled persons into mainstream society and repairing damage inflicted by modernisation policies and market forces, as evidenced in rising levels of drug abuse, HIV/AIDS, migration and environmental pollution.

In Search of an Alternative Regional Order

The Asia-Pacific region has endured the controlling influence of hegemonic power since the Second World War. The end of the Cold War offered a unique opportunity to explore and set a new and comprehensive agenda for change. Paradoxical though it may seem, the unilateralism exhibited by the United States since September 11 may in fact indicate the decline of empire. The phenomenal rise of the Chinese economy will almost certainly reshape the regional order, not only economically but also politically. The question is whether Asia-Pacific responses can be calibrated to the geopolitical realities of an increasingly multipolar world. To do this with any prospect of success will require a new mindset when it comes to rethinking regional interrelationships. In this context, Japan and Australia as regional powers will need to collaborate with others in ASEAN+3 and the ASEAN Regional Forum (ARF) to devise the regional and global infrastructure that can establish a system of comprehensive security for the region. To this end, a coherent strategy will need to be devised that mobilises the energies not only of states but of markets and civil society and confers on all three elements of the region's political economy a role in the design of the emerging regional and global architecture.

Three key tasks flow from this analysis. The first is to connect in more coherent and mutually beneficial fashion the region with the global order. Here, the critical objective is to reform and revitalise global institutions, in particular the UN system, which will increasingly be called upon to respond to transnational threats to security. The second task is to mobilise the international community through the United Nations and other global and regional fora to develop initiatives that might arrest, if not reverse, present trends pointing to a new and dangerous nuclear arms race. The third task is to move towards a new regionalism in Asia Pacific by reinvigorating and retooling the existing architecture.[15] This will no doubt require the more effective participation of civil society, not least through Track Two and Track Three processes that monitor decisions and enhance accountability.[16]

Therefore, the search for alternative pathways to regional stability and prosperity must involve a range of actors across the political and societal spectrum. But which actors are most likely to have the will and the capacity to play a positive role? At one level, we can observe governments like South Korea working hard to develop a more constructive relationship with the North, while others in Southeast Asia are trying to steer the region towards greater independence and a different security agenda. Regional security in any case depends on increasing economic interdependence, thus underscoring the important role the market can play in security-building. The civil societies of the region may also have a role to play. Many civil society organisations and movements are increasingly operating not only within but across national boundaries.[17]

What is perhaps most striking about the present conjuncture is the need for common reflection and sustained dialogue – a process that needs to engage not only states and inter-governmental organisations, but the business and epistemic communities of the region, and the rapidly developing network of non-governmental organisations. The kind of dialogue that needs to take place and the active measures to promote it will almost certainly play a critical role in shaping the future of the Asia-Pacific region. The context for these discussions includes globalisation, the 'war on terror', alliances with the world's sole superpower and their place in Asia. The aim is to consider alternatives to global and regional insecurity, with a view to proposing workable long-term alternatives, rather than short-term palliatives. In the following chapters, the authors, though they pose different questions and examine even the same questions from different vantage points, nevertheless share the same intellectual preoccupation: how to interpret the competing principles of hegemony and human security as they have applied in the post-Cold War period, and might more appropriately apply in the future.

THE LOGIC AND STRUCTURE OF THE BOOK

This study has developed directly out of the imperatives sketched in the preceding analysis and a desire to elucidate the new pressures on existing global and regional institutions, especially since the events of September 11. The authors have sought to connect the threads of these crucial national, regional and global debates and weave them into a comprehensive and timely analysis of Asia Pacific as it responds to the challenges of the new millennium.

The contributors to this book, all experts in their respective fields, include Australian scholars whose area of expertise has centred on great power relations both in a global and regional setting, regional security, including alliances systems, as well as global security, including the role and functioning of the UN system and the prospects for international disarmament and arms control. Japanese scholars provide insightful perspectives on the nature and significance of regional pressures and threat perceptions, on the ambiguities of the US military role in Asia Pacific and most importantly on the recent and prospective evolution of Japanese security policy, not least in relation to the present debate on the Japanese Constitution (the 'peace' clause) and the implications of proposed changes both for Japan itself and for its neighbourhood.

We have added other voices: from Malaysia – to analyse the meaning of China's meteoric rise to economic superpower; from Pakistan – to provide a theoretically informed analysis of America's pugnacious unilateralism; and from Papua New Guinea – an Australian voice that seeks to invest middle power with new meaning and content. Both Japanese and Australian contributors offer an intriguing juxtaposition of the theoretical and practical implications of hegemony on the one hand and human security on the other.

In Part I of this book three authors mount a critical investigation of the central issue of hegemony in the East Asian context. Medium-term East Asian regional futures crucially turn on the fundamental question of US hegemony that has framed the rise of both postwar Japan and post-Maoist China. Assessments of US hegemony in East Asia vary considerably, depending on the concept of hegemony employed and the particular interpretations of the trajectory of US power in recent years.

Mustapha Kamal Pasha explores this situation of global flux in the post-September 11 world. Pasha is more concerned to illustrate how the hegemon is using the 'war on terror' as the necessary 'global crisis' that then requires the continuation and broadening of the imperial role. There are no spatial limits to this 'new imperium', which is being constructed in a global state of emergency. It is a binary division of the world between friends and enemies that subordinates all other values to the defence of the 'homeland' or (Western) civilisation.

Pasha introduces a new way of seeing the boundaries and divisions of this divided world by focusing our attention on what he calls Islamic cultural zones (ICZ). This analytical tool allows him to explain the urgent need for bridging seemingly conflictual worlds to ensure respect for human dignity and advancement of human security, one of the major themes of the book.

If we are to look more closely at how American hegemonic power is given form and amplified throughout this region then we must carefully analyse the significance of the alliance system that operates in Asia Pacific. This is precisely what Nick Bisley sets out to do by focusing on the 'lynch-pins' of the US alliance system, Japan and Australia. His basic argument is that these Cold War alliances are outdated as a means to stabilise relations in contemporary Asia Pacific. As for Japan and Australia, they risk distancing themselves from their neighbours as they cling to these outdated shibboleths whilst the region indicates a general distancing from US hegemonic intentions.

The powerful American alliance system was originally established during the Cold War as the superpower sought to contain communism in East Asia by first curbing the influence and impact of Chinese communism. It is this history and its current implications, especially for an understanding of China's present and future role in the region, that concern Chandra Muzaffar as he explores the strategies and priorities of US hegemony in Asia Pacific.

Muzaffar argues that there is a self-interested ambivalence about some elements of America's political and military elite which, whilst celebrating China's embrace of the market, still harbour fears of China's phenomenal economic ascendancy. Could it challenge American power and influence? This new 'containment policy' focuses on China's human rights record (which undoubtedly leaves a great deal to be desired) and its expanding military budget to build a fearful picture of a rising power which may challenge US dominance. Somewhat controversially, Muzaffar contends that fears about China's economic and military power are grossly exaggerated. He suggests that the spectre of a looming Chinese threat is a deliberate strategy pursued by influential elements of the American elite intent on maintaining America's global hegemony.

Part II of the book is focused on a contemporary debate of great complexity, which has serious implications for security in the Asia-Pacific region and beyond. The repercussions of proposed amendments to Article 9, the peace clause, in the Japanese Constitution have certainly been discussed elsewhere. However, there seemed to be a gap in the literature requiring a deeper and more penetrating analysis of the evolution of Japan's social and political fabric, which has far-reaching ramifications not only for Japan's external relations but also for regional and global security. It is with this in mind that the present volume offers three nuanced perspectives on this crucial issue. Each of them in similar yet insightfully contrasting ways connects politics, culture and security, the domestic and the international.

Michael Seigel is convinced that the changes to the Constitution are problematic for Japan's place in a volatile region. He begins by explicating the 'security dilemma' – developing the proposition that our very efforts to achieve security can, unless great care is exercised, lead to the conflict we seek to avoid. He presents us with an overview of the competing perspectives on security and international relations that emerged during the bloody twentieth century. His key contention is that we cannot afford continuing acceptance of these failed premises, at a historical moment which has given us infinitely more powerful weapons, and in a context where global crises are increasingly interconnected.

Seigel carefully examines (and calls into question) the arguments usually advanced to support changing Article 9 of Japan's Constitution. He analyses the proposed text for constitutional change viewed from the perspective of China and the two Koreas, countries that may fear the rise of a militarised and more nationalistic Japan. He is at pains to show that pre-emptive strikes on foreign military bases perceived as a threat to Japan would now be a part of this new security thinking. Solving Japan's security dilemma may require a new approach to the Constitution, which challenges some of the basic historical assumptions on which the modern Japanese state operates.

Jiro Yamaguchi offers a perceptive historical survey of postwar Japanese thinking on the US-imposed Constitution, on wider security issues and the American alliance. He takes us through the reform process that has been a part of Japanese politics since the early 1990s, from Hosokawa's political reforms to Hashimoto's administrative reforms and Koizumi's structural reforms. He uses this background to posit an insider's informed analysis of the Koizumi government's efforts to amend Article 9 of the Constitution.

Yamaguchi warns that excision of Article 9 means justifying Japan's wartime and colonial past, which will deeply disturb many Asian countries. He is concerned that the political debate in Japan has moved away from rationality into polemic underlined by a resurgent nationalism. He goes on to argue that under Prime Minister Koizumi's watch some of the most important principles of postwar Japanese politics have come under challenge. For the first time a Self-Defense Force (SDF) contingent was sent to Iraq (a theatre of war) to support the US military operation. Koizumi continued to visit the Yasukuni shrine knowing how this would be construed as provocation by China and Korea. Under his leadership Japan has become more enmeshed in American strategy, and simultaneously more isolated in Asia.

In his chapter, Yoshikazu Sakamoto offers a political analysis, informed by a critical re-reading of the generational history of Japan's postwar experiences, and anchored in the philosophy of self-determination and democratisation on a global scale. He challenges the attempt by the Japanese state to deny the voices of 'abandoned people', both within its borders and those outside in Asia, who have been, and continue to be, critically affected by its policies and its nationalistic rhetoric.

Sakamoto presents us with a challenging re-conceptualisation of the dilemma facing Japan. He first draws attention to the spontaneous effort of the Japanese people that arose in the postwar years and created an autonomous movement aimed at building 'a peace-oriented democracy rooted in Japanese soil'. Sakamoto suggests that the push for peace originated primarily from the Japanese people at the very time that the United States was increasingly concerned to make Japan an integral part of its containment policy in the late 1940s. This impetus for peace, he argues, has since been weakened by changed circumstance, historical forgetting, domestic political power plays, and also by the lure of the American nuclear umbrella.

By carefully defining the contradictions inherent in the gradual shift away from the original pacifist and democratic movement, Sakamoto challenges those who would purely seek to 'defend the Constitution'. He suggests that Japanese pacifism based on the Constitution contains a double-standard which must be clearly acknowledged.

His argument is that those who are committed to the retention of Article 9 need to address the inconsistencies of supporting a huge self-defence force whilst favouring neutrality; of calling for an end to nuclear weapons and proliferation whilst sheltering under the US umbrella; of supporting troops for peacekeeping but continually relaxing the definition of peacekeeping to include such conflicts as the current war in Iraq.

Part III of the book analyses in greater depth and detail the roles that Japan and Australia are playing in the region and on the global stage. The central question addressed here is: can Japan and Australia, two significant regional powers, contribute, individually and together, to a more effective system of regional security and cooperation?

Michael Hamel-Green in his chapter charts a worrying drift away from multilateralism and cooperative security by middle powers like Japan and Australia. He suggests that the alliance with the United States has seen both countries weaken their support for the disarmament agenda at the United Nations. His careful analysis of voting trends in the UN General Assembly is invaluable evidence in support of his case.

Both countries appear to be embracing directly or indirectly approaches that accept the US emphasis on coercive, selective and military methods of achieving compliance with non-proliferation norms. This is evident in their active participation in the Proliferation Security Initiative (PSI) interdiction scheme, and their involvement in US missile defence programs. Both countries continue to be involved in the non-UN sanctioned US-led Iraq intervention.

Hamel-Green documents the many proposals and new initiatives for nuclear disarmament that can be supported at both a regional and a global level by member-states. Many of these encourage a more positive role for Japan and Australia as middle powers that might mobilise the international community through the UN system. Working together at the United Nations and at a regional level, they could help avert the looming arms race in East Asia.

Focusing on the specific circumstances of the Pacific Islands, Allan Patience traces the effects of neo-colonial arrogance and makes a plea for a new and heightened role for both Japan and Australia in the South Pacific, which he argues is facing a debilitating crisis of governance. Patience documents the failure of recent Australian policy in Papua New Guinea and proposes a better-informed and cooperative regional strategy involving Japan (possibly China and Malaysia, Indonesia or the Philippines) that would curb Australia's hubris and repair some of the damage already done. His is an argument for 'niche diplomacy' in the South Pacific. For him, niche diplomacy comes into play when states that are not inherently powerful nonetheless exercise an influencing – perhaps a leadership – role on specific regional or global issues. Niche diplomacy, he contends, has become increasingly evident in the post-Cold War climate of growing global multipolarity, and may take on an even greater salience in the wake of the post-September 11 events.

Patience is acutely aware of the extent to which both Japan and Australia have become estranged from their neighbours. He suggests that their middle power identity needs to be reinvented so as to enable them to address more effectively issues of poverty, governance failure and aid delivery. Small states in the South Pacific are weak states and several are becoming failed states. Papua New Guinea, for example, faces deep-seated law and order problems, corruption at all levels of government, and failure of basic services, including health, security and education. It is here, in the South Pacific, Patience suggests, that Japan and Australia have an opportunity to overcome their estrangement from the region and to win the respect and cooperation of their neighbours and the rest of the world. The emphasis is on negotiating neo-colonial undercurrents and eschewing patronising politics in the construction of more convivial regional architecture.

Having earlier dissected the contrasting meaning of hegemony and human security, and what this means for the region, the book finally brings these threads together in Part IV by exploring how states and civil society are attempting to manoeuvre in a multipolar world. Whilst the focus is on the influential role that Japan and Australia may play in a volatile region, there is a much wider applicability to such an analysis. The complex *problématique* of governance in the era of globalisation requires that we necessarily shift our analytical gaze first to the United Nations, the principal global institution mandated to oversee the system of global security. Here we immediately observe that the United Nations is at crisis point. For many it is now a case of the organisation being restructured to deal effectively with an intricate set of policy and organisational challenges or risk becoming largely irrelevant.

Post-Cold War expectations were for a 'peace dividend' as expensive nuclear arsenals were dismantled. Hope lay in foundations for a more peaceful 'new world order' with the United Nations at the centre of a more united world community. States faced pressure to work through the United Nations to guarantee 'collective security' for all. States were expected to use force only if acting in line with the UN charter and on behalf of the international community.

Ensuing crises in Somalia, Kosovo and Rwanda began to tarnish this dream of a more united and peaceful world community, which was finally shattered by the terrorist attacks on the United States in September 2001. The momentum shifted dramatically as the 'war on terror' began.

Tetsuya Yamada offers an analysis of the United Nations and of the major proposals (put forward by the UN Secretary-General and others) for constructing a more effective approach to global governance. Yamada remains unconvinced that a reformed and revitalised United Nations can seriously challenge the power of the hegemon. He argues that the very structures of the international system were built by hegemonic power and that these institutions are still captive to this reality. He is, therefore, less optimistic that any proposed restructuring of the United Nations will result in a significant shift in the prevailing power paradigm. Yamada judges the effectiveness of the UN system by studying its record in maintaining or restoring peace and security. By comparing Somalia, Bosnia and Rwanda he evaluates what the United Nations has done and what it has failed to do during the past 15 years. Yamada then goes on to examine the future role of the United Nations. He explores the implications of the two reports on UN reform, *A More Secure World: Our Shared Responsibility* (2004), and *In Larger Freedom: Towards Development, Security and Human Rights for All*,[18] and evaluates the outcomes of the World Summit held in September 2005.

In her chapter, Shigeko Fukai focuses on defining more carefully what we mean by 'sustainable peace and human security'. If this concept is to challenge and replace older, more restrictive definitions of military security, then its core meaning must be clearly articulated.

Fukai opens her chapter with a quote from US Secretary of State Condoleezza Rice who derides the idea of an 'illusory international community' and argues that US foreign policy should be focused primarily on national interest. Implicit in this kind of statement is the assumption that there is an inevitable conflict between the pursuit of national interest and commitment to the interests of an international community. Fukai questions this assumption. She contends that, in the face of rapidly worsening global environmental degradation and social inequity, we are now compelled to think in terms of longer-term and more enlightened self-interest and to construct foreign policy based on a broader conception of national interest that incorporates global public interest at its core.

Fukai elucidates the vision of sustainable peace that has been constructed by the contributions of diverse disciplines since the early 1970s when the Club of Rome brought down their preliminary but seminal judgement on the 'limits to growth' on our planet. She updates these arguments and takes us on an intellectual journey aimed at challenging some of the prevailing economic 'myths' on which the present global system of production and 'over'-consumption is seemingly premised.

In one way or another, Fukai's contention is that the 'wretched of the earth' will eventually demand a fairer distribution of the earth's scarce resources. Fukai argues insistently that the political elites of the current system disregard this demand at their peril. Because experience indicates that if change is not possible by peaceful means, and in the face of acute deprivation, resentment builds to the point where some may choose violence as the only alternative. Fukai thus makes a case for the disarmingly simple, yet politically complex proposition that the international community and the member-states must begin to articulate and apply the twin concepts of sustainable peace and 'human security'.

Joseph Camilleri concludes this study by drawing together the key themes running through the preceding contributions. One of these, he contends, is the continuing influence of the US alliance infrastructure set up during the Cold War years. Japan and Australia, he suggests, are intriguing case studies of this phenomenon precisely because they are constrained in their responses to change, their domestic political culture is extremely sensitive to alliance management, and they are yet unlikely to pursue independent policies of regional management outside of the alliance.

Camilleri goes on to assess the challenges facing the state and civil society in both countries, and explores the more imaginative policy options open to them in relation to three key signposts: relations with the United States, reform of the UN system, and cooperative regionalism. In response to the post-Cold War realities of a multipolar world, Camilleri suggests that it is timely for both Japan and Australia to undertake a careful re-examination of the alliance with the United States. This would enable both countries to develop a more independent security policy, to better reflect their goals and aspirations, while at the same time contributing to global and regional security.

Camilleri casts a discerning eye over the emerging regional edifice in Asia Pacific (ASEAN, APEC, ARF, ASEAN+3 and ASEM) and finds that though much has been achieved, much crucial re-tooling and refurbishing remains to be done. The existing regional architecture needs 'a more solid normative foundation, a stronger institutional base and a more coherent set of functions' he argues. Among other proposals, he offers the intriguing idea of an updated normative framework that would be encapsulated in a formal charter or 'declaration of principles'.

To summarise, the overall analysis offered in this book is that in the post-September 11 world we are slowly but steadily moving towards multipolarity as the hegemon's authority declines. The United Nations is at a pivotal point in its existence and middle powers like Japan and Australia will no doubt help to shape its future. China's star is rising and this region has to contend with all the ramifications of this complex reality. Human security is a concept whose time is approaching, certainly one that warrants close and sustained attention. It offers the international community a broader philosophical and political purpose and gives added ballast to the emerging regional and global multilateralism that is a feature of the post-Cold War period. It poses perhaps the two most intriguing and critical questions of the moment: can civil society and epistemic communities, operating across cultural and civilisational boundaries, play a more influential role in defining the goals and processes of regional cooperation in Asia Pacific? Can states, multilateral organisations and civil society develop a more effective partnership in the pursuit of these goals?

NOTES

1. Nathaniel Peffer, 'Regional Security in Southeast Asia', *International Organization*, 8 (3), 1954, pp. 311–315.
2. For a comprehensive exposition of this two-tier approach to regional representation see Joseph A. Camilleri, *Regionalism in the New Asia-Pacific Order: The Political Economy of the Asia-Pacific Region*, Vol. II, Cheltenham: Edward Elgar, 2003, pp. 28–35. For a political emphasis of Asia-Pacific regionalism also see Dennis Rumley, 'The Geopolitics of Asia-Pacific Regionalism in the 21st Century', *The Otemon Journal of Australian Studies*, 31, 2005, pp. 5–27.
3. For our purposes Asia Pacific includes the following countries: Australia, Brunei, Cambodia, China, Japan, Hong Kong, Indonesia, DPRK (North Korea), ROK (South Korea), Laos, Malaysia, Burma (Myanmar), New Zealand, Philippines, Papua New Guinea, Singapore, Taipei, Thailand, Vietnam.
4. This is a variation of the Polanyian perspective to two competing world order models: US hegemony or 'Pax Americana' that relies on 'hard' power, versus interregionalism and 'civilian' power. See Björn Hettne, 'Karl Polanyi and the Search for World Order', available at Karl Polanyi Institute of Political Economy, Concordia University, http://artsandscience.concordia.ca/polanyi/pdfs/Hettne-2004.pdf (sighted on 11 December 2005).
5. For further reading see Antonio Gramsci, *Selections from the Prison Notebooks*, New York: International Publishers, 1971, also Perry Anderson, 'The Antinomies of Antonio Gramsci', *The New Left Review,* 100, 1976, pp. 5–78, Anne Showstack Sassoon (ed.), *Approaches to Gramsci*, London: Writers and Readers, 1982; for historicised application of Gramscism, including hegemony, see Randall D. German and Michael Kenny, 'Engaging Gramsci: International Relations Theory and the New Gramscians', *Review of International Studies*, 24, 1998, pp. 3–21; also for the ideological legitimisation of hegemony see Robert W. Cox, 'Social Forces, States and World Order: Beyond International Relations Theory',

Millennium: Journal of International Studies, 10 (2), Summer 1981, pp. 126–155, and in particular his 'transnational managerial class' concept, see Robert W. Cox, *Production, Power, and the World Order: Social Forces in the Making of History*, New York: Columbia University Press, 1987, pp. 359–360.

6. Most notable proponents of the 'ascendancy' school include Charles Krauthammer, 'The Unipolar Moment', *Foreign Affairs*, 70 (1), 1990–91, pp. 23–33, Robert Kagan, 'The Benevolent Empire', Foreign Policy, 111, 1998, pp. 24–35, S. Mallaby, 'The Reluctant Imperialist: Terrorism, Failed States and the Case for American Empire', *Foreign Affairs*, 81, 2002, pp. 2–7, Stephen G. Brooks and William C. Wohlforth, 'American Primacy in Perspective', *Foreign Affairs*, 81, 2002, pp. 20–33, A. Wolfson, 'Conservatives and Neo-Conservatives', *The Public Interest*, Winter 2004, pp. 32–48, and Michael Cox, 'September 11th and U.S. Hegemony – Or Will the 21st Century be American Too?', *International Studies Perspectives*, 3 (1), 2002, pp. 53–70, and 'American Power Before and After 11 September: Dizzy with Success?', *International Affairs*, 78 (2), 2002, pp. 261–276. But liberal theorists such as G. John Ikenberry, 'American Power and the Empire of Capitalist Democracy', *Review of International Studies*, 27, 2001, pp. 191–212, and Joseph S. Nye, *The Paradox of American Power*, New York: Oxford University Press, 2002, and also former US National Security Advisor, Zbigniew Brzezinski, *The Choice: Global Domination or Global Leadership*, New York: Basic Books, 2004, seek to 'tame' US hegemony through institutional reforms.
7. See Chalmers Johnson, *The Sorrows of Empire: Militarism, Secrecy, and the End of the Republic*, New York: Metropolitan, 2004.
8. Peter Van Ness, 'Hegemony, not Anarchy: Why China and Japan are not Balancing US Unipolar Power', *International Relations of the Asia-Pacific*, 2, 2002, pp. 131–150.
9. See Immanuel Wallerstein, *The Decline of American Power: The U.S. in a Chaotic World*, New York: New Press, 2003 and Immanuel Wallerstein, *Alternatives: The US Confronts the World*, Boulder, CO: Paradigm, 2004, also see Richard B. Du Boff, 'U.S. Hegemony: Continuing Decline, Enduring Danger', *Monthly Review*, December 2003, at: http://www.monthlyreview.org/1203duboff.htm (sighted on 22 November 2005), Jonathan Friedman and Christopher Chase-Dunn (eds), *Hegemonic Decline: Present and Past*, Boulder: Paradigm, 2005, Christian Reus-Smit, *American Power And World Order*, Cambridge, UK: Polity, 2004, Alex Callinicos, *The New Mandarins Of American Power: The Bush Administration's Plans For The World*, Cambridge, UK: Polity, 2004.
10. An international poll for the BBC of 11 countries – including the United States – found that 57% felt the United States was wrong to invade Iraq, see BBC News, 'Poll suggests world hostile to US', 16/06/2003, at http://newsvote.bbc.co.uk/2/hi/americas/2994924.stm (sighted on 22 November 2005). A year after the Iraq war discontent with the United States intensified according to a worldwide public opinion survey by Pew Research Centre for the People & the Press, *A Year After the Iraq War*, Washington DC, 16 March 2004.
11. Douglas Paal, *Nesting the Alliances in the Emerging Context of Asia-Pacific Multilateral Processes*: A U.S. Perspective, Washington: Asia/Pacific Research Center, July 1999.
12. The White House, 'President Bush: 'No Nation Can Be Neutral in This Conflict', Remarks by the President To the Warsaw Conference on Combating Terrorism at: http://www.whitehouse.gov/news/releases/2001/11/20011106-2.html (sighted on 12 December 2005).
13. Prior to September 11 US regional strategy rested on its Defense Department's East Asia Security Reports (EASR) of 1990, 1992 and 1998. United States Department of Defense, *The United States Security Strategy for the East-Asia-Pacific Region*, Washington DC, 1998.
14. The Commission's definition of human security is: 'to protect the vital core of all human lives in ways that enhance human freedoms and human fulfilment. Human security means protecting fundamental freedoms – freedoms that are the essence of life. It means protecting people from critical (severe) and pervasive (widespread) threats and situations. It means using processes that build on people's strengths and aspirations. It means creating political, social, environmental, economic, military and cultural systems that together give people the building blocks of survival, livelihood and dignity'. Commission on Human Security, *Human Security Now*, New York, 2003, p. 4.

15. Significant region-wide inter-governmental organisations have emerged in Asia since the end of the Cold War. ASEAN (membership: Brunei, Cambodia, Indonesia, Laos, Malaysia, Myanmar, Philippines, Singapore, Thailand, Vietnam) is the principal engine of East Asian multilateralism, its approach to regionalism is unique in that its emphasis is on longer time horizons, informal structures and processes, consensual decision making, comprehensive notions of security, and commitment to non-interference in the internal affairs of member countries. ASEAN+3 consists of the ten ASEAN countries plus China, Japan and South Korea, and is the most significant political expression of 'pan-Asian' consciousness and of East Asian economic interdependence. ASEM, the Asia-Europe Meeting (EU and ASEAN+3), aims at closer commercial, financial, technological and cultural links between the two regional formations. ARF (ASEAN Regional Forum) is the centrepiece of the multilateral security cooperation architecture in Asia Pacific. APEC (Asia-Pacific Economic Cooperation group) aims at trade-liberalisation, and was set up by an Australia–Japan initiative in 1989 (membership includes Australia, Brunei Darussalam, Canada, Chile, China, Hong Kong, Indonesia, Japan, Korea, Malaysia, Mexico, New Zealand, Papua New Guinea, Peru, Philippines, Russia, Singapore, Taipei, Thailand, United States and Vietnam).
16. Some leading regional Track Two institutions include Council for Security Cooperation in the Asia Pacific (CSCAP), Pacific Economic Cooperation Council (PECC), APEC's Business Advisory Council (ABAC), Network of Asian Think-tanks (NEAT), Council on East Asian Community (CEAC), Asia Cooperation Dialogue (ACD), Institute for International and Strategic Studies (ASEAN-ISIS). The leading regional Track Three organisations include the Third World Network, Focus on the Global South, International Movement for a Just World, Asia-Pacific Research Network, Centre for Asia-Pacific Women in Politics, Asian Human Rights Commission, Asia Monitor Resource Centre.
17. A small example of such initiatives are the Joint Australia–Japan Workshop, 'Searching for Equitability and Peace in the Post-9/11 World: Exploring Alternatives for Australia and Japan', co-organised by the Institute for Social Ethics, Nanzan University, and the School of Social Sciences, held at Nagoya, on 12–15 September 2005 (see M.S. Michael and L. Marshall, *Securing the Region post-September 11*, Melbourne: Politics Program, La Trobe University, 2005), and the UN-backed Global Partnership for the Prevention of Armed Conflict (GPPAC) Northeast Asia Regional Conference in Tokyo, February 2005, which brought together fifty NGO representatives and researchers from Seoul, Beijing, Shanghai, Hong Kong, Taipei, Vladivostok, Ulan Bator, and Japan. Several other proposed initiatives are contained in a number of chapters.
18. See UN Doc A/59/565, *A More Secure World: Our Shared Responsibility* – Report of the High-level Panel on Threats, Challenges and Change, 2 December 2004; and UN Doc A/59/2005, *In Larger Freedom: Towards Development, Security and Human Rights for All* – Report of the Secretary-General, 21 March 2005.

PART I

Hegemony and East Asia Relations

2. Hegemony, Perilous Empire and Human Security

Mustapha Kamal Pasha

This chapter visualises the emergence of a contradictory world order – a perilous empire – in the wake of 11 September 2001, crystallised by an irresolvable tension between the foundational compulsions of sovereignty and unilateralist aspirations of an *empire without hegemony* under the aegis of the United States. Resting on global exceptionalism, the drive towards empire without securing consent of the subordinated seeks to reshape the international society of states and redefine its organising logic: sovereignty. A key site for examining both the contradictions of the present constellation and the effects of global exceptionalism, are the Islamic cultural zones (ICZ) after September 11, especially concerning human security. These highly diverse geographical zones, stretching from North Africa to South, Central, and Southeast Asia are characterised by Muslim majority populations or a substantial Islamic presence (not including the Islamic diaspora in North America or Europe), with a recognisable Islamic identity in quotidian practice, sensibility and awareness. Recognising considerable variance at both levels of religious commitment within and between the ICZ as well as political expression conditioned by faith, this chapter offers a broad sketch of the principal threats to human security, focusing on its cultural aspects.

The tension between sovereignty and empire – two opposing, if mutually constitutive, designs of world order – is expressed more tangibly in new challenges posed by an undeclared 'state of emergency' and the doctrine of pre-emption. Attempts to build a new imperium under the conditions of emergency not only threaten the international society of states, but extend and deepen the assault on global human security already under serious threat from global neo-liberalism. The ICZ are especially vulnerable in the present international political climate. In the face of exacerbating internal tensions and conflicts, their vulnerability is heightened. Any project of empire-building aimed principally at the Islamic world reinforces the vicious cycle of structural and direct violence.

To situate this discussion more systematically, the chapter proceeds in three sections. The first section examines the major implications of September 11 on world order and human security, including the effects of the so-called 'war on terror'. The second section links the effects of the 'war on terror' with the newly assigned status of ICZ as a strategic site for the actualisation of a global 'state of emergency'.[1]

In the context of already existing political and cultural divisions within ICZ, the 'war on terror', especially its ideological accompaniment – the crusade for democratisation of the Islamic World – widens internal strife. In the third and final section, the impact of these trends on human security in the ICZ is briefly explored. The discussion is merely illustrative, suggestive of broad and more complex political trends, not a unified picture.

BETWEEN SOVEREIGNTY AND EMPIRE

World orders are neither universal nor eternal.[2] Particularism and historical contingency remain their abiding elements.[3] The post-Second World War constellation has shared these principal elements, characterised by partial and uneven realisation of the principle of sovereignty. In this mapping, nations are unequal and the rules of international society have applied unequally to different regions and cultural zones.[4] Paralleling the international society of states based on the principle of sovereignty, empire's nagging presence is a constant reminder of the impossibility of sealing off one epoch from the next or conviction in evolutionary progress. Hence, decolonisation did not efface empire nor make the world safe for universalising sovereignty. Changes in the political form did not translate into radically transformed structures of economic or political domination/subordination, recognised during the euphoric phase of decolonisation.[5]

Asymmetry and hierarchy, inequality and injustice, inclusion and exclusion have underscored international relations, showing a tenuous co-existence between overlapping and contradictory principles, often disrupting the neat parsimony of historical orders. Naturalised by hegemonic paradigms or the hegemony of particular powers, world orders appear eternal and universal.[6] In essence, world orders are generally impregnated with rival principles, surreptitiously or overtly competing for supremacy.

Recent claims about dramatic shifts in world politics in the wake of September 11 shadow recent assertions signifying the emergence of a post-sovereign, post-Westphalian world order.[7] The world after September 11, however, appears to depart in significant ways from the universe projected in either theories of globalisation or postmodern constructions of international relations.[8] A number of images now compete for recognition in the aftermath of September 11, discarding novel claims that not long ago were beginning to fiercely challenge the self-same verities of political realism.[9] Talk of the loss of sovereignty, given the pressures of globalisation, has been pervasive amongst former area specialists, scholars of development and underdevelopment, or international relations experts.

The intensity and speed with which the image of a new imperium has secured presence in the contemporary imagination apparently accentuates the dramatic turn of events since September 11, but perhaps paradoxically, this comfort is secured by familiar tropes in international relations. Hence, the ease with which old binaries have been recycled, traditional notions of security invoked, and danger reinscribed into the quotidian practices of international interaction tends to affirm the resilience of hegemonic paradigms and their innate capacity to reappear as soon as their death has been proclaimed.[10] In this view, the banishment of human security, in the wake of September 11, from the recently expanded repertoire of international relations, becomes more explicable. Notwithstanding the failure of traditional conceptions of security, both to account for September 11 and to address the sources of global insecurity, the return of global militarism and theoretical rationales readily assembled after the dramatic events demonstrate the scope and depth of hegemonic thinking. This is a cautionary reminder of resisting the temptation to announce paradigm change with signs of trendy shifts in intellectual climate, only to discover their swift absorption into established (and establishment) thinking or marginalisation without much fanfare or protest. The relative facility with which political economy, and more lately, constructivism have been embraced and reworked within hegemonic structures of thought illustrates this point. Alternatively, the fate of Marxism, dependency theory, and lately, postmodernism, either through wilful neglect or quiet burial, also sensitises us to the perils of premature celebrations attending the presumed demise of hegemonic paradigms. In this wider context, talk of a total break with the past after September 11 must be qualified by a careful scrutiny of the conceptual repertoire used to rationalise this claim. Doubtless, there is a discontinuity between the worlds before September 11 and after, but there is also considerable continuity in hegemonic thinking as well, concealed in current attempts to normalise traditional security.

In varied discourses, the image of a decidedly unilateralist project under the aegis of the United States is being accorded hegemonic status.[11] It is important, however, to recognise some qualitative differences between the old and the new understandings of empire. Though talk of empire in the guise of hegemony has its historical antecedents, especially in the post-Soviet world of US supremacy and global neo-liberalism undergirding it,[12] the post-September 11 cosmos has a fundamental element unseen in real time. Unlike previous imperial orders, predicated on particularistic ideas of social and cultural organisation (despite well-advertised universalistic aspirations designed to rationalise those orders), the post-September 11 order possesses three distinctive and different elements: its *global* scale, its *temporal* horizon, and its *totalising* effect.

While appreciating the continuing impact of September 11, it is equally significant to appreciate that the blueprint of such an order predates September 11.[13] For a long time, both the propensity towards US unilateralism and neo-liberal globalisation has been fairly well settled within the architecture of international relations. What distinguishes the post-September 11 period, though, is the unleashing of contradictions produced by the global 'state of emergency'. With the United States finding 'itself subject to the recoil of the violence of globalisation,' other structural features of the international system are being reworked.[14] In appearance, the entire edifice of the post-Second World War order is crumbling. A more accurate representation is the sharpening of tensions between sovereignty and empire, with new paradoxes and ambiguities. At the risk of over-simplification, the urges of empire seem to overshadow the requirements of sovereignty.

Concerning the distinctive properties of the new constellation, first, the new imperium recognises no spatial limits. It appears to be premised on a notion of a global 'state of emergency' based on a binary division of the world into friends and enemies, subordinating most other values and claims to the self-defined needs of security of the homeland or (Western) civilisation.[15] At no previous time in human history, perhaps, has the scale of imperial ambition been greater, reinforced by an absence of countervailing power, either political or technological. Resistance to this unprecedented global reach remains either too sporadic or diffuse to be effective.

The globalisation of the 'state of emergency' dissolves traditional distinctions between the inside and the outside, erasing in one stroke the worlds conceived in the name of sovereignty. The prospect of a unilateralist global empire constrained neither by cultural modesty nor self-restraint, gives world politics a remarkably uncertain trajectory. In the absence of a viable internal or external opposition, uncertainty turns into the frightening image of global totalitarianism despite pronounced gestures towards the coming of global democracy.[16] In this context, the distinctive features of a global 'state of emergency' are noteworthy. According to John Armitage, the 'orthodox modern State of Emergency was a situation declared by the state, in which strategies and tactics of the military were employed legally, typically because of a number of occurrences of civil disorder such as terrorism, the methodical use of carnage and coercion to attain political aims.'[17] By contrast, the 'hypermodern political conception,' which informs the present (global) 'state of emergency':

> is an 'excessive' conception that places a premium on the fundamentally extreme codes of an increasingly militarized lawlessness and lack of political order. It is a disproportionate state response and military compulsion based on a fervently legal or civilian, not to say civilising, mission currently and habitually referred to by political leaders as the 'War on Terrorism'.[18]

Secondly, the 'war on terror' (and the global 'state of emergency') defies historicity and temporal specificity. Rather, no end is envisioned nor is it in sight. The search for hidden and known enemies proceeds, with the likely prospect of discovering (and inventing) new ones, thus rationalising the need for the endless character of the emergency. Even the most grandiose ambitions of historical empires have been tacitly conceived primarily as temporal orders based on historically tempered arrangements that would produce the ascent into heaven, the end of history, the final frontier or eternity.[19] By contrast, the new constellation is devoid of time considerations. The reinforcing logic of a divided world, unbridgeable conflict against the enemy, between civilised and barbarian, or good and evil, flattens time into space.

Finally, there is no escape from the 'state of emergency'. Totalising, it spans humankind in its entirety, collapsing age-old distinctions between centres and peripheries. A single line of exclusion/inclusion cuts across the globe, adjusting its reach according to local exigencies. With sovereignty under suspension, the walls come down. Paradoxically, the global 'state of emergency' is an admission of the full maturation of a truly global era, but also an era globalised only to retain distinctions and civilisational hierarchies, and in essence, defined by those distinctions. Not mutuality and social interconnectedness, but discrimination on a global scale.[20]

Seemingly, an actualised totalising imperium threatens not only the emerging post-Westphalian order offered by globalising currents (including the effects of the transnationalisation of capital and state, integration of markets, global communications, and international migration), but sovereignty and its institutional realisation in both multilateral organisations and informal norms widely accepted as global common law.[21] Belief in military force as the ultimate arbiter of global affairs now returns, but purged of any ambivalence drawn from Kantian liberalism or even the self-limiting rationalism of classical realism. Hence, as soon as we mistakenly believed the international relations community was poised to partially accept notions of a borderless world, talk of borders and policing appeared to strike back. But the form of borders and policing departs radically from the strictures of sovereignty, projecting the enemy/friend divide on the global scale. This is, indeed, a borderless world, defined not by globalisation, but by empire. Not only is the optimism of hyper-globalisers about the arrival of an integrated, homogenising global society challenged, a Manichean *Weltanschauung* of a divided world acquires respectability in the corridors of Northern power.

If this image is partially credible, the world now is neither separated by a presumed ideological East–West conflict nor the North–South divide of wealth and misery, privilege and plenty, but a displacement of a clash of civilisations between the West and Islam, echoing Samuel Huntington.[22] But unlike Huntington's geo-cultural mapping, the presumed clash is *de*-territorialised. Symbolic and real, either as a legitimating tool for global reach or an actual consolidation of the idea of cultural conflict, the Manichean logic underpinning this scenario becomes transparent.

In their nakedness, these projections of a post-September 11 world order recognise the magnitude of the attacks in New York and Washington and expected US response. Extant proclamations by state managers in the hegemonic North, however, take us much further. Removing political legitimacy from the imperial design, the exercise of military force becomes its own legitimating rationale. Yet, the subordination of the principle of sovereignty to the compulsions of a new empire introduces considerable stress and uncertainty into world politics. Similarly, despite convergence between the mutual disciplinary aims of neo-liberal globalisation and the global 'state of emergency', both produce effects neither anticipated nor easily tamed. Both expose contradictions inherent to liberalism, whose underlying rationale works to privilege civilisational security against intimate barbarians, or to lift humanity from its barbaric state into an expanding market-driven paradise of wealth and plenty. Requiring disciplinary powers to realise these elusive goals, neo-liberalism and the 'state of emergency' must both shelve procedures trumpeted as the hallmark of a liberal imaginary and preferred world. We will return to this question in the conclusion.

Despite its differentiated realisation on a world scale and the structural imperatives of both hierarchy and inequality in the world system, the principle of sovereignty had promised considerable stability and protection to political and cultural diversity in global affairs. Although sovereignty itself rests uncomfortably on the foundations of an order more akin to empire, it surreptitiously affords the weaker actors (states) the possibility, if not the certainty, of survivability. The sheer recognition of political communities as *separate* political entities in the international society of states is a significant factor helping acknowledge, albeit nominally, the principle of unity-in-diversity. With that principle severely tested and shaken by an unending global 'war on terror', but more tangibly, by the doctrine of pre-emption and its enforcement, the prospect of a totalising empire surpasses the negative Orwellian dystopia in spatial scale. The interjection of compliance as the chief prerequisite for membership in the global community and global surveillance to ensure it, gives world politics a character more alarming than the Hobbesian image of a state of nature. Failure to comply (which also means accepting a particular logic of political and economic organisation) can mean not simply censure or sanction but extinction, as exemplified in Afghanistan and Iraq. It is in this context that the post-September 11 world order becomes recognisable, presenting new perils to the weaker members of the international society of states. In the absence of countervailing resistance to a totalising empire, the prospects for human emancipation as an ideal, or human security more immediately, become further removed from the terrain of a realisable world.

To return to the contradictions of the imperial project, a few points are noteworthy. First, in practice the global 'state of emergency' contradicts the compulsions of neo-liberal globalisation. The former seeks to divide the world in the name of unifying it. The latter principally aims to unify the world. Though division is an incontestable consequence, it is not the organising aim of neo-liberal globalisation. In this sense, powerful contradictions appear, drawing upon the difficulty of reconciling the enemy–friend distinction with the image of one-world under neo-liberal global capitalism. The global 'state of emergency' relies on the state of exception, with its own logic. As Giorgio Agamben suggests, '[o]ne of the paradoxes of the state of exception lies in the fact that in the state of exception it is impossible to distinguish transgression of the law from execution of the law, such that what violates a rule and what conforms to it coincide with any remainder.'[23] Second, the absence of hegemony in a 'state of emergency' in the interests of domination makes neo-liberal globalisation more susceptible to internal dissent in the marginalised areas of global political economy. Tensions within the Northern Tier of the global political economy, sometimes characterised as inter-imperialist rivalry, however, clearly suggest a deeper fault line between rival designs of globalisation, either *with* or *without* hegemony. While there is a basic consensus on the (neo-liberal) constitution of the global political economy in the Northern Tier, there are fundamental differences over the exercise of force as the principal means of realising global neo-liberalism. It is erroneous to read these differences as inter-imperialist rivalry, a tendency linked to an earlier phase in the career of capitalism.

REVISITING SEPTEMBER 11

The significance of September 11 for world order is usually asserted, but not carefully examined.[24] Given the unprecedented nature of the attacks in New York and Washington, observers of different hues have treated September 11 in self-evident terms. The significance of September 11 lies in the event itself, the brazenness of the attacks, the presumed targets of Northern economic and military might, and the devastation inflicted on civilians. In what way, though has the world changed after September 11? Closer scrutiny of this question opens up the possibility of re-examining some basic assumptions about the nature of world order.[25] In appearance, the multilateral world of interdependence has suffered an irreversible setback with the ascendancy of an unbridled form of unilateralism. Globalisation, in turn, faces insurmountable obstacles in appeals to homeland security and preemption. These images simplify the contradictory nature of our contemporary times, marked by pressures in different directions.

Clearly, the unilateralist thrust of the current US administration portends threats to comprehensive security both in form and substance. As noted, international society has rested uncomfortably on a symbolic embrace of the principle of sovereignty, despite uneven instantiation of that principle. In substantive terms, a rejection of established arrangements, especially those consolidated during decolonisation, have been put into question with the presumed incapacity of international society to guarantee 'sovereign' existence of entities that seek to be its integral part. The doctrine of preemption appears to supersede the notion that sovereignty can reside in the world community, the latter now based on arbitrary enforcement by the most powerful member of the international society. Occupation and regime change in Afghanistan and Iraq underscore the seriousness of the threat to multilateralism.

However, it is an obvious case of historical amnesia to erase countless instances of preemption, an essential ingredient of imperial design. The disciplinary practices of empire are not excesses to be lamented, but recognised as its defining elements. What gives current iterations of the doctrine of pre-emption its unprecedented character, is the *context*, *scale*, and *speed* of its materialisation. The soothing promises of multilateralism; time-space compression or globalisation, the assumed arrival of a global civil society; and the end of the Cold War presented an image of a brave new world. Violence and conflict were simply atavistic blemishes on modernity. In due course, the obstacles would vanish and an integrated world would emerge: better, enlightened and universal. The disappointment and surprise of an explicit enunciation and enforcement of pre-emption can be better contextualised against this promising forecast. These responses reveal the self-illusory character of liberalism, failing to recognise the inherent tension between securitisation and sovereignty.

The fate of globalisation is also not as straightforward as it may seem.[26] Taking globalisation as a multi-dimensional process of social connectedness on a world scale, unilateralist attempts to simultaneously seal borders, build 'national' fortresses, and draw a Manichean line between enemies and friends are both self-defeating and inherently unrealisable. In this regard, though, September 11 may help rationalise the rule of the exception.[27] The main target of securitisation, thus, is the Muslim community, both inside and outside Western 'national' borders. Islamophobia (the fear of Islam) and militarism are intertwined, bordering on psychosis. This mood appears to pervade the European, especially British, scene. As William Dalrymple notes, 'Islam has now replaced Judaism in Britain as Britain's Second religion, and it sometimes feels as if Islamophobia is replacing anti-Semitism as the principal Western statement of bigotry against the "Other"'.[28] Not without historical parallels, particularly the unlawful internment of Japanese Americans during the Second World War, the shift from tacit to explicit classification of immigrant Muslims as a potential threat to national security signals a climate of closure. However, to the extent that Muslims are generally viewed as people outside modernity, and by implication, beyond the pale of globalisation, the enactment and enforcement of new security laws, for instance, is not viewed with much disdain at the epicentre of power. With renewed fervour, the march of neo-liberal globalisation can continue, not to be dampened by September 11. By isolating Muslims as both a domestic and global problem, globalisation can be redefined. To the extent that the ICZ are outsiders to civilisation in this perspective, they need not pose an insuperable problem for neo-liberal globalisation, only a serious military threat.

However, geopolitical thinking conditions political economy. In direct and subtle ways, the emphasis on border policing and pre-emption has reintroduced traditional security concerns at the expense of human security, the latter viewed as 'a condition of existence in which basic materials needs are met, and in which human dignity, including meaningful participation in the life of the community can be realized.'[29] Challenging the state-centric, cold logic of realism, human security affirms the centrality of the 'human' in providing security. A return to *raison d'être* reduces the protection of human life and dignity at the individual and communal levels to secondary or tertiary concerns. The self-justifying logic of the 'state of emergency' overrides international moral and ethical imperatives linked to ideas of mutuality, interdependence, and global sustainability. In this regard, cultural (and religious) distinctiveness defining particular societies can be easily subordinated to perceived threats. The civiliser–barbarian dichotomy can return with little pretence of regard towards principles of difference, autonomy or tolerance. You are either with the imperial power or against it.

The 'war on terror' illustrates the perils facing the world community over the question of human security. Essentially defined as a stateless threat to humanity, terrorism secures justification to dismantle states. The chief casualties of state death invariably are ordinary people unable to escape domestic tyranny or externally imposed political will. In both Afghanistan and Iraq, suffering has principally fallen on the dispossessed. A unilateralist stance on eliminating global terrorism addresses neither the sources of violence presumably directed at civilisation, nor helps establish international consensus against global terrorists.

Policy interventions in the wake of September 11 have generally reinforced the status of hegemonic ways of thinking about world order. The simplifying logic of clash between world communities, either in hardcore realism or in its disguised expression as civilisational conflict, now occupies centre-stage in policy circles, especially perspectives closer to state power. Return of the old binaries (good versus evil, civilised versus barbarian, saved versus damned) suggests the intermingling of (Christian) religious imagery with the fundamentalist rhetoric of secularism. The potential opening in world politics after the end of the Cold War to global cultural awareness and tolerance has been rapidly dissipated with the materialisation of a 'global risk society.'[30] Against this background, the ICZ acquire notoriety and salience, a strategic site for the play of contradictions in the emerging world order. Again, and, in a contradictory fashion, the dictates of militarism and neo-liberalism tend to clash as the next section tries to show.

ISLAMIC CULTURAL ZONES AND THE GLOBAL 'STATE OF EMERGENCY'

In a number of ways, the ICZ have graduated from peripheral zones in international relations to becoming strategically pivotal to the consolidation of a new order marked by the undeclared global 'state of emergency'. First, the binary world proposed in both cultural and political mappings of empire is directly linked to Islam. Notwithstanding liberal overtures to the need for distinguishing 'good' from 'bad' Muslims, as Mahmood Mamdani perceptively notes,[31] Muslims are the principal global target of suspicion, mistrust, scrutiny, and surveillance. Reduced to the status of an undifferentiated 'Other', the ICZ have become the recognisable *outside* of an inside (the civilised community of nations). This binary worldview, however, is at odds with the real significance of political Islam in the new imperial design, underlining the contradictory nature of the present constellation.[32]

There is an obvious tension between the worldview sanctioned in the imperial imagination and the practical discomforts of empire-building. In the ICZ, this contradiction is the source of considerable discontent. The persistent demonisation of Islam contradicts the political marriage between 'national' elites in the ICZ and Northern power. From the perspective of Muslim majorities, political servitude and cultural rejection appear to go hand in hand. This helps explain why the quest for human dignity in the ICZ emanates both from perceived political weakness of its elites and the apparent denial by many in the North of the Islamic ethos as a valid signifier of cultural identity. Since the Islamic revolution in Iran, this sentiment has been at the core of politics in the ICZ. After September 11, the usually defensive recognition of Islamic identity in the face of Western military power has deepened.

The third reason for the significance of the ICZ is more obvious. These are frontline regions for *testing* the doctrine of pre-emption, a crucial plank in the imperial design. As Afghanistan and Iraq have demonstrated, the global 'state of emergency' knows no borders. Attempts to extend the doctrine to other ICZ (Syria and Iran, for example) are seen as a precursor for similar efforts directed at 'rogue' states. Yet, pre-emption is not without its own contradictions. Imperial management is a risky and costly business. To make it feasible, it must rely on sovereign authority or collapse under the weight of excessive burdens, both material and human. Hence, in one of the more stark paradoxes of the current constellation, sovereignty is invoked as a palliative to cure the ills originating from campaigns of transgressing it. Hence, the dismantling of sovereign authority necessitates its Lazarus-like return. The enormous difficulties of nation and state-building are not merely coincidental; they express the palpable failure of this doctrine of pre-emption and the importance of legitimate authority in governance. Even repressive political arrangements require order.

Finally, the ICZ are the terrain of the new ideological war between the seemingly progressive, secular West, on the one hand, and a regressive, fundamentalist Islam, on the other. As with earlier imperial designs, the emerging order borrows lines from the familiar script.[33] Building upon a civilised–barbarian binary construction, for instance, the global 'state of emergency' is rationalised as yet another crusade against savages or a newer version of the 'idea of progress', bringing enlightenment to dark continents, emancipating the hapless populations of their self-inflicted sorrows. Hence, regime change is presented as an actual design of freedom, with democratisation and secularisation as its most potent ingredients. The ideational and political impact of this civilising project on ICZ is neither insignificant nor unidirectional.

The latest liberal civilising project, like its predecessors, is based on a self-contradiction. It seeks to repudiate (Islamic) cultural principles different than its own, an objective directly contravening the putative essence of a liberal imaginary informed by tolerance, multiculturalism, and respect for pluralism. The campaign of imposing 'democratic' structures in the ICZ compromises the temper of a democratic vision stressing, even in its weakest formulations, the need for an elective affinity between ends and means. Enforcement and human security collide in fundamental ways.

RETHINKING HUMAN SECURITY IN THE ISLAMIC CULTURAL ZONES

To contextualise, human security must be understood in its particularised form in the ICZ, taking into account both its universalistic aspects and culturally coded, historically specific manifestations. The penchant to reduce human security to material procurement neglects the most salient aspect of the concept. In the ICZ and elsewhere, safety from chronic dangers such as hunger, disease or political violence is intertwined with the desire to seek protection against radical disruptions in the patterns of ordinary life. These patterns are culturally embedded, drawing upon received orders of religious and lay practice. Hence, the principal perceived threat may not be poverty, but cultural destitution, the inability to reproduce a form of life consistent with self-identity, both social and communal. This perspective allows the possibility of releasing analyses of ICZ from the trivial dichotomies of tradition–modernity or sacred–secular.

On the other hand, there is also a need to repudiate an excessive focus on the centrality of religious belief in understanding broader cultural dynamics. An appreciation of diversity within the ICZ, especially the range of cultural practices spanning the Islamic world, may help dispel hyper-orientalised explanations of social and political reality. The orientalist propensity to see religion as the all-pervasive factor in human affairs in the ICZ negates the possibility to recognise either the heterodox mixes of religious and non-religious elements in the constitution of social reality or the historicity of living religion. While the significance of Islam to different facets of the social and personal worlds in the ICZ is undeniable, it is neither self-evident nor self-explanatory. Politics and political economy are equally salient constitutive elements of the Islamic universe. The assumption of an unchanging Islam through the ages also mischaracterises the varieties of its materialisation under radically altered historical conditions either as a political ideology or political movement. Appreciating its historicity, one is better situated to understand the nature of contemporary political movements bearing the banner of religion.

In these terms, the elasticity of the concept of human security, with flexible boundaries and conflicting meanings, may not be totally a hindrance.[34] At the most basic level, stressing the need to shift attention away from the state to the human level contains sufficient merit. It helps recognise the *conditions of actual social existence* and the *necessity to secure* those conditions for fulfilment of what is intrinsically human. Threats to fulfilment are heterodox, including both the character of structures that persist and human action channelled through those structures. At another level, by combining ideational, cultural, and material elements, human security affirms holism. Hence, what strikes initially as a boundless concept, the refrain of critics,[35] can also be viewed as its principal asset. In two ways, especially, human security in this expanded form, serves useful purposes, in addition to overcoming the conceptual limits of traditional security. First, it reveals the narrow constrictions of possessive individualism and material civilisation.[36] Neo-liberalism tends to reduce human fulfilment to access to the market and realisation of latent, if unspecified, material interests through exchange. Business civilisation is seen as being normatively superior to its rivals. Human security alerts us to limiting compass and content of the notion of human fulfilment. Though often cast as mere provision of 'basic needs,' a discernible strength of the concept lies in emphasising the indivisibility of forms of life and their material supports. Hence, more positively, this aspect of human security affirms culture and its centrality to notions of human fulfilment. One crucial dimension of a culturally embedded notion of human fulfilment is dignity. Without securing forms of life, invariably realised and realisable in cultural practice, there is nothing of value to secure. In this sense, the neo-liberal project of the 'good life' thoroughly stands in opposition to human security at its core.

The link between neo-liberalism and the new imperium, however, is neither transparent nor unmediated. Both rely on the idea of enforcement, the one through multilateralism, the other through unilateralist fiat. The inherently divisive logic of the global 'state of emergency', however, can frustrate the consolidation of neo-liberalism by opening up fresh cracks in the Southern Tier of the global political economy through excitement of religious and cultural sensitivities, as observable in the ICZ. To be sure, these sensitivities are neither primordial nor traditional, but an inescapable part of the repertoire of the modern world.

Neo-liberalism has already produced unbridgeable fractures of unequal condition in the ICZ. The binary logic of the 'state of emergency' deepens these fractures, linking compliance to the ideological imperatives of neo-liberalism, though with attendant contradictions. Hence, the political divide drawn between 'us' and 'them' finds resonance in embracing or resisting neo-liberal globalisation. Resistance is a constitutive element of worldwide neo-liberalism, not a reaction to modernising processes.[37]

Yet, neo-liberalism covers a vast array of practices, ideas, and objectives. Distinctive, though to neo-liberalism are four common elements: market fundamentalism, consumerism, welfare retrenchment, and liberal governance. Faith in the market is clearly the primary feature of neo-liberalism, the belief in the virtues of unrestrained exchange and the commoditisation of virtually all aspects of human life. Elevated to a religious system, market fundamentalism aims to liberate society from itself, particularly from other belief systems requiring society to tame individual material desires and their spillover into the personal sphere. Resting on a materialist ethic, self-realisation becomes achievable through consumption. Other societal obligations are reduced in scale and content. The empty container of the self can be filled with little assistance from embedded social relations, of family, community, and politics.[38] The attractiveness of the neo-liberal design is based principally on a presumed nexus between consumption and selfhood, an expanding universe of self-fulfilment via the market. However, this image mischaracterises the centrality of sociability to selfhood. Market fetishism obfuscates the simple fact that the more enduring aspects of human self-fulfilment lie outside exchange, from family ties to membership in community and social relations relatively untouched by the logic of exchange.

The hegemony of consumption proposed in the neo-liberal design coheres nicely with a diminution in both social welfare and liberal governance. Self-help and individual sovereignty displace attachments to distributive good and responsibility. The cares of the self override cares of others, of community or society. Neo-liberalism empties deliberation out of citizenship, replacing it with *virtual* politics. Satiated and fulfilled in the world of consumption, the citizen can enjoy the spectacle of politics without experiencing it as a constitutive struggle to be social.

Abstract and idealised, the world of neo-liberalism has been materialised quite unevenly on a global scale. In the ICZ, in particular, there is considerable variance in the intensity and range of the neo-liberal impact. The shared element, however, is the plight of the already marginalised. Human security has been under constant threat in nearly all the ICZ, but especially for those states with poor redistributive capacity and declining political legitimacy. These regions are also the locale of new Islamic political movements, seeking to challenge the perceived secularised sectors of state and civil society. For the most part, these new movements challenge the old religious order and its complicity with power, domestic or foreign. Elevated to salience in the new strategic design of empire, these movements become the prime target for erasure. In this sense, the social ground paved by neo-liberalism for new varieties of political Islam paradoxically emerges as the principal site for imperial enforcement. Without historical awareness of the contradictory nexus between neo-liberalism and the global 'state of emergency', the ICZ appear simply as backward zones in need of forced reconnection. As Susan Roberts, Anna Secor and Matthew Sparke point out:

> what distinguishes this moment of neoliberal geopolitics is that the notion of enforced reconnection is today mediated through a whole repertoire of neo-liberal ideas and practices, ranging from commitments to market-based solutions and public–private partnerships to concerns with networking and flexibility to mental maps of the planet predicated on a one-vision of interdependency.[39]

In this context, the post-September 11 constellation presents specific threats to human security in the ICZ. A few considerations are relevant here. First, internal cultural divisions between various sections of the population within the ICZ reflexively mirror the cultural divide affirmed by the 'state of emergency'. While there is no one-to-one correspondence between an assumed clash of fundamentalism on a global scale and its local expression, its repeated enunciation is reflected in the gulf separating the globalising *local* elites and the marginalised populations seeking redress by embracing the appeals of political Islam. Cultural conflict at the local level signifies deepening fractures within ICZ. Class, ethnic and gender conflicts readily collapse into culture wars, played with passionate intensity. Increasingly, the conflation of various shades and forms of social conflict with cultural conflict stresses the difficulty of inoculating politics. The 'war on terror' accentuates the conflated nature of political phenomena in the ICZ.

These phenomena are amenable to a better understanding in an historical context, which has been marked persistently by conflict and ambivalence between the worlds of Islam and their Western counter-part. Islam has mostly served as the historical other in European/Western consciousness. In turn, Occidentalist understandings, particularised in current variations of political Islam, see the West as powerful and ruthless or as a decaying civilisation. The 'war on terror' recycles these natural attitudes, with potentially extended and deadly political repercussions.

The inability to recognise contemporary forms of political Islam as modern phenomena misguides analyses of either sovereignty or empire. To a considerable degree, the aspirations of political Islam emanate from a recognition that Muslim elites have embraced the principle of sovereignty, without demonstrating their capacity to actualise it within global political economy or the world community of interacting states, cultures, and civilisations. Nationalism ultimately produced a partial realisation of that principle. Political Islam seeks to realise sovereignty in an alternative idiom, with secular arrangements having failed. In this sense, political Islam is inherently *modern* at its core. In this context, Islamic political movements are ultimately *national* in character. The notion of a transnational Islam confronting Western civilisation and neo-liberal globalisation, therefore, requires qualification to allow analyses of the meanings, dynamics, and impacts of political Islam in varied settings.

Failure to recognise political Islam as a modern phenomenon also detracts from our understanding of its own complicity in empire, as Timothy Mitchell has argued.[40] However, there are various tendencies within political Islam, which stand in different relationships to empire. A more complete picture would recognise political Islam as a synthesis of cultural and political currents, not simply the latter. It is in the cultural domain, especially, that the oppositional character of political Islam is attenuated. The perceived threats posed by the 'war on terror' in the ICZ are not simply about sovereignty, but forms of life, though the two are impossible to separate.

The national character of Islamic political movements directs scrutiny towards contingent, historically specific and spatially trapped processes of change and transformation. Though spatial confines remain porous, they are not open-ended. The desire to materialise the promise of sovereignty guides not only so-called secular modernists, but political Islam as well.

The new cultural crusade isolates radical secularism as the preferred ideal for adoption in the ICZ. Forgotten in zealous enunciations of this ideal are different historical trajectories experienced by religion in its relations to Western modernity: (1) the Protestant/Calvinist compromise; (2) asceticism; and (3) compartmentalisation of the social world into separate spheres, just to name a few. Often, the lines between one and the other have been blurred in both doctrinal and cultural practice. While all three options co-exist within the ICZ, a significant marker of living Islam and the contradictory and ambivalent status of religion in Muslim social life, the first option has been singled out as the only pathway allowing realisation of modernity and the fruits of neo-liberal globalisation. The transformation of religious salvation into an earthly vocation of hard work in the service of God promised by the Protestant/Calvinist compromise can also be read as disciplinary neo-liberalism, finding cumbersome resistance in the ICZ. Hyper-globalisers may not articulate this ideal in these terms, but the script is not entirely opaque or undecipherable.[41] The potential effects of actualising this vision present a frontal assault on human security in the ICZ. A key aspect of this one-dimensional view is its inability to '*recognize* the equal value of different cultures; that we not only let them survive, but acknowledge their *worth*'.[42]

CONCLUSION

The post-September 11 world order reveals basic tensions produced by the undeclared global 'state of emergency'. Neo-liberal globalisation has sought consensus as the preferred element in materialising its aims, despite the rhetoric of anti-globalisation. The social layers of incorporation, though thin, are significant. Hegemony does not rest on the erasure of dissent, but its formalisation. The enemy–friend distinction, however, exposes even these layers to wider internal scrutiny weakening the global reach of neo-liberalism. Beside direct forms of violence produced by the actualisation of the undeclared global 'state of emergency' by the Bush/Blair coalition, the 'war on terror' is undermining the capacity of local regimes to legitimise their embrace of neo-liberal globalisation. Restless populations seeking economic justice and political expression also read externally directed secular democratisation as an assault on their culture and faith. The perceived and real disruption in the patterns of ordinary life, an intrinsic aspect of human security, translates into not only destitution and marginalisation, but desperation. In a general climate of global risk and uncertainty, desperation can often become a surrogate for politics.

On an orientalist reading of Islam, the new crusade for democratisation directed at the ICZ conflates the idiom of political expression, which evades Western liberalism, with an assumed absence of a desire for human emancipation.[43] Denying agency to the dispossessed populations in the ICZ, their faith and culture become easy targets for erasure or displacement. In this sense, the assault on human security could not have been more unmediated, merging the struggle to secure a better life with the quest for cultural security.

Mapping the post-September 11 terrain presents a picture of both the risks attending the rapid erosion of sovereignty, and the contradictions between securitisation and neo-liberalism on a global scale. As the chapters that follow show, there are no linear pathways from here to there. Perhaps, this recognition can open up spaces for envisioning alternative designs more sensitive to the question of human security.

NOTES

1. The idea of a global 'state of emergency' draws from the special section on 'The State of Emergency' in *Theory, Culture & Society*, 19 (4), 2002, especially Michael Dillon, 'Network Society, Network-Centric Warfare and the State of Emergency', *Theory, Culture & Society*, 19 (4), 2002, pp. 71–79. In this context, also see Michael Dillon, 'Sovereignty and Governmentality: From the Problematics of the "New World Order" to the Ethical Problematic of the World Order', *Alternatives*, 20, July/September 1995, pp. 323–368.
2. Kenneth Boulding, 'The Concept of World Order', *American Behavioural Scientist*, 34, May/June 1991, pp. 581–593.
3. Robert W. Cox, *Production, Power, and World Order: Social Forces in the Making of History*, New York: Columbia UP, 1987.
4. This feature of sovereignty has been reified, especially by Robert Jackson. See Robert Jackson, *Quasi-States: Sovereignty, International Relations and the Third World*, Cambridge, UK: Cambridge UP, 1990.
5. For a classical statement, see Kwame Nkrumah, *Neo-Colonialism: The Last Stage of Imperialism*, New York: International Publishers, 1965.
6. Steve Smith, 'The United States and the Discipline of International Relations: "Hegemonic Country, Hegemonic Discipline"', in Mustapha Kamal Pasha and Craig N. Murphy (eds), *International Relations and the New Inequality*, Oxford: Blackwell, 2002, pp. 67–85. Also see Steve Smith, 'The End of the Unipolar Moment? September 11 and the Future of the World Order', *International Relations*, 16 (2), 2002, pp. 171–183.
7. James N. Rosenau and Ernst-Otto Czempiel (eds), *Governance Without Government: Order and Change in World Politics*, Cambridge, UK: Cambridge UP, 1992.
8. On globalisation, see David Held, Anthony McGrew, David Goldblatt and Jonathan Perraton, *Global Transformations: Politics, Economics and Culture*, Stanford, CA: Stanford UP, 1999; Saskia Sassen, *Losing Control? Sovereignty in an Age of Globalization*, New York: Columbia UP, 1996; Jan Aart Scholte, *Globalization: A Critical Introduction*, New York: St. Martin's Press, 2000; and Mohammed A. Bamyeh, *The Ends of Globalization*, Minneapolis: University of Minnesota Press, 2000. On postmodern intervntions, see notably James Der Derian and Michael J. Shapiro (eds), *International/Inter-textual Relations: Postmodern Readings of World Politics*, Lexington, MA: Lexington Books, 1989; Jim George, *Discourses of Global Politics: A Critical (Re) Introduction to International Relations*, Boulder, CO: Lynne Rienner Publishers, 1994; and Christine Sylvester, *Feminist Theory in a Postmodern Era*, Cambridge, UK: Cambridge UP, 1994.
9. Michael Cox, 'Whatever Happened to American Decline? International Relations and the New United States Hegemony', *New Political Economy*, 6, 2001, pp. 311–340.
10. Mustapha Kamal Pasha, 'Fractured Worlds: Islam, Identity, and International Relations', *Global Society: Journal of Interdisciplinary Studies*, 17 (2), 2003, pp. 111–120.
11. Robert Vitalis, 'Black Gold, White Crude: An Essay on American Exceptionalism, Hierarchy and Hegemony in the Gulf', *Diplomatic History*, 26, 2002, pp. 185–213.
12. John Agnew and Stuart Corbridge, *Mastering Space: Hegemony, Territory, and International Political Economy*, London: Routledge, 1995.
13. In this vein, the pre-September 11 report of the Project for a New American Century (PNAC), released in September 2000, presents an important blueprint. See *Rebuilding America's Defenses: Strategy, Forces and Resources for a New Century. A Report of the Project for the New American Century*, September 2000, http://www.newamericancentury.org/RebuildingAmericasDefenses.pdf (sighted on November 25, 2005).
14. Dillon, 'Network Society', p. 77.
15. William E. Connolly, 'The New Cult of Civilizational Superiority', *Theory and Event*, 2 (4), 1999, pp. 1–6.
16. On a background to global totalitarianism, see Giorgio Agamben, *Homo Sacer: Sovereign Power and Bare Life*, trans. Daniel Heller-Roazen, Stanford, CA: Stanford UP, 1998. Also see Michael Hardt and Anthony Negri, *Empire*, Cambridge, MA: Harvard UP, 2000.
17. John Armitage, 'Introduction', special section on 'The State of Emergency', *Theory, Culture & Society*, 19 (4), 2002, p. 27.

18. Ibid., p. 28.
19. R.B.J. Walker, 'After the Future: Enclosures, Connections, Politics', in Richard Falk, Lester Edwin J. Ruiz, and R.B.J. Walker (eds), *Reframing the International: Law, Culture, Politics*, New York and London: Routledge, 2002, pp. 3–25.
20. R.B.J.Walker, 'International/Inequality', in Mustapha Kamal Pasha and Craig N. Murphy (eds) *International Relations and the New Inequality*, Oxford: Blackwell Publishers, 2002, pp. 7–24.
21. Joseph Nye, 'Limits to American Power', *Political Science Quarterly*, 117 (4), 2002/03, pp. 545–559.
22. Samuel P. Huntington, *The Clash of Civilizations and the Remaking of World Order*, New York: Simon and Schuster, 1996.
23. Agamben, *Homo Sacer*, p. 57.
24. For a thoughtful collection on the meaning of September 11, see Craig Calhoun, Paul Price and Ashley Timmer (eds), *Understanding September 11*, New York: New Press, 2002.
25. A dissenting view to mainstream analyses can be found in Noam Chomsky, *9-11*, New York: Seven Stories Press, 2001. For an account that challenges both mainstream and critical perspectives, see Immanuel Wallerstein, 'U.S. Weakness and the Struggle for Hegemony', *Monthly Review*, 55 (3), 2003, pp. 23–50.
26. Michael Mann, 'Globalization and September 11', *New Left Review*, 112, November/December 2001, pp. 51–72.
27. On the concept of the exception and its role in securing sovereign authority, see Carl Schmitt, *The Concept of the Political*, trans. George Schwab, New Brunswick, NJ: Rutgers UP, 1976. In this vein, also see Nehal Bhuta, 'A Global State of Exception? The United States and World Order', *Constellations*, 10 (3), 2003, pp. 371–391.
28. William Dalrymple, 'Islamophobia', *New Statesman*, 19 January 2004, p. 18.
29. Caroline Thomas, *Global Governance, Development and Human Security: The Challenge of Poverty and Inequality*, London: Pluto Press, 2000, p. 6.
30. Ulrich Beck, 'The Terrorist Threat: World Risk Society Revisited', *Theory, Culture & Society*, 19, August 2002, pp. 39–55.
31. Mahmood Mamdani, 'Good Muslim, Bad Muslim: A Political Perspective on Culture and Terrorism', *American Anthropologist*, 104 (3), 2002, pp. 766–775. Also see Louise Cainkar, 'Arabs, Muslims and Race in America — No Longer Invisible: Arab and Muslim Exclusion After September 11', *Middle East Report*, 32 (3), 2002, pp. 22–29.
32. Timothy Mitchell, 'McJihad: Islam in the U.S. Global Order', *Social Text*, 73, Winter 2002, pp. 1–18.
33. Philip Wander, 'The Rhetoric of American Foreign Policy', *The Quarterly Journal of Speech*, 70, November 1984, pp. 339–361.
34. The literature on human security is voluminous. For useful background discussion of the concept, see Jorge Nef, *Human Security and Mutual Vulnerability: The Global Economy of Development and Underdevelopment*, 2nd ed., Ottawa: International Research Development Centre Press, 1999; Caroline Thomas and Peter Wilkin, *Globalization, Human Security and the African Experience*, Boulder, CO: Lynne Rienner Press, 1999; and Fen Osler Hampson, *Madness in the Multitude: Human Security and World Disorder*, Ontario: Oxford UP, 2002.
35. Roland Paris, 'Human Security: Paradigm Shift or Hot Air?', *International Security*, 26 (2), 2001, pp. 87–102.
36. Stephen Gill, 'Globalisation, Market Civilization and Disciplinary Neoliberalism', *Millennium: Journal of International Studies*, 23 (3), 1995, pp. 399–423.
37. Mustapha Kamal Pasha, 'Globalization, Islam, and Resistance', in Barry K. Gills (ed.), *Globalization and the Politics of Resistance*, Houndmills, Basingstoke, Hampshire: Macmillan Press, 2000, pp. 241–254.
38. On the notion of embeddedness, see Karl Polanyi, *The Great Transformation*, New York: Farrar and Rinehart, 1944.
39. Susan Roberts, Anna Secor, and Matthew Sparke, 'Neoliberal Geopolitics', *Antipode: A Radical Journal of Geography*, 35 (5), November 2003, p. 889. In this context, also see Thomas L. Friedman, 'Roto-rooter', *The New York Times*, 16 April 2003, p. 27, cited in Roberts, Secor and Sparke, 'Neoliberal Geopolitics'.

40. Mitchell, 'McJihad'.
41. See Thomas L. Friedman, *Lexus and the Olive Tree*, New York: Farrar, Straus & Giroux, 2000.
42. Charles Taylor, 'The Politics of Recognition', in Amy Gutmann (ed.), *Multiculturalism: Examining the Politics of Recognition*, Princeton, NJ: UP, 1994, p. 64. Emphases in original.
43. Noah Feldman, *After Jihad: America and the Struggle for Islamic Democracy*, New York: Farrar, Straus & Giroux, 2003.

3. Still Anchoring an American Asia Pacific?

Nick Bisley

AMERICA'S ASIA PACIFIC

For many in the region and beyond, it has long been an article of faith that the forward projection of American military force, and its political framework – the series of bilateral alliances and security agreements the United States has with a range of key states – has been vital to the strategic stability of Asia Pacific.[1] Among a diverse political, economic, social and geographic landscape, in which there is more distrust than amity, America has been the most important stabilising force. Erstwhile Singaporean Prime Minister Lee Kuan Yew pithily described the United States as 'the least distrusted power' in the region. It was precisely this, along with its massive preponderance of military power, which, so goes the standard story, kept the People's Republic of China (PRC), the Democratic People's Republic of Korea (DPRK) and the Soviet Union in check through the latter phases of the Cold War and beyond.

While not utterly unproblematic, the orthodox account is reasonably compelling and was certainly accepted by many key powers in the region. ASEAN states, as well as Japan and South Korea, were deeply concerned when the United States appeared to flirt with isolationism in the early 1990s. To assuage the concerns felt by their alliance partners the United States released the 1995 and 1998 Nye Reports setting out the strategic rationale for continuing to project force in a Cold War fashion in a post-Cold War Asia Pacific.[2]

In the past seven years or so the strategic environment in the region, and in the international system, has changed considerably. Elements such as the economic and military rise of the PRC, the continuing predominance of the United States, September 11, the pursuit of ballistic missile defence (BMD) by the United States and some of its allies, and the proliferation of nuclear weapons are only some of the more significant aspects of these changes. In response to changing circumstances, and particularly in reaction to the challenges made evident by September 11, as well as to technological developments and the preferences of key policy makers, the United States is beginning to reorganise its global strategic posture and doctrine.[3] While we have yet to see how this will be fully operationalised, a number of things are clear already. First, the United States is to move away from its 'two-war' policy whereby its military deployments and acquisitions were intended to be able to fight two conventional wars at the same time. Second, it is going to adopt a lighter and more agile strategic posture. Again, precisely what this means is unclear in concrete terms, but however viewed, the global deployment of high numbers of troops in foreign lands is unlikely to last.

Any significant restructuring or reorganisation of America's strategic posture will involve a commensurate amendment to the political framework within which the strategic policies operate. In Asia Pacific, the political dimension of American grand strategy has been and continues to be its series of bilateral alliances and security agreements. The Japan–US alliance is without doubt the most important, but the alliances with Korea and Australia are of considerable weight as well. The curious fact of American power in the region is that in spite of the changes that have occurred since the early 1980s, and which have accelerated through the 1990s, the bilateral alliance framework is still deemed to be the most appropriate policy approach by US planners. Although the broad approach is being maintained there have been some subtle yet significant developments. Although not the focus of this chapter, the US–ROK relationship is faring poorly; it is not beyond repair but relations are at a low ebb and show no meaningful sign of improvement in the short-term.[4] On the other hand, the alliances with Australia and with Japan have both been strengthened in recent years. In Koizumi's Japan and Howard's Australia, George Bush has two enthusiastic partners and two popular political leaders who share the American view of their own respective roles and of the broader American strategic presence in Asia Pacific and beyond.

The purpose of this chapter is to consider these developments in the context of Asia-Pacific regional order. The buttressing of these two relationships, occurring as it does at a time of ever-rising Chinese confidence and military spending, and given that it involves a decisively more muscular approach to defence and security policy in Japan, is a significant development in the international relations of Asia Pacific. The statement made following the US–Japan Security Consultative Committee meeting in Washington in February 2005 makes clear how this is viewed on both sides of the Pacific: 'the US–Japan Alliance, with the US–Japan security arrangements at its core, continues to play a vital role in ensuring the security and prosperity of both the United States and Japan, *as well as in enhancing regional and global peace and stability*'[5] (italics added). This chapter considers whether the enhancing of America's alliances with Japan and Australia increases regional stability and security. The conclusion reached is that while the alliances *can* continue to provide the stabilising force that they have done in the past, however, the *way* in which the alliances are being enhanced casts very serious doubt on their ability to provide assurances to the region. Indeed, it is far from clear that the current trajectory of US policy in the region is going to be appropriate to the circumstances of Asia Pacific in the twenty-first century.

Alliances and Regional Order

At the outset, it is worth making a few general remarks about the American role in the region. There are a wide range of ways in which one can interpret the character of American power in Asia Pacific.[6] While this chapter does not have time to weigh into this important matter in any real depth, one must recognise that although the alliance system plays an important role in regional order, it is only one part of the broader set of forces which shape the character of the region, such as economic relations and socio-cultural forces like nationalism and the lingering influences of colonialism. When analysing American power in the broader sense, one needs to consider the full range of American influence which includes a substantial private economic dimension in the form of banking and finance, trade and investment, and of course that significant though rather protean element, soft power. Our concern here is with the alliances, and thus the focus is on this branch of formal American state power.

American power provides the structural coercion which underpins regional order in Asia Pacific. The alliances are the political framework that ensures the continuation of the levels of consent needed to facilitate such a considerable forward projection of military force. The point is that alliances are a means to advance coercion and mobilise and reinforce consent for a given military balance. As such, they tend to structure political and strategic dependence into their members' policies. For our concerns here, we should also recognise that alliances involve two further important elements. First, alliances breed the twin dilemmas of entrapment and abandonment, whereby members can become either entangled in conflicts they might otherwise avoid or can find their security guarantees, on which they rely, reneged upon. Second, as any scholar of Japanese and Australian defence policy can attest, alliances require management. Specific commitments are subject to the vagaries of international politics and of course to the demands of domestic pressure. Striking the balance between the often competing demands of international and domestic pressure can be a particular challenge.

There are, of course, a set of relatively clear purposes to the alliance system. First, members perceive that the alliances provide them with a sense of security reassurance. Alliance partners find their own security enhanced, and through the range of agreements, the scope of military force, and willingness to deploy, alliance members find the broader context of security relations to be reassuring. The second aim of the system, and one which is perhaps the greatest legacy of its Cold War origins, is deterrence. The system seeks to deter regional powers from using force in times of crisis, and more broadly to deter regional powers from seeking to supplant the United States as the predominant power in the region.

The system's third aim is to contain the PRC. While it is unlikely that such an aim would ever be enunciated by members, there can be little doubt that America's military presence in the region is intended to contain China's military influence and particularly to deter it from using force to resolve the Taiwan problem. A similar further purpose, although one which is of reduced significance, is to keep Japan in check. Even the most hardheaded PRC nationalist who decries American hegemony believes that the current strategic balance in the region is preferable to one in which Japan is the dominant military power.

During the Cold War, Australia and Japan were seen as strategic anchors of this alliance system whose purpose was to contain and ultimately defeat the perceived communist menace. Clearly, Japan was the more important relationship, although Australia's proximity to the troublesome region of Southeast Asia, its loyalty and the advantages of its location for satellite communications gave it added heft. Today, given the strengthening of both alliances, can one say that these alliances still anchor an American Asia Pacific? Do they enhance the broader stability and security of Asia Pacific?

ALLIANCE ENHANCEMENT IN A CHANGING ASIA PACIFIC

Japan

Following a period in the 1980s and 1990s when the US–Japan alliance appeared to be adrift,[7] the alliance has been reinvigorated under Koizumi Junichiro's prime ministership. This strengthening of the alliance is the central plank of a broader transformation of Japanese security and defence policy in which Koizumi is intent on building on the improvements that began with the 1996 defence guidelines, and moving Japan away from its past attitude to security and defence policy toward a more assertive foreign policy stance.

In response to perceived changes in international security and capitalising on changes in domestic politics,[8] Japan's security and defence policy has recently taken a distinctly militarised turn.[9] This more assertive policy has a number of aims, the most basic of which is the enhancement of Japan's security in the face of what is perceived to be a more complex world. The recent strengthening of things involves a range of moves which are at once military and political. The highest profile has been the Japanese involvement in the 'war on terror' and its consequent deployment of SDF forces in support of America's intervention in Afghanistan and, more controversially, to Iraq. In these two actions, Japan made clear that it would take controversial military actions beyond traditional limits to enhance the alliance and advance its security aims. In participating in these actions, Japan has nailed its colours firmly to the mast of the US global strategic posture.

The second element of alliance enhancement is the adoption of a new National Defense Program Outline in late 2004.[10] It reaffirms the centrality of the alliance to Japan and to its vision of the region (an important departure from previous outlines) and, more importantly, it places Japan's security policy firmly in the hawkish camp on both China and the DPRK. Specifically it enhances the alliance by prioritising intelligence sharing, technology exchange and enhanced inter-operability between US and Japanese forces. The third element involves the continuation of significant Host Nation Support for US forces, in spite of ongoing domestic problems which have prompted the signing of a new Status of Forces agreement intended to smooth American responses to concerns about the behaviour of local troops.

Finally, the most contentious aspect has been Japan's December 2003 commitment to America's BMD programme.[11] Not only does it have significant operational elements which tie Japan ever more closely to the American military command and control system, it has significant political consequences. The decision to acquire such a BMD system increases Japan's dependence on the United States,[12] escalates tensions with China and poses serious questions for the existing interpretation of the defensive character of Japan's alliance role.

In spite of some continuing niggles, the alliance is in better shape than in many years and now formally embraces the idea that collective action is central not only to Japan's defence but to the security and stability of the region. Japan sees that the risks, both political and strategic, of this enhanced role and increased use of military assets are worth taking to secure its place in the region and the international system.

Australia

The Australia–America alliance has been, and continues to be, the cornerstone of Australia's security and defence policy, although it was subject to some strain in the 1980s and the 1990s. Upon coming to office, John Howard's conservative coalition government sought to tighten relations with the United States, both economically and politically. It was not able to advance this ambition until the election of the conservative Bush administration in 2000 and, most importantly, the transformation in American foreign policy that resulted from the terrorist attacks of 11 September 2001.

Since then the broader Australian–US relationship has flourished and the basis of this has been Australia's commitment to America's foreign policy aims and the enhancement of the alliance.[13] Beyond the steadfast political support and broader array of activities that have burnished relations, Australia has undertaken a number of important actions, both military and political, that have strengthened the political, strategic and operational aspects of the relationship. The most important aspect of this has been Australia's commitment to the 'war on terror'. Australia invoked ANZUS for the first time in its history in 2001 (mirroring NATO's invocation of Article 5) and sent SAS troops to fight in Afghanistan as well as ADF ships and logistics support for the campaign. More contentiously, Australia has made very public its support for the American-led intervention in Iraq. This involved not only a high profile diplomatic support role (adding much needed multinational credence to a pretty thin coalition) but also committed 2,000 troops to the invasion.

The open-ended commitment to the 'war on terror' has been matched with a series of other decisions to further strengthen the alliance. First, Australia, somewhat surprisingly, has signed on to America's BMD programme. While it does not appear that Australia is going to acquire and deploy a system, it is committed to participating in the programme under development. Second, Australia is moving to enhance its inter-operability with American military forces. This refers not only to the broader strategic realities of American predominance but also to the decision to structure future hardware acquisitions and training on the assumption of joint operation. From the purchase of M1 tanks to participation in the F35 JSF Australia has put its lot firmly in line with American military systems.

As Camilleri's chapter in this volume discusses, this reinvigoration has been part of a broader policy aimed to enhance the full range of the relationship. From the Free Trade Agreement to the excellent personal relationships that Bush and Howard, as well as other key elites, enjoy (notably Australia's former ambassador in Washington, Michael Thawley), virtually all aspects of the relationship have become more firmly entrenched. One must recognise that many in Australia are uneasy about this enhancement, with concerns that Australia has reduced its policy flexibility, that it has undermined its relations with its East Asian neighbours, and that it has increased its prospects of becoming a terrorist target being some of the more prominent.[14] The past five years have seen a considerable transformation of Australia's defence and security policy. Australia is now more willing than it has been since Vietnam to use force to advance its policy ends, to deploy combat troops a long way from home, and to participate in risky actions with the United States to advance America's global aims which may not necessarily fit in to traditional understandings of Australia's national interests.

STRONGER ALLIANCES – A MORE SECURE REGION?

These two alliances have been the foundations of a relatively stable American-brokered regional order. In the fluid and quite combustible circumstances of Asia Pacific, it would appear self-evident that efforts to strengthen these relationships would result in a more stable regional setting. Yet the appeal of such an intuitive position may be too beguiling. It is possible that stronger alliances may stabilise the region, but it is contingent on the way in which the alliances are enhanced and on the kind of role that they play. The alliances have changed in terms of both strategic purpose and operational function; equally, the character of Asia Pacific has been transformed and it is not clear that the fit between the newly strengthened alliances and the security setting of Asia Pacific are as appropriate as they could be. The purpose of this final section of the chapter is to explore this proposition. The reinforcement of the two alliances, the clear step to a more assertive policy for Japan and for more risky commitments for Australia, have not directly undermined or reconfigured regional relations. Yet there are good reasons to doubt that this is an optimal security strategy either for each state or for the region as a whole.

New Region – Old System?

The character of both the international system and Asia Pacific has fundamentally changed since the alliances were first established. If one looks at the political, economic and institutional character of the region, it is almost entirely different. Where in the past the region was dominated by authoritarian states, today it is inhabited by a growing number of democracies, many of which appear to be well consolidated. More importantly, where once the region was divided between those that were part of the capitalist economy and those that were not, virtually all have now embraced global capitalism. Equally, in the early phase of the Cold War even those states that were a part of the system tended to favour a mercantilist approach to economic development; today an overwhelming majority are relatively open and outward-looking. Finally, the region is now criss-crossed with a series of embryonic multilateral efforts to cooperate in the economic and security spheres. The political, economic and institutional structures of Asia Pacific are entirely different from when the alliances were first formed.

The alliance system was created as a means to project America's containment policy to Asia Pacific. The bilateral relationships were thought to be the best means for the United States to contain the perceived threat posed by the Sino–Soviet presence. For the allies, the security guarantees of the system were the primary benefits. As the region evolved through tri-polarity and beyond, the bilateral system was maintained as the respective members preferred the benefits which it extended, and the broader uncertainty and mistrust in the region generated a preference for the status quo. Today, the security environment of the region has some clear lines of continuity but also some significant differences from that which existed even ten years ago.

The two most obvious lines of continuity are the continued division of Korea and the dispute across the Taiwan Strait. Even here, there have been some important developments in recent years which have shifted the security environment and the prospects for the resolution of these conflicts: the DPRK has gone nuclear and Taiwan is now a consolidated democracy. But it is the changes to the region which have a more important impact on the broader security setting and strategic balance to which states feel they need to respond. Of the many shifts (beyond those mentioned briefly above), the following are of particular importance: the success of Chinese modernisation and its economic and diplomatic consequences; the incorporation of Vietnam, Laos and Cambodia into ASEAN; nuclear proliferation; the increased perception of vulnerability to terrorism; the growth of 'new' security challenges, especially infectious diseases, organised crime and environmental problems; and resource security, especially energy dependence. In short, the security setting of Asia Pacific rests on subtly different foundations now – threats are less clear, more diffuse and more elusive – therefore one has good reason to doubt whether bilateral military means are the best way to enhance regional security and stability.

One of the alliance system's greatest strengths has been the support it garnered from most in the region. Beyond the basic point that the strategic setting which it was intended to stabilise has fundamentally changed, one can no longer be certain that the states of the region prefer the predominance of the United States to all other scenarios. Of the many factors that have made the system appear increasingly obsolete, China is the most important. China's economic growth, and its foreign policy transformation,[15] have substantially changed regional attitudes toward China. This will be discussed further below. As the PRC has made good its normalisation programme, few in the region actively distrust it. More importantly, as Muzaffar's chapter in this volume eloquently discusses, many in the region feel that China should be treated as a status quo power and not contained. The alliance system is one still based primarily on a containment footing and its target is the PRC. Whatever American conservatives may say about China and its military modernisation programme, their words resonate with few in the region.

To a certain extent, the enhancement of the alliances is a response to new circumstances, but it is not clear that they are an appropriate response. In part, this is because these changes, while continuing to provide a deterrence element, also appear to be creeping toward the realm of collective security. This should not be over-stated, but the nature of the alliances now is such that partners are expected to contribute to security actions in ways that would never have occurred in the past. More importantly, the alliances are now central elements of America's global security strategy. This means that alliance partners are expected to contribute to and participate in wide-ranging activities with a global scope and with ramifications well beyond the region whose security they ostensibly serve. Given that the character of the region's sources of insecurity has changed, that the focus of the alliances are now global as well as regional, alongside the noticeable shift in regional preferences, it is not clear that the logic of alliance enhancement is especially compelling from a regional point of view.

Being Bound to Ally

In his now famous work on soft power, Joseph Nye declared that, in the wake of the Cold War, the United States was 'bound to lead' due to its predominance in both forms of power. Not examined in the book, however, was the other way in which the United States was bound.[16] In many respects, the United States was 'bound' to continue its dominant position in the international system because it had little option. The configuration of military, economic and political interests which had produced predominance tied America into its leadership position. In just such a fashion both Australia and Japan are 'bound to ally' with the United States. They are both bound in the sense that they are surely going to continue to ally with the United States given their history and present preferences, but also they are bound in the sense of being tied to the United States. This 'bound to ally' syndrome is the function of political necessity but has been further entrenched by recent operational linkages. In both perceived and real terms, especially both sides' commitment to BMD and the focus on inter-operability of military force, both Japan and Australia appear to have locked themselves into their alliance relationships in the longer run.

While the operational aspects are ties that bind, they also induce a political posture in which autonomy is more difficult to negotiate. 'Bound to ally' syndrome means that policy choices for both have become increasingly limited. More importantly, it reduces the flexibility of decision makers to respond to regional developments. If one considers the policy response that Australia and Japan would have to develop to a crisis in the Taiwan Straits or an American pre-emption somewhere in East Asia, one can gain some sense of the problems which binding poses. The extent to which this acts as a constraint will depend on Washington's attitude toward policy deviation. Given the current climate, it is very hard to imagine Japan or Australia having much latitude for regional difference. Indeed Australia's attempts to carve out policy space in regard to Taiwan and the EU embargo on arms sales to China have already earned it rebukes.

Being bound to ally means that a state's flexibility to deal with crises in the short term and with changes in the structure of its interests in the medium to long term can be seriously curtailed. Perhaps more importantly, given the global character of American strategy – and the way in which Asia Pacific appears to be seen to be part of the globe rather than a region in its own right – being bound to ally brings two distinct challenges for alliance partners. First, states can considerably increase the risks of being ensnared in conflicts and crises of little or no immediate interest. The traditional dilemma of alliance entrapment is ramped up given the double movement of tightening cooperation by the partners and the global focus of the United States. Second, there is the distinct risk of a reduction in attention to regional problems. There can be no doubt that Asia Pacific is a part of a larger international system, and that its fortunes are shaped by global forces, yet the region has specific and pressing security challenges which require close and careful attention. Being bound to ally to a partner that requires participation in its global strategy means that states run the very real risk of failing to spot or respond appropriately to local challenges or worse, spotting them and not being able to take appropriate action due to alliance commitments whether operational or political.

The China Factor

China's rise has transformed the political and economic landscape of Asia Pacific and this has caused most in the region to shift, if only subtly, their foreign policy preferences. Without question, the central element in any evaluation of the region is the question of Sino–American relations. Some feel that the military modernisation programme will radically shift the strategic balance and that China will actively seek to challenge American strategic predominance. This is a prospect that no one in the region relishes, but nor is it one in which others, in the region's interests, are unambiguously on America's side. Whatever gloss one wishes to put on it, the projection of American power is intended, under the current administration, to prevent any other power coming to a dominant position. This has potentially damaging long-term consequences for the region. America is clearly focussing on containing China and doing what it can to prevent the PRC from becoming the pre-eminent military power in the region. Regardless of whether this is the aspiration of the PRC leadership, the United States continues to make the military the central platform of its strategic response to China's transformation. This containment policy is structured through the alliances. Yet, as many have argued, it is far from clear that a military response to China's rise is the most effective means of securing the region.[17] At the most basic level this runs the risk of creating a self-fulfilling prophecy whereby concerns about China enhance PRC insecurity which fuels a more militarised approach to defence and security policy within the PRC which in turn prompts a classic security dilemma response from the United States.

For Japan and Australia, this is an especially worrying development. Both have extensive economic interests in China which will be placed at risk in any confrontation (whether overt or indirect) whereby they appear to be on the American side. While most in the region, and this is particularly so of Japan and Australia, would prefer not to have to choose between the United States and China, it is very hard to see how, given their alliance commitments, they could do otherwise.

More broadly, the shift in regional perception on the treatment of China is clear. There is certainly not a consensus in the region which concurs with the hawkish interpretation of Chinese intentions. Rather, there is a distinct preference among most in the region to avoid treating China in a way which encourages a more assertive policy. China has managed a remarkable economic transformation and its future success (and that of the CCP) is predicated on continuing this challenging process. America, and its allies, appear committed to the belief that this will produce a military power that, by dint of its existence, will challenge American interests. The rest of the region has adopted a hedging strategy and both Japan and Australia have denied themselves this option. Other regional powers, such as South Korea and Singapore, recognise that China is not necessarily atavistic, that it has sufficient interests at risk to constrain the more nationalist elements and that China has a recent foreign policy record that gives some comfort to those who take a status quo view of China's intentions. In solidifying themselves in what looks to be an alliance system with an anti-China bias, the United States, Australia and Japan may be contributing to the instability they seek to diminish and may be locking themselves out of regional multilateral security efforts which take a consequentialist US-exclusionary posture.

New Security – Old Dilemmas

The alliance system is still focused on traditional security problems, particularly the territorial disputes of Taiwan and Korea and the perpetuation of US military predominance. Important though these may be, the system has little interest in or scope for coping with the very pressing security problems posed by 'new' challenges such as infectious diseases, organised crime and resource security. For many in the region, these are far more pressing sources of fear and insecurity than territorial disputes. As a traditional security alliance system, it is unlikely that it would ever address these matters, or that it would offer much even if it were to be so reconfigured.

In traditional thinking, that central concept of international relations, the security dilemma, maintains its place at the heart of action. One can never really know the motives behind, for example, Chinese deployment of missiles in Fujian province. Thus, one must be prudent and assume the worst; this is the tragedy of international relations. Many have argued that such thinking is outmoded. While in Asia Pacific one can find reason for its continued relevance, there is also a raft of new security problems (alluded to above) which do not fit easily into this traditional thinking. The Sixth Fleet is of little use in containing an avian influenza pandemic. Yet, the security setting of Asia Pacific is a nasty combination of the new and the old. Ultimately, states in the region have to face both elements of the traditional inter-state security problems and often acute transnational unorthodox threats. The problem is that these challenges require almost contradictory efforts to resolve them. While there is some scope for dual movement, the limited character of defence spending in Japan and Australia means that money spent on military programmes with the United States is money not spent on other means to secure themselves and the region from new security problems for which military approaches are often inappropriate. The actions of Japan and Australia illustrate how states respond to this complex environment given the geographic, political and economic constraints. Bandwagoning with the major power represents what they believe to be the optimal strategy, yet it provides cold comfort for many of the more pressing and acute crises that exist or lie just over the horizon.

Perhaps the most pointed aspect of the 'new' security dilemma relates to terrorism and is, in essence, a new version of an old problem. Traditionally alliance partners have had to cope with the challenges of entrapment or abandonment that alliances engender. When one enters an alliance there is the possibility that you will be dragged into conflicts that you would otherwise have avoided, or, worse, that in spite of alliance guarantees you will be abandoned.[18] For alliance partners managing these possibilities is a perennial challenge. For Japan, these fears have long existed; equally, for Australia there has always been doubt in some people's minds about the genuine character of the security guarantee. If Australia were really attacked, would America really risk itself to defend this far off land?

As Hughes correctly points out, historically, Japanese security policy makers have negotiated this dilemma relatively well.[19] But the enthusiasm with which both Japan and Australia have embraced the Bush doctrine and participated in the 'war on terror' has manifestly increased the entrapment problem, for example, clearly ratcheting up the likelihood of terrorist attack. Equally, it does so with regard to North Korea and Taiwan. Both sides may be willing to wear this risk, but its knock-on effects for the region should not be underestimated.

Stability and Instability in an Uncertain Region

While the belief that stability in the region depended on US troop presence was well founded in the Cold War period, there are good reasons to question whether a substantial reduction or removal of troops would necessarily lead to wholesale regional instability. The region is marked by a considerable degree of uncertainty and lingering mistrust between key players, most notably Japan and China. There can be no doubt that the PRC and the DPRK share a considerable portion of the blame for destabilising the region over, respectively, the Taiwan Straits and the nuclear issue, but the American military presence and the policy of the Bush administration have themselves contributed to a growing sense of insecurity. It is not unreasonable to conclude that American force projection is not providing the level of comfort that some argue that it does.

In entrenching a military and political system which retains a focus on the containment of China and the perpetuation of American military dominance of the region, the alliance strengthening of Japan and Australia cannot be said to have enhanced the stability and security of Asia Pacific. This is not to say that they have destabilised it, but the assumption that the bilateral alliance system is the optimal means to improve regional stability and security can no longer go unchallenged. The region has witnessed a distinct shift in which the growth in power and influence of China, coupled with normalised policy to its regional neighbours, has encouraged many, especially ASEAN states, to move slightly away from their previous position favouring an American brokered status quo. Given that the US approach is predicated on a relatively confrontational approach to China, this slight movement has become more distinct. The region does not want to see a growing rivalry between China and the United States (this was one of the primary motives behind the formation of the ARF), but if pressed most will not side with the United States over the PRC. Moreover, the PRC's actions have promoted rather than undermined regional trust. For most, this move is slight, the jury is still very much out about the PRC, but the signs thus far are promising. One indicator for region watchers is the Spratlys. If China is genuine about its normalised footing then it has little choice but to adopt a peaceful and moderate resolution to the Spratlys dispute. For regional stability, the most important element is not perpetuating US military predominance but working to increase trust and amity between the major powers, and particularly between China and Japan and the United States and China. Under the current system, this is virtually impossible.

Australia and Japan have positioned themselves such that they have little option but to be with the United States. Their regional security interests therefore will be more heavily influenced by preferences in Washington than within the region. If Washington adopts accommodative policies, this will not prove too problematic, but if Washington is assertive, then their lives will be more complex. However viewed, for Tokyo and Canberra their flexibility to respond to crises has been constrained, and their capacity to contribute to regional multilateral groupings is limited, as they are perceived to lack autonomy and may find themselves increasingly isolated if moves to squeeze the United States out of regional matters increase. Equally, pressure will come from the United States to stay out of such developments. In short, it is hard to concur that enhancing these alliances enhances regional security. They do improve each party's specific short-term interests but the regional consequences are at best ambivalent.

The answer to the question which gives this chapter its title is clearly yes, the strengthened alliances do continue to provide key structural support elements to American military hegemony in the region. However, the tightening of the alliances combined with a more assertive United States which is undertaking a distinctly global strategic posture, makes many in the region uneasy. This is particularly the case with regard to its approach to China. The problems of alliance rigidity and the means through which the United States perpetuates its military presence provide good reasons to doubt that the alliance system will continue to have the stabilising effect that it has had for the past thirty years. The specific problems of the transformation of the regional international system and the requirements of the alliances, the limits imposed by being 'bound to ally', concerns about provoking China and regional conflict and the lack of fit with the pressing problems of new security challenges provide solid reasons to be sceptical of the stabilising prospects of the system. Japan and Australia anchor an American Asia Pacific, but this anchor can no longer be thought of as the key force stabilising a fractious and often times distrustful region.

NOTES

1. See Robert G. Sutter, *The United States and East Asia: Dynamics and Implications*, Boulder, CO: Lynne Rienner, 2002, and Douglas T. Stuart and William T. Tow, *A US Strategy for the Asia-Pacific*, Adelphi Paper 299, London: IISS, 1995.
2. Department of Defense, *The United States Security Strategy for the East Asia-Pacific Region 1998*, Washington, DC: USGPO, 1998.
3. To get a flavour of change see United States Department of Defense, 'Transformation – About Us', at http://www.defense.gov/transformation/about_transformation.html (sighted on 18 September 2005); it is expected that the Quadrennial Defense Review due out later this year will provide the most important indication of what this will involve.
4. Donald P. Gregg, 'The US and South Korea: An Alliance Adrift' in M.H. Armacost and Daniel I. Okimoto (eds), *The Future of America's Alliances in Northeast Asia*, Stanford: Asia-Pacific Research Centre, 2004.
5. US Department of State 'Joint Statement of the US-Japan Security Consultative Committee', 19 February 2005, at: www.state.gov/r/pa/prs/2005/42490.htm (sighted on 18 September 2005).
6. Recent examples include Michael Mastanduno, 'Incomplete Hegemony: The United States and Security Order in Asia', in Muthiah Alagappa (ed.), *Asian Security Order: Instrumental and Normative Features*, Stanford, CA: Stanford UP, 2003, pp. 141–70 and Peter Van Ness, 'Hegemony, Not Anarchy: Why China And Japan Are Not Balancing US Unipolar Power', in *International Relations of the Asia-Pacific*, 2 (1), pp. 131–150.
7. Funabashi Yoichi, *Alliance Adrift*, New York: Council on Foreign Relations Press, 1999.
8. Robert Pekkanen and Elis Krauss, 'Japan's "Coalition of the Willing" on Security Policies', in *Orbis*, 49 (3), Summer 2005, pp. 429–444.
9. Richard Tanter, 'With Eyes Wide Shut: Heisei Militarisation and the Bush Doctrine', in Mel Gurtov and Pete Van Ness (eds), *Confronting the Bush Doctrine: Critical Views from the Asia-Pacific*, London: Routledge Curzon, 2005, pp. 153–180; Alan Dupont, *Unsheathing the Samurai Sword: Japan's Changing Security Policy*, Sydney: Lowy Institute, 2005 and Christopher W. Hughes, *Japan's Re-emergence as a 'Normal' Military Power*, Adelphi Paper No. 368-9, Oxford: Oxford UP/IISS, 2004.
10. Japan Defense Agency, 'National Defense Program Outline for FY 2005 and After', at www.jda.go.jp/e/defense_policy/japans_defense_policy/4/ndpgf2005/1.pdf (sighted on 24 September 2005). For a general assessment see David Fouse, 'Japan's FY 2005 National Defense Program Outline: New Concepts, Old Compromises', *Asia-Pacific Security Studies*, 4 (3), March, 2005.
11. See 'Statement by the Chief Cabinet Secretary', Prime Minister of Japan and his Cabinet at www.kantei.go.jp/foreign/tyokan/2003/1219danwa_e.html (sighted on 24 September 2005).

12. Hughes, *Japan's Reemergence*, pp. 110–114.
13. See William T. Tow, 'Deputy Sheriff Or Independent Ally? Evolving Australian-American Ties In An Ambiguous World Order', *Pacific Review*, 17 (2), 2004, pp. 271–290, and Rod Lyon, *Alliance Unleashed: Australia and the US in a New Strategic Age*, Canberra: ASPI, 2005.
14. For example see Mark Beeson, 'Australia's Relationship with the United States: The Case for Greater Independence', *Australian Journal of Political Science*, 38 (3), 2003, pp. 387–405, and Owen Harries, 'Don't get too Close to the US', *The Australian*, 17 February 2004.
15. Evan S. Medeiros and M. Taylor Fravel, 'China's New Diplomacy', *Foreign Affairs*, 82 (6), November/December 2003.
16. Joseph S. Nye, *Bound to Lead: The Changing Nature of American Power*, New York: Basic Books, 1990.
17. For example, Lanxin Xiang, 'Washington's Misguided China Policy', *Survival* 43 (3), 2001, pp. 7–23.
18. Glenn H. Snyder, *Alliance Politics*, Ithaca: Cornell UP, 1997.
19. Hughes, *Japan's Re-Emergence*, pp. 21–29.

4. Containing China: A Flawed Agenda

Chandra Muzaffar

China has been on the radar screen of US foreign policy makers and political strategists since 1949. That was the year that the Chinese Communist Party seized power in the world's most populous nation through a popular revolution. For the next three decades, the United States of America was concerned about curbing the influence of Chinese communism, especially in Asia. However, since the beginning of the 1990s it has focused more on ensuring that China does not emerge as a superpower capable of challenging US supremacy and its global hegemony.

In this chapter, we shall first show how the United States sought to check the spread of Chinese communism. Both the successes and the failures of this enterprise will be examined. We shall then turn to the current, more complex phase in United States–China relations. On the one hand, corporate America is one of the principal beneficiaries of China's economic dynamism. On the other hand, the political and military elites in the United States, deeply perturbed about China's ascendancy, are seeking to curb and contain China's power and influence within the region and in the world. The chapter will conclude that there is no reason to contain China. But there is every reason to check Washington's global hegemony.

CURBING CHINESE COMMUNISM

Various Moves

For American leaders in 1949 the 'loss of China' – the overthrow of the Kuomintang regime of Chiang Kai-shek, a staunch US ally, by the communists – was a catastrophic blow. It conditioned to a great extent various US moves and manoeuvres in different parts of Asia for the next 20 years or so. It was one of the main reasons behind 'President Truman's decision in 1950 to order the Seventh Fleet to defend Taiwan and police the Taiwan Strait'.[1] China was also a factor in explaining General Douglas MacArthur's decision to march north to the Chinese border in 1951 in the midst of the Korean War, thus provoking Chinese intervention. Even US intervention in Vietnam which began in an oblique manner in the fifties and intensified in the early sixties was motivated in part by a fear of China acquiring greater influence in Southeast Asia if North and South Vietnam were united under Ho Chi Minh's communist rule. US involvement in Indonesia in the late fifties until the mid sixties was also shaped to a considerable degree by the China factor. As the Kahins observed in their 1995 work entitled *Subversion as Foreign Policy*, 'To a striking degree the massive involvement of the United States in Indonesia was part of a piece with the composite pattern of anti-communism, loss-of-China prescription, and opposition to neutralism that was so prominent in its relations with other Southeast Asian countries'.[2]

The string of military bases that the United States either established or reinforced in various Asian countries after 1949 was also in a sense a response to the perceived threat of Chinese Communism. By the end of the sixties, the United States had bases in a number of countries, from Japan and South Korea to Taiwan, and from Thailand to South Vietnam and the Philippines. Two of these countries, the Philippines and Thailand, were part of an eight nation anti-communist military alliance initiated by the United States, called the Southeast Asia Treaty Organisation (SEATO). Set up in 1954, SEATO also included (apart from the United States), Britain, France, Australia, New Zealand and Pakistan.

At the same time, the United States forged close political and economic ties with a whole range of countries in Asia including those that were outside SEATO. Opposition to communism was one of the reasons why some of these countries – such as Malaysia – gravitated towards the United States. The United States for its part attempted to strengthen the economic foundations of these countries – Japan, South Korea, Taiwan, Thailand, Malaysia and Singapore, among others – to show the world that capitalism offered a better alternative to communism. Investments from the United States and other Western capitalist economies, American technologies and easy access to the huge American consumer market were all meant to accelerate the development of anti-communist Asia.

Those governments which were not communist but refused to be drawn into the US's anti-communist alliances, both formal and informal, often earned the wrath of Washington. Two outstanding examples of this were the Sihanouk government in Cambodia and the Sukarno government in Indonesia in the late fifties and sixties. Because of his refusal to join SEATO and his determination to develop ties with China and the Soviet Union while maintaining good relations with the United States, Sihanouk became the target of US machinations – specifically, CIA engineered manoeuvres – to topple him. Finally, the CIA succeeded in 1970. Similarly, concerted efforts were made by the CIA and successive US administrations to depose Sukarno, whose desire to remain outside both the United States and Soviet orbits irked many people in Washington. As with Sihanouk, they eventually managed to oust Sukarno in 1965.[3]

It is worth noting that it was only after Sukarno was overthrown that Washington gave enthusiastic support for the formation of another regional grouping, the Association of Southeast Asian Nations (ASEAN), in 1967. In the initial stages, ASEAN brought together five states, namely, Indonesia, Malaysia, Singapore, Thailand and the Philippines. Unlike SEATO, ASEAN gave no emphasis to military cooperation. The focus was on economic and cultural cooperation, buttressed by political cooperation aimed at creating peace and stability within the region. However, the five ASEAN states, we should remind ourselves, were staunchly anti-communist. Indeed, right up to 1974, none of them had any diplomatic relations with China. In addition, the United States was very keen on making sure that it remained that way since its Vietnam adventure was turning into a mess and it was apparent by the early seventies that the United States was on the verge of suffering a major defeat at the hands of the Vietnamese.

Success or Failure?

It is appropriate to ask at this point: did the United States succeed in containing the spread of Chinese communist influence in Asia in the fifties right up to the seventies? US intervention in the Korean War, specifically its provocative stance vis-à-vis China only served to entrench the division between communist North Korea, on the one hand, and South Korea, on the other, which, to all intents and purposes, was a client state of the United States. Its massive military involvement in Vietnam could not prevent the unification of North and South Vietnam under communist leadership, but a communist leadership which all along had been more nationalist than communist: a critical characteristic of the Vietnamese liberation movement which the political strategists in Washington had missed. As in the case of Vietnam, the United States failed to stop communist governments from coming to power in both Laos and Cambodia.

But outside the Korean peninsula and Indo-China, the United States, at first glance, appears to have had some success in keeping much of Asia non-communist. Did it not help to thwart the rise of the Indonesian Communist Party (PKI), an ally of the Chinese Communist party, by orchestrating a right wing coup and installing a military junta in power in 1965? Didn't the United States blunt the appeal of the communist ideology by facilitating – as we have seen – the rapid economic development of a number of countries in the region?

While there is certainly a grain of truth in both these rhetorical questions, a closer examination of the situation in each country in Asia will reveal that the main reasons that explain why communism was kept at bay are more complex and contextual. A few examples will suffice. In Indonesia, for instance, the role played by Islamic organisations in mobilising mass sentiment against communism – given its association with atheism in the popular mind – was a far more crucial factor in the demise of the PKI than the CIA engineered coup itself. Islam also acted as a bulwark against the spread of communism in Malaysia. An ethnic factor perhaps had an even more decisive impact. Since the majority of the communists in the country were Chinese immigrants or descendants of immigrants, the indigenous Malay community viewed the armed communist insurgency as an alien attempt to wrest power from the 'sons of the soil'. Besides, the government had also succeeded in overcoming the underlying political, economic and cultural grievances that had fuelled the insurgency. Similarly, by attending to some of the grievances of the peasantry, the Philippine government especially in the fifties and sixties managed to weaken the communist movement in that country. Catholicism also played a role. In Thailand, communism was never a major challenge. Nonetheless, the overwhelming moral authority of the monarchy ensured that belief systems which were at variance with its notion of order and hierarchy could not develop a mass following.

As for the link between the economic progress of various countries in Asia and the containment of communism, US support was far less important than certain endogenous inputs. In South Korea and Taiwan, land reform and state-led economic growth accompanied by distribution provided the real impetus for transformation. It is a matter of some irony that both these achievements were not in accord with American-style capitalism. In the case of Singapore, an incorruptible, competent leadership capable of planning and executing policies for the people was the single most important factor that created prosperity in the little island republic. Likewise, Malaysia's economic success was due mainly to a judicious mix of growth and equity achieved over long decades of relative ethnic harmony and political stability.

What all this implies is that neither American economic policies in the region nor its military and political interventions were decisive in checking the spread of communism. The attempt to forge a military alliance to curb the ideology's expansion was also an abysmal failure. SEATO was pronounced dead and laid to rest in 1977. The numerous military bases that the United States established in Asia were equally ineffective. If anything, they merely served to incense and antagonise the local population. Okinawa was a case in point. The Clark and Subic bases in the Philippines were closed down in the late eighties partly because of 'people power'.[4]

CONTAINING CHINA

Economic Transformation

It is one of the great ironies of history that after more than 27 years of American military, political and economic efforts to defeat Chinese communism, the ideology, specifically its economic dimension, was vanquished by the Chinese ruling elite itself! The modernisers within the leadership, with Deng Xiaoping at the helm, who managed to wrest power from the dogmatists following the death of Mao Tse Tung and the end of the disastrous Cultural Revolution in 1976, introduced some fundamental changes to the economic system. Private ownership of farms and small and medium-sized enterprises was allowed by law; entrepreneurs could retain their profits; private savings were encouraged; and domestic and foreign investments in various sectors of the economy were given a boost. As a result of these changes, much of China was transformed into a market economy.

In the course of the last 25 years, this market-oriented economy has witnessed phenomenal progress. It has grown at an average rate of 9.5 per cent per annum for more than two decades, making it the world's fastest developing economy. Indeed, in terms of purchasing power parity, China is already the world's second largest economy.[5]

Cheap, quality Chinese goods are found everywhere, from Latin America and Africa to Europe and the United States. China has also become a huge global factory producing goods for some of the biggest multinational corporations in the world. 'For example, most Dell Computers sold in the United States are made in China, as are the DVD players of Japan's Funai Electric Company.'[6]

The East Asia specialist Chalmers Johnson notes that 'China's trade with Europe in 2004 was worth 177.2 billion, with the United States 169.6 billion and with Japan 167.8 billion.'[7] Because China's trade with the United States has been growing rapidly – by some 34 per cent in 2004 – the west coast parts of Los Angeles, Long Beach and Oakland have become 'the three busiest seaports in America'.[8]

It goes without saying that big American corporations view China today as a gigantic jar of honey which they have just begun to savour. But there are other influential and powerful actors who are becoming increasingly critical – and wary – of China. Some of them have drawn up elaborate strategies on how to contain China.

Negative Perceptions: Human Rights

We have attempted to classify these negative perceptions of China into three categories. First, there are criticisms that revolve around China's human rights record. Then, there are those fears about China as a military threat to its neighbours. Finally, there is concern within certain circles that China, because of its growing economic clout, poses the most formidable challenge ever to the United States' global hegemonic power. These three categories are by no means watertight compartments. A group that condemns China for its suppression of freedom of expression may also harbour misgivings about its alleged military build-up and at the same time may believe that China is preparing itself to become the next superpower. After elucidating the arguments in each of the three categories, we shall subject them to scrutiny.

Accusations about China's gross human rights violations have a long history dating back to the birth of the communist state in 1949. However, since the economic transformation of China, these allegations have become more specific and more focused. The continuing political dominance of the Chinese Communist Party, the absence of electoral competition and a multi-party system, state control over the media and the judiciary and glaring weaknesses in the observance of the rule of law are some of the issues that human rights caucuses in the United States, academics and politicians from both the Republican and Democratic parties, often target.[9] In more recent years, some of these groups, reinforced by influential Christian networks, have deplored the lack of religious freedom in the country. They point to the curbs and controls imposed by the state upon the Catholic and Protestant churches and upon the spiritual movement known as the Falun Gong.

There is a strong factual basis to many of the allegations hurled at the Chinese government about its lack of respect for the civil and political rights of the people. It is irrefutably true that the Communist Party controls all the major institutions of state and society. And yet, an objective evaluation of the situation will persuade us that perceptible changes are taking place in China. In certain parts of China, the Party has allowed grassroots elections for village councils to be held. The candidates are individuals without any affiliation to the Party. Some mayors and city councillors organise town hall-style meetings where a whole range of issues are debated. Environmental groups have emerged even in rural areas to protest against state projects such as dams that impact adversely upon the lives of vulnerable peasant communities.[10] There are also instances of well-educated professionals challenging corrupt public officials in the media and exposing abuses of power. Even in the sphere of religion, 'household' churches that refuse to toe the Communist Party line are tolerated in an environment where all religions, from Buddhism and Taoism to Christianity and Islam are experiencing a revival of sorts. Besides, the teachings of Confucius – China's greatest sage – which were sidelined during the Mao decades, have now gained considerable respectability and are offered as university courses.

The unwillingness of the Washington political elite and most human rights advocates in the United States to acknowledge that China is gradually embracing certain political and social freedoms has begun to pique Chinese leaders. They suspect that constant attacks upon China's human rights record may be a ploy to discredit the nation so that it will not gain legitimacy and credibility as a leader of the world community. This is one of the reasons why the Chinese government has now chosen to retaliate against US criticisms by publishing its own annual report on US human rights violations.[11]

Negative Perceptions: Military Threat?

Just as the United States accuses China of human rights transgressions, it also often alleges that China poses a military threat to its neighbours. As we have hinted, since Chiang Kai-shek installed himself in Taiwan in 1949, US political, military and security elites have projected the island in the eyes of the world as the primary target of China's military agenda. It is because of China's aggressive policy towards Taiwan, these elites argue, that tensions rose over the Taiwan Straits in 1954 and 1958 and then again in 1996. The fact that China fired missiles into the sea near two major Taiwanese ports between July 1995 and March 1996, to which the United States was forced to respond by dispatching the USS Nimitz and the USS Independence, shows clearly that Beijing has no qualms about using military force to regain control over Taiwan. If anything, the anti-secession law passed by the National People's Congress in March 2005, which states unequivocally that China would resort to 'non-peaceful means' to reunify Taiwan with mainland China after all other means have failed, is conclusive proof of Beijing's intention.[12]

There have been other situations where Beijing has flexed its muscles, Washington elites point out. It has allegedly adopted a belligerent stance over the Spratly and Paracel islands in the South China Sea. These islands are claimed in part or whole by six other governments, Vietnam, Taiwan, the Philippines, Malaysia, Brunei and Indonesia. In fact, China and Vietnam clashed twice in 1974 over the Paracels, and in 1988 over the Spratlys.

All this indicates – China critics are fond of saying – that China's neighbours are not safe or secure. After all, Beijing has increased its military budget by 12.6 per cent in 2005, bringing it to 29 billion dollars. In the last 15 years, its military expenditure has been increasing steadily in the name of the modernising its armed forces.[13]

While concern over China's militarisation and the challenge that this poses to the region has been expressed by American leaders of various stripes, it is the neo-conservatives (neo-cons) surrounding President George Bush who have been particularly vocal. They are convinced that China is building its military power in order to dominate the rest of Asia. This constitutes 'a direct threat to Taiwan and China's other democratic neighbours – and to America's vital interest in a balance of power in Asia'.[14]

China, as one would expect, has a very different perspective on all the issues pertaining to its alleged military role in Asia. Taiwan is an integral part of China.

Right from 1949, the Beijing leadership had made it unambiguously clear to the world that it would never ever tolerate the idea of a separate, independent Taiwan. The United Nations itself conceded to the Chinese view in 1971 when it returned the China seat in the United Nations to its rightful occupant – after it had been unjustly usurped by Taiwan for 22 years mainly because of the backing of the United States. Indeed, when the United States established full diplomatic relations with Beijing in 1978, it recognised that indisputable fact in international law that there is only one China and Taiwan is part of it. US administrations since then have by and large accepted this political reality – except that the Bush presidency, it is obvious, is less enthusiastic about it than its predecessors.[15] Be that as it may, as far as international law and established political and diplomatic norms are concerned, China has every right to ensure that its territorial integrity and national sovereignty are respected, even if that means using force – as a last resort – to bring about the reunification of Taiwan with mainland China.

By the same measure, China's territorial claims over the Spratlys and the Paracels by themselves are no indication of its military ambitions in the region. A cursory study of Chinese history will reveal that the Chinese have always been preoccupied with the sanctity of their borders and have from time to time gone to war to enforce their territorial claims. This is what happened for instance in the early part of the fifteenth century during the period of the Ming Dynasty when the Chinese armada – the biggest and the most advanced in the world at that time – embarked upon a series of global voyages under the famous Admiral, Zheng He. The only naval battles that the armada was involved in were confined to areas that were contiguous to China's borders – in the Spratlys and Paracels; in parts of northern Vietnam; and in Yunnan. From other parts of Southeast Asia, what the Chinese kingdom expected was an acknowledgement of its political suzerainty. This is why Zheng He, who went right up to East Africa and Arabia and perhaps even further, did not use the formidable naval power at his command to conquer alien territory or to establish bases on foreign soil.[16] Fast forward to the twentieth century, even China's brief war with India in 1962 was also about border regions and boundaries.

Based partly upon its historical record and partly upon its current political conduct in Asia, Beijing has always maintained that its neighbours have nothing to fear from its increased military spending, which has been prompted largely by the United States stance vis-à-vis Taiwan. Even with these increases, China's military expenditure of 29 billion dollars for 2005 amounted to a fraction of the US military budget of 400 billion for the same year. By way of comparison, Japan's military expenditure in 2005 totalled 47 billion dollars.

It is not China that has been belligerent towards its neighbours. It is the United States that has been aggressive towards China. In April 2001, for instance, a US plane spying upon a Chinese battleship collided with a Chinese military aircraft in mid-air resulting in the death of its pilot. Beijing considered it an act of provocation but avoided a confrontation with the United States over the incident.[17] For even more compelling evidence of the US's belligerent attitude towards China, one has to look at its ballistic missile defence (BMD) programme. The BMD programme is essentially 'a new space-based, high-tech grand strategy for transforming the military and securing global dominance for decades to come.'[18] The proponents of BMD such as the US Defense Secretary, Donald Rumsfeld, see China as one of the principal hurdles to total US global dominance and are convinced that an ultra-sophisticated weapons programme will deter the former from even contemplating challenging the latter.[19] To contain China, Rumsfeld and others in the Bush administration are now encouraging some of China's neighbours to strengthen their military muscles. Japan has been asked to set aside its pacifist Constitution and accelerate its rearmament. Given the uneasiness between Japan and China which erupted yet again in April 2005 over Japan's distorted presentation of its massacre of the Chinese people before and during the Second World War in a school text, a rearmed Japan can only send shivers down the Chinese spine. The United States has also promised India that it will extend whatever help it can to enable China's southern neighbour to become a major world power.[20]

There is no doubt at all that containing China militarily is high up on Washington's Asian agenda. This is not because China is a threat to any of its neighbours or to the United States. Projecting China as a military threat is part of the US strategy of perpetuating its own military dominance. It is to ensure that any nation that is not an ally or a client that may have some military potential is clubbed and clobbered before it raises its head. After all, for the neo-cons, US global hegemony is the prised trophy of American victory in the Cold War. It is a trophy they would want to hold on to at all costs. Besides, military hegemony also means ever-escalating military expenditure and bigger and bigger contracts for the arms merchants.

Negative Perceptions: Economic Clout

This brings us to the third major argument for containing China propounded by the neo-cons and their ilk. It is because of China's rapid economic ascendancy that the United States feels threatened. We have already caught a glimpse of China's economic dynamism. What we have yet to fathom is why this economic dynamism is viewed with so much trepidation in certain circles.

For some years now in their burgeoning bilateral trade, the United States has been recording larger and larger deficits as against China's bigger and bigger surpluses. In 2004, for instance China registered a 162 billion dollar trade surplus while for the single month of June 2005 the figure was already 17.6 billion. These huge surpluses are due mainly to US imports of cheap Chinese textiles and apparel.[21]

Since these huge trade deficits result in the loss of manufacturing jobs, quite a bit of anger has developed against China among both American workers and some owners of capital. They feel that it is because the Chinese currency, the Yuan, is grossly undervalued – its July 2005 de-pegging from the dollar and slight appreciation notwithstanding – that China is able to export its goods so cheaply. They argue that China should therefore allow the Yuan to appreciate much more.

America's trade deficit has been exacerbated by its federal budget deficit. This deficit began to grow under the Reagan presidency in the eighties and was caused to a great extent by his tax cuts and military expenditure.[22] This twin deficit – trade and budget – is primarily responsible for the US's massive debt which has worsened under Bush. As of 15 August 2005, its outstanding public debt stood at more than 7.9 trillion dollars.[23] The United States today is the world's largest debtor nation. A substantial chunk of this debt is owed to countries in East Asia such as Japan, China, South Korea and Taiwan. This is yet another reason why the United States feels that it has become increasingly vulnerable to Chinese economic power.

To add to the woes of the US economy, China is attempting to buy up American multinational corporations. The most high profile of these was the bid by the China National Offshore Oil Corporation (CNOOC) to take over the giant American oil company, UNOCAL. Though the CNOOC offered a better price – 18.5 billion dollars – than its American rival, Chevron, both the US House of Representatives and the US Senate went all out to stop the purchase.[24] The failure of the Chinese take-over bid shows that the American political elite has become extremely alert to what they perceive as China's looming economic challenge.

There is yet another related aspect of China's present economic drive which has set alarm bells ringing in Washington. Since the Chinese economy is expanding rapidly, its energy needs have increased by leaps and bounds – which was one of the reasons behind its UNOCAL bid. But more than purchasing foreign oil companies, the Chinese strategy is to forge agreements and establish solid economic links with energy-producing countries and regions. China has very good relations with a number of such countries in the African continent, which supplies China with almost one third of its oil needs.[25] Latin America is another region of the world where the Chinese are active finalising sales agreements. They have agreed 'with Brazil's state controlled oil company to finance a $1.3 billion gas pipeline between Rio de Janeiro and Bahia once technical studies are completed'.[26] Under new agreements made with the government of Venezuela, 'China will be allowed to operate 15 mature oil fields in eastern Venezuela. China will invest around $350 million to extract oil and another $60 million in natural gas wells'.[27] In September 2004, China and Kazakhstan entered into a $3.5 billion pipeline agreement. Even more significant, on 28 October 2004, Beijing and Tehran signed a $100 billion dollar agreement which 'entails the annual export of some 10 million tons of Iranian liquefied natural gas (LNG) for a 25 year period, as well as the participation, by China's state oil company, in such projects as exploration and drilling, petrochemical and gas industries, pipelines, services and the like'.[28] At the same time, Iran will also be exporting 150,000 barrels of crude oil per day to China for 25 years at market prices. Needless to say, these newly forged Beijing–Tehran links have created a great deal of consternation in Washington. Washington is equally dismayed that its long time ally, Saudi Arabia, has granted to a Chinese oil company 'the right to explore for natural gas in Saudi Arabia's al-Khali Basin and Saudi Arabia has agreed to build a refinery for natural gas in Fujian (China) in exchange for Chinese investment in Saudi Arabia's bauxite and phosphate industry'.[29]

How has Beijing itself defended its trade, investment and economic ventures in the last few years? It rightly attributes its penetration of the American and other markets to its ability to produce cheap but quality goods and products which cater to consumer tastes. It is able to do this for an obvious reason: an abundance of skilled, productive labour and not because of its currency, per se. Likewise, China views its quest for energy as a legitimate economic activity. It is seeking access to oil and gas. It has no intention of controlling the level of production or the pattern of distribution of these resources which it recognises is the sole prerogative of the nation which owns them.

This is the nub of the matter. Unlike China, the United States has, for the last so many decades, sought to control, directly or indirectly, the production and distribution of oil and gas at some of the most strategic energy centres on earth. It explains to a great extent why it has embarked upon wars, established military bases, propped up puppet regimes and manipulated politics in certain regions. This is especially true of its role in the Middle East – the world's most important oil exporting region – since the Second World War.[30] From the overthrow of Prime Minister Mohamed Mossadegh in oil rich Iran in 1953 to the invasion and occupation of oil rich Iraq in 2003, it is the same old story of the assertion and re-assertion of hegemonic power over and over again. There is no need to repeat that it is because of its determination to perpetuate and expand its global hegemony that Washington has deliberately chosen to portray China's economic ascendancy as a threat to its well-being. China, on the other hand, has tried on a number of occasions to assure the United States that its rise is not a threat to anyone. As one of its leaders put it recently, 'China's development is an opportunity instead of a threat to the world. That is becoming the consensus of the international community.'[31]

CONSEQUENCES – AND CONCLUSION

If, in spite of Chinese assurances, Washington continues to regard Beijing as a threat that should be contained economically, politically and militarily, it is quite conceivable that tensions between the two nations will increase rapidly. In such a situation, Taiwan could be the flash point of an actual conflict. Other Asian nations might be drawn into the conflagration. Japan is a prime candidate. So is South Korea. Even India – the present thaw in Sino–Indian relations notwithstanding[32] – could gravitate towards Washington in the event of a Sino–US conflict. ASEAN states would also be forced to take sides.

Of course, there are analysts who argue that a war between the United States and China is most unlikely because of the power and potency of globalisation. As we have seen, American investments are flowing into China and vice versa. Bilateral trade is increasing. Technology transfers are multiplying. China, in other words, is becoming more and more integrated into the Washington-helmed global economy. As one of these analysts puts it, 'That fundamental reality of the global economy explains why we won't be going to war with China. The Pentagon can plan for all it wants, but it does so purely within the sterile logic of war, and not with any logical reference to the larger flows of globalisation'.[33]

It is doubtful whether globalisation alone will be enough to dissuade the Pentagon, the neo-cons and other influential actors and lobbyists in Washington from pursuing their agenda of curbing and controlling China. For containing China, as we have shown, is not just a question of putting China in its place. It is a camouflage for perpetuating and enhancing US global hegemony. To reiterate, it is a goal which is driven by its own logic – the logic of power. Hegemony seekers, like the neo-cons, will not subordinate this passionate commitment of theirs to other considerations. In fact, this is explicitly articulated in Washington's National Security Strategy of September 2002 which makes it clear that the United States will not brook any challenge to its global hegemony – a hegemony which it views as permanent and perennial.[34]

This is why the root of the problem that confronts humankind today is Washington's global hegemony, not China's ascendancy. It is checking Washington's hegemony, not containing China, that is the real challenge facing us all at this hour.

How will we respond to this global challenge?

NOTES

1. See Chalmers Johnson, *Blowback: The Costs and Consequences of American Empire*, London: Time Warner Books, 2002, p. 23.

2. See Audrey R. Kahin and George M. Kahin, *Subversion as Foreign Policy*, Seattle: University of Washington Press, 1997, p. 16.
3. Ibid.
4. See Chandra Muzaffar, 'The Interface between Southeast Asia and the US: A Contemporary Analysis', paper presented at an international conference on the theme 'Their America: The US in the Eyes of the Rest of the World' organised by the New School in New York City, 18–19 October 2004.
5. See Chalmers Johnson, 'No Longer the 'Lone' Superpower', at www.commondreams.org/views05/0315-24.htm (sighted on 15 March 2005).
6. Ibid.
7. Ibid.
8. Ibid.
9. For an example of such criticism see Amnesty International, 'China', *Amnesty International Report 2004*, London: Amnesty International Publications, 2004, pp. 153–156.
10. See 'A New China Rises', *Time*, 27 June 2005.
11. State Council of the People's Republic of China, *The Human Rights Record of the United States in 2004*, Beijing: State Council of the People's Republic of China, 2005.
12. See 'China Passes Anti-Secession Bill', *New Straits Times*, 15 March 2005.
13. Ibid.
14. See Ross H. Munro, 'China: The Challenge of a Rising Power', in Robert Kagan and William Kristol (eds), *Present Dangers: Crisis and Opportunity in American Foreign and Defense Policy*, San Francisco: Encounter Books, 2000, p. 68.
15. Ibid.
16. This view of Admiral Zheng He is now being challenged by certain biased Western historians who are out to present Chinese naval power in the fifteenth century as 'imperialistic' and 'militaristic'. See for instance Geoff Wade, *The Zheng He Voyages: A Reassessment, Asia Research Institute, Working Paper Series*, No. 31, at www.ari.nus.edu.sg/docs/wps/wps04_031.pdf (sighted on 17 September 2005).
17. See 'Jiang Blames US for Collision', *New Straits Times*, 4 April 2001.
18. See Chalmers Johnson, *The Sorrows of Empire*, United Kingdom: Verso, 2004, p. 83.
19. Ibid.
20. See 'India, US make a tectonic move', *The Australian*, 23 July 2005.
21. See 'U.S. Trade Deficit widens', *San Francisco Chronicle*, 13 August 2005.
22. See 'I.M.F. Warns That U.S. Debt Is Threatening Global Stability', *New York Times*, 8 January 2004.
23. See 'U.S. National Debt Clock', at www.brillig.com/debt_clock (sighted on 15 August 2005).
24. For a background analysis to the UNOCAL affair see 'Why Beijing Wants to Take Over Unocal', *New Straits Times*, 28 June 2005.
25. Quoted in 'China May Have to Think Again on Africa', *New Straits Times*, 14 July 2005.
26. Johnson, 'No Longer the "Lone" Superpower', p. 11.
27. Ibid., p. 12.
28. See 'China Rocks the Geopolitical Boat', *Asia Times Online*, 6 November 2004, at http://atimes.com/atimes/Middle_East/FK06Ak01.html (sighted on 17 September 2005).

29. See Chietigj Bajpaee, 'Setting the Stage for a New Cold War: China's Quest for Energy Security', Power and Interest News Report (PINR), at www.pinr.com/report.php?ac=view_report&report_id=272 (sighted on 3 March 2005).
30. See various articles in Chandra Muzaffar, *Muslims Dialogue Terror*, Malaysia: International Movement for a Just World, 2003.
31. Quoted from 'China Says its Rise is Not a Threat', *New Straits Times*, 29 July 2005.
32. For an optimistic view of Sino-Indian ties see 'On the Threshold of a New Asian Century', *New Straits Times*, 15 April 2005.
33. See Thomas P. M. Barnett, *The Pentagon's New Map*, New York: Berkley Books, 2004, p. 229.
34. See Richard A. Falk, *The Declining World Order: America's Imperial Geopolitics*, New York: Routledge, 2004, especially pp. 230–231.

PART II

Japan's Security Dilemma

5. Questioning the Rationale for Changing Japan's Peace Constitution

Michael T. Seigel

Since 1947, Japan has had a Constitution that renounces war and relinquishes the right of the country to possess the means of war. Compromises on these principles over the years have given Japan one of the strongest military forces in the world. The use of that force, however, remains highly restricted by the Constitution.

A process has been underway in the Diet to shift from this impasse. Recent years have seen numerous moves at government level to promote constitutional revision. On 20 January 2000, constitutional review committees were established in both chambers of the Diet. Both committees presented reports in April 2005. The Liberal Democratic Party (LDP) set up a committee to draft a proposal for a new Constitution in December 2004 under the leadership of former Prime Minister Yoshiro Mori. That committee finalised its draft on 28 October 2005. The leading opposition party, the Democratic Party of Japan (DPJ), established its own committee in December 1999 and published the proposal from this committee on 31 October 2005. Thus, by the end of October 2005, each of the two houses of the Diet and both major political parties had produced documents with concrete proposals for constitutional revision, all of which included changes in the peace clause.

In the election for the lower house of the Diet (the House of Representatives) held on 11 September 2005, the LDP won fully sixty per cent of the seats and the ruling coalition (the LDP and Komeito)[1] won more than two thirds.[2] Given this victory, the most significant proposal was the one that came from the LDP.[3]

The LDP draft does present itself as peace oriented, repeating the first paragraph of Article 9 verbatim ('Aspiring sincerely to an international peace based on justice and order, the Japanese people forever renounce war as a sovereign right of the nation and the threat or use of force as means of settling international disputes').[4] However, as constitutional lawyer Asaho Mizushima points out, the 'pacifism of the Constitution lies in the second paragraph of Article 9 . . . It is the position a party takes on the second paragraph that determines its position on the pacifism of the Constitution.'[5] The second clause of Article 9 of the current Constitution states that in 'order to accomplish the aim of the preceding paragraph, land, sea, and air forces, as well as other war potential, will never be maintained. The right of belligerency of the state will not be recognized.'[6] The LDP draft replaces this with four paragraphs, the first and third of which are as follows:[7]

> 1) In order to secure the peace and independence of our country and the safety of the country and the people, a self-defence army is maintained under the command of the Prime Minister.
> 3) The Self-Defense Army, in addition to activities carried out to fulfil the tasks determined in paragraph 1, in accordance with what is established in law can carry out activities in international cooperation in order to secure international peace and safety, to maintain public order in emergency situations, and to protect the life and liberty of the people.[8]

The breadth of this makes possible pre-emptive strikes and a range of activities in the international sphere including collective self-defence, humanitarian interventions, and peacekeeping operations in conflict situations – all of which are prohibited under the current Constitution.

THE RATIONALE FOR CONSTITUTIONAL REVISION

The numerous rationales given for changing the peace clause can be grouped into three categories. One, which will not be taken up here, is associated with the fact that the Constitution was imposed on Japan. The other two categories, national defence and international cooperation, are the focus of this chapter.

These two categories are not always immediately apparent in the debate. One argument frequently brought forward is that the Constitution should be revised to recognise the existence of the Self-Defense Force. This is based on the understanding that the Self-Defense Force is unconstitutional – a commonly held view that is asserted in the report of the Constitutional Review Committee of the lower house, where it is described as 'the accepted view of constitutional scholars'.[9] The argument is that the Constitution needs to be adjusted to the reality of the Self-Defense Force. This is the position, for example, of the DPJ whose statement argues that repeated 're-interpretations' of the Constitution to justify the existence and activities of the Self-Defense Force have made it a 'hollow' document or a 'dead-letter' and that to restore its effectiveness it must be revised to recognise the Self-Defense Force.[10] However, with this argument, reasons are required as to why the solution should be changing the Constitution rather than abolishing the Self-Defense Force.[11] Reasons given for this are ultimately reducible to the categories mentioned above.

It is also argued that the more than fifty years that have elapsed since the Constitution was enacted have brought so many changes to the world that the

Constitution must be updated to adjust to these changes. However, the concrete changes that are said to require a constitutional revision generally have to do with threats that Japan faces and the need for Japan to carry its share of the burden of peacekeeping in the world. Thus, this argument too is ultimately reducible to the two aspects that are the focus of this chapter – national defence and international cooperation.

Actually, the world situation changed radically soon after the Constitution came into effect. The idea of the peace clause was originally proposed to Prime Minister Shidehara by Shiratori Toshio, an indicted A class war criminal, and by Shidehara to MacArthur as a kind of a *quid pro quo*, as Jiro Yamaguchi points out in Chapter 6, for maintaining the emperor system.[12] Less than two years after it came into force, the People's Republic of China came into being, radically altering the geo-political situation for Japan. However, at that time Japan resisted pressure from the United States and chose to maintain the peace Constitution.

The Defence Rationale

The idea that there are current threats to Japan's security has been an important part of the debate on constitutional revision. CNN Tokyo Bureau Chief Rebecca MacKinnon has said that North Korea's 'threats have reinforced a growing sense of vulnerability in Japan. In the eyes of most Japanese, North Korea remains a long-term military threat.' MacKinnon quotes Masashi Nishihara as saying, in reference to North Korea:

> This has been a great concern for the Japanese people . . . This has contributed to the change in Japanese consciousness of the need to defend their own nation. Since they have long range missiles that can reach Japan, we have to . . . have our own system which can cope with such threats from North Korea.[13]

A spate of anti-Japanese demonstrations in China in April 2005, along with China's increasing military and economic clout, also gave rise to apprehensions in Japan.

Given that, even with the Constitution as it stands, Japan already has one of the strongest military forces in the world, the argument that Japan needs to change its Constitution in order to build up its defence capacity may not seem convincing. Nevertheless, the argument has persuasive force in the public arena in Japan, in part because many Japanese are unaware of the strength of the Self-Defense Force, and in part because there is a wide understanding that the Constitution excessively constrains use of this force (by, for example, not permitting pre-emptive strikes).

The military options open to a country in face of external threats are to build up enough military might to resist the threat self-reliantly or to establish alliances that will provide protection. In terms of self-reliant defence, the current Constitution prohibits pre-emptive strikes and, in regard to alliances, it prohibits the exercising of collective self-defence (that is, participating militarily in the defence of an ally when Japan itself is not under attack).[14] In terms of its defence posture, these are the only actions prohibited by the Constitution, and therefore, whether overtly or not, they are what is at issue when constitutional revision is considered in terms of defence. With regard to pre-emptive strikes, the idea that Japan should consider possessing 'the capability to attack foreign missile bases to pre-empt potential launches against the country'[15] had been proposed by the Prime Minister's Council on Security and Defense Capabilities. The LDP draft proposal, in defining the function of the proposed Self-Defense Army broadly as being 'to secure the peace and independence of our country and the safety of the country and the people,' abides by this proposal.

With regard to collective self-defence, it has been repeatedly argued that Japan must strengthen its alliance with the United States. Tomohisa Sakanaka, in his address to the Diet on March 25, 1994, argued for an abrogation of Article 9 on the grounds that 'it is impossible today for a country to achieve security alone and participation in collective self-defence is essential. Japan's Constitution therefore must be adjusted to this reality.'[16] Riichi Furugaki also argues that 'the security environment surrounding Japan has changed drastically, especially after the Cold War. These changes require Japan to review the Constitution and the interpretation of the right of collective self-defence. Japan cannot defend itself without collective self-defence in the current security environment.' It is primarily, of course, the defence relationship with the United States that these thinkers have in mind. The 'importance of the Japan-U.S. security arrangement', says Furugaki, 'will never decline in the conceivable future. In order to enhance the credibility of U.S. nuclear deterrence for Japan, Japan needs to share more military responsibility . . . by exercising collective self-defense with the United States.'[17]

International Cooperation

'International cooperation,' whatever it is taken to mean, has been a major factor driving the process of constitutional revision. The report of the upper house of the Diet, the House of Councillors, in discussing whether 'now, fifty years after the Constitution was enacted, it is still applicable to the conditions of international society,' assessed the new issues to which the current Constitution may not be applicable in the following way:

> With regard to pacifism, it is not sufficient to simply relinquish warfare as a means of solving international disputes. The intention of positively contributing to peace in international society should be made clear. A clause dealing with international cooperation should be included in the text of the Constitution clearly showing

the rationale for Japan's international cooperation and specifying cooperation in activities carried out jointly by international society . . .

For Japan, based on the experience of war, a pure pacifism that totally rejects armed forces, the means of war, has set the tone. In the twenty-first century, in place of this kind of pure pacifism, a forward-looking strong pacifism is needed. The shape that our country should aim to take in the twenty-first century is one of positive pacifism. It should aim at being a country of peace and humanitarianism, a country that contributes to international society.[18]

Here, the phrase 'positive pacifism' is used in a way that would include using military force to establish peace.

The LDP draft proposal also stresses international cooperation not only in the paragraph of Article 9 already quoted but also in the preamble:

We, the Japanese people, earnestly desiring an international peace founded on justice and order, cooperate with other countries for the realisation of this. While recognising variety in value systems, we carry out unceasing efforts in international society to eradicate oppressive government and human rights abuses.[19]

If this is understood to include the possibility of military means, and there is nothing in the draft to remove this implication, it suggests the possibility of a very aggressive policing role.

PROBLEMS AND DILEMMAS

Addressing the rationale for constitutional revision, then, will require addressing all three aspects: the defence rationale, collective self-defence, and international cooperation.

Dilemmas of the Defence Rationale

Behind the arguments for defence is the rationale that governments, having the responsibility to defend the nation, must anticipate threats to the life, territory and sovereignty of the nation and the people, and develop the capacity to respond to those threats, stopping them through deterrence if possible before they eventuate.

While it may seem beyond question, this rationale like all others, is historically conditioned. It is conditioned particularly by the failure of policies of disarmament and appeasement in the inter-war years to avert the Second World War and by the success of deterrence in the Cold War. However, it should not be overlooked that Chamberlain and those who advocated appeasement in the 1930s were learning their own historical lessons. The July crisis of 1914 had shown that responding to perceived threats with deterrence could actually lead to conflict. As Garrett L. McAinsh points out:

none of the Great Powers had really wanted a general European War in 1914. The war appeared to have been caused not by some militaristic plot, but by the unwillingness of everyone concerned to back down in the crisis which preceded it... the lesson of history seemed to be that patience, compromise, even a willingness to retreat – in other words appeasement – stood a far better chance of preserving peace than did stubborn rigidity in the face of foreign provocation.[20]

The failure of Munich has been raised frequently in the postwar years, but we risk much if we learn the lessons of Munich[21] and forget the lessons of the July crisis.

Deterrence in the Cold War also cannot be seen as an unqualified success. It might be better to say that during the Cold War deterrence produced the second most damaging set of outcomes is that it possible to entertain – in terms of proxy wars, deep rifts in international society (as well as in many countries, and in domestic society), the development of massively destructive and indiscriminate weaponry, the proliferation of this weaponry around the globe and the lack of any guarantee that it will not fall into criminal or terrorist hands, the orientation of many parts of the economy towards military pursuits, and much else. The Cold War has had an extremely regrettable impact on the world and it should not be forgotten that for more than a quarter of the world's population, it is not over.

There are essentially two problems with the approach of anticipating threats and developing responses, namely that the threat perception itself may be erroneous and that the measures taken to respond to the threat may provoke even more serious problems than the ones they were intended to avoid.

Problems with Perceiving Threats

History is littered with examples of threat perceptions being erroneous.

Much of Australian history has been characterised by a fear of invasion, particularly of an Asian invasion. Numerically incapable of defending themselves, Australians have always sought the support of a strong ally – Britain until the Second World War, and since then the United States. To win the support of this ally, Australia has sent its own forces to that ally's wars (Sudan in the 1880s, South Africa in the Boer War, Europe and the Middle East in the First World War, North Africa and Europe in the Second World War, and since 1945 to Korea, Vietnam, the Gulf War, Afghanistan and Iraq). Australia has paid a very high price for its fear of invasion, yet there seems to be no evidence at all that Australia has in fact ever been in danger of invasion (except, of course, in the Second World War, but even then, Japanese attacks on Australia were more related to Australia's strategic significance than to a desire for Australian territory).

The domino theory is another case of a threat that was perceived as very real at the time but has been discredited in later years. This theory led the United

States into the Vietnam War, and the outcome was that Vietnam, Laos and Cambodia all became communist countries, the very situation that the United States had sought to avoid – in spite of the fact that, as Chandra Muzaffar points out in Chapter 4, Ho Chi Minh (originally a nationalist rather than a communist) modelled the first Constitution for independent Vietnam on the US Constitution![22]

As the case of the domino theory and the Vietnam War shows, erroneous threat perceptions can turn into self-fulfilling prophecies. In the early decades of the twentieth century, there was a widespread fear of what was called the 'Yellow Peril'. Insofar as this influenced the treatment of Japan at, and subsequent to, the Paris Peace Conference, and insofar as this treatment was a contributing factor in provoking Japan towards the confrontational expansionism that characterised its policies in the 1930s, this too became a self-fulfilling prophecy.

The fact that threat perceptions can be erroneous and can become self-fulfilling prophecies should be an important part of the debate in Japan about constitutional revision – especially when that debate revolves around threats to Japan. We may look at the domino theory and at notions of race wars and the 'yellow peril' as outmoded, quaint, erratic, biased, but these ideas seemed very real to the people who held them and were part of the dominant worldview for many decades. In any era, our perceptions of threats are always likely to be grounded in some degree of preconception and prejudice. Janeen Webb and Andrew Enstice argue, for example, that behind Australia's fear of invasion was the fact that Australians themselves acquired the land through invasion ('peoples who occupy land they or their parents have taken from its original inhabitants are likely to be keenly aware of the possibility of displacement in their turn').[23] They also mention a fear that atrocities committed against Chinese in Australia would provoke an invasion to take vengeance,[24] and that often fears were deliberately provoked by people with a political agenda.[25] In a book published in 1926 arguing that in the future Japan would invade Australia, Fleetwood Chiddell produces no evidence at all of actual Japanese intent towards Australia[26] but argues that since England undertook colonial expansion when the population and the lifestyle the people aspired to could not be sustained by the land available, Japan would clearly do the same thing (the 'same forces that made England a colonising Power are at work in Japan').[27] Clearly, our perceptions of threat can arise from many sources including projections from our own past wrongs, projections of our own style of reasoning onto others, and manipulation by people who have an interest in creating tension.

One area where our perceptions are particularly prone to be inaccurate is in determining the meaning of arms build-ups in other countries. For example, one piece of evidence Chiddell does give of Japan's expansionist intent is the strength of its navy:

> The indication of warlike purposes is so unmistakeable in the maintenance of a navy utterly disproportionate to the wealth of the country and to the range of territory it is required to defend, that the onus of proving harmless intent lies upon those who believe in it.[28]

Chiddell takes an immediate leap from the possession of a strong navy to 'warlike purposes.' However, there are numerous feasible explanations for the strength of Japan's navy. There was, even at that stage, an awareness of the possibility of war with the United States. Much of Japan's economic growth had been achieved in the area of armaments, particularly in the period from the Russo–Japanese War to the end of the First World War, and cutting back on arms production would have significant economic consequences. A further reason was the desire of the navy and the army to increase their strength in the domestic political scene. James Joll points to similar factors in the arms build-up that led up to the First World War.[29] The fact that these arms build-ups did constitute a factor in the background to war does show their seriousness. Whatever the intent, they create war potential and therefore constitute a threat. But the more accurately and comprehensively arms build-ups are understood, the greater the chance of dealing with them without provoking an escalating cycle of threat and counter-threat.

Responding to Threats – The Problem of the Security Dilemma

Responding to threats, either by building up defence capability or by entering into alliances, can create a security dilemma. Other countries perceive the arms build-up or the alliance as a threat. If their response is an arms build-up or an alliance of their own, then tensions mount. The outbreak of the First World War is often given as an example of the security dilemma, but there are more proximate examples. According to Don Oberdorfer, the nuclear threat that Japan now faces from North Korea is a response to such provocation: 'North Korea's nuclear ambitions date back to the 1950-51 Korean War, when it came under the threat of a nuclear attack by U.S. forces,' and to the 1970s 'when it was revealed that South Korea was engaging in a secret nuclear weapons program.'[30]

Another example may be the recent joint military exercises between China and Russia, purportedly carried out in response to the terrorist threat but considered by many to be a response to the increased American presence in Central Asia since September 11.[31] The very presence of US forces in Afghanistan and Uzbekistan has provoked a response that is seen as a threat by the United States and its allies – the very kind of escalation that emerges with a security dilemma.

Japan and the Security Dilemma

For almost sixty years, Japan has been protected from the security dilemma by the peace Constitution. Under the present Constitution, no Japanese government could carry out a belligerent act against another country. This has given Japan the opportunity to build up a very strong military without that constituting a direct threat to other countries. This is not to say that neighbouring countries do not watch Japan cautiously. But as long as Japan's Constitution is unchanged, Japan's military strength will not constitute a direct threat. This may have resulted in there being little awareness in Japan of the risks involved. While it is frequently mentioned that constitutional revision runs the risk of creating tensions in Asia, there has been little systemic and explicit discussion of the security dilemma in the mainstream press or in the public pronouncements of politicians in regard to the issue of constitutional revision.

Japan currently has one of the highest levels of military spending in the world ($42 billion in constant 2003 US dollars in 2004 according to SIPRI,[32] or almost $46 billion according to the CIA World Factbook,[33] thereby ranking fourth in the world according to SIPRI or third according to the CIA). If Article 9 is changed, if Japan becomes a country capable of military action overseas, then Japan's military potential will immediately come to constitute a threat to its neighbours of vastly different proportions than it does now. For the security and stability of the region, a change in Article 9 would constitute the equivalent of an instantaneous arms build-up of enormous proportions. An Agence France-Presse report on interviews conducted with security experts in Japan after one of the reports of the Prime Minister's Council on Security and Defense Capabilities concluded that 'Japanese moves to overhaul its "defense-only" security policy that could enable it to launch pre-emptive strikes on foreign missile bases will trigger a wave of unease across Asia' adding that 'Any suggestions that Japan is taking a higher military profile have unnerved China and other Asian countries that were invaded by Japan during World War II.'[34] If Japan's Constitution is changed, that in itself is likely to start an arms race in the region – with all the risks that that entails.

Dilemmas of Collective Self-defence

What would be the outcome for Japan of an arms race? The question is whether Japan could really compete – given China's population, resources and current economic growth, and Japan's aging population, declining birth-rate and dependence on imports? Although one goal of some who promote constitutional revision is to reduce Japan's dependency on the United States, it seems likely that abandoning Article 9 would actually increase that dependence. Indeed, why else would the United States be promoting a revision of the Constitution? Warren I. Cohen points out that the United States emerged from the Second

World War with a completely different attitude to that which guided it at the end of the First World War: this 'time they would create a world order conducive to the interests of the United States, which would allow it to increase its wealth and power, and carry its values to every corner of the globe.'[35] If there has been any change of this under the Bush administration, it is in the aggressiveness with which that goal is pursued. The United States would not be interested in a change in Japan's Constitution if it did not see such a change as a means to pursue this goal.

In spite of the prominent place that discussion of external threats has had in the debate on the Constitution, there is good reason to doubt whether that is really what is driving the decision making with regard to Article 9. There seems little reason to believe that Japan is more vulnerable to attack now than it was at the height of the Cold War. Further, it was not some external threat that gave rise to the current trend towards constitutional revision but the Gulf War and what was considered a lacklustre performance by Japan in pulling its own weight in ousting Saddam Hussein's forces from Kuwait. The limited participation of Japan in Iraq and Afghanistan has stimulated the discussion further. Both the historical context of the discussion and the pressure from the United States suggest that what is driving the movement towards constitutional revision is the plans the United States has for integrating Japan into its global strategy rather than the 'threats' that are proffered in the public forum in Japan.

Enhancing the level of Japan's participation in the alliance has long been a goal of the United States. Alan Renouf reports that in the negotiations for the ANZUS Pact in 1951 the United States proposed that Japan be included, one reason being that it would 'provide an international framework which would enable Japan to get around the anti-military provisions of the Japanese Constitution.'[36] More recently, the comments of Richard Armitage in Tokyo that Article 9 of the Constitution obstructs the Japanese–American Alliance,[37] the comments of Colin Powell at an Asia Society dinner in New York on 11 June 2002 about Japan contributing 'more to its own defense as well as to peace and security worldwide,'[38] and papers of various US think tanks promoting the idea that Japan should have a relationship to the United States like that of the United Kingdom[39] all indicate pressure on Japan to adopt a more pronounced international military role.

In Chapter 3, Nick Bisley refers to 'entrapment and abandonment' as the two risks entailed in alliances. Like the security dilemma, these are risks from which Japan has been protected by its peace Constitution. Australia's experience may be enlightening. Australia's defence relationship with Britain was one in which there was a great disparity in the strength of the alliance partners. There is a perception among Australians (reflected in such popular movies as *Breaker Morant* and *Gallipoli*) that Australian soldiers were not treated as equals to British soldiers in the Boer War and in the two World

Wars, and were sacrificed far more readily. Yet Australia had no option (or perceived itself as having no option) but to send its soldiers to these wars. Yet in Australia's hour of direst need, and indeed while Australian troops were still in Tobruk fighting for Britain, Britain decided to abandon Australia to the Japanese.[40] In the Second World War Australia was defended not by Britain but by the United States, and the United States protected Australia not because of any alliance, but because of the advantages it provided in terms of military strategy. It is not inconceivable that abandoning the peace clause of the Constitution would place Japan in a similar relationship with the United States that Australia had with Britain.

There is a third dilemma in alliances, and that is the question of how alliances affect other international relationships. How have Australia's relationships with England and the United States, and Japan's relationship with the United States, affected their relationships with other countries in Asia? This is taken up in other chapters and will not be dealt with here.

Dilemmas of International Cooperation

Collective self-defence and collective security are conceptually quite distinct. Collective self-defence refers to alliances in which countries agree to come to one another's aid in case of attack. Collective security refers to the wider approach to security spelled out in Article 51 of the UN Charter. 'International cooperation', on the other hand, is not a term with a specific definition. It is broad enough to cover all forms of cooperation including collective self-defence, collective security, and all forms of international collaborative activity from development aid and disaster relief to organising international sporting events. It does not necessarily mean global or even multilateral cooperation. Bilateral cooperation would still be international cooperation.

As used in the LDP's proposed draft, what exactly would it entail? Insofar as it implies military action, two important questions are (1) whether it would be restricted to UN Peacekeeping Operations or could include such things as humanitarian interventions, and (2) whether it would be restricted to UN authorised activities or could include activities not authorised by the United Nations. The importance of this distinction is clearly shown by the dispatch of the Self-Defense Force to Iraq – nominally to work for the reconstruction of the country but clearly in fact to support, albeit in a non-combat capacity, a unilateral military action by the United States that has not been authorised by the United Nations.

The experience of Iraq makes clear that even when the concepts are quite distinct, in reality there can be a great deal of ambiguity. At the beginning, the US attack on Iraq was, at least purportedly, an act of self-defence on the part of the United States, responding to a threat from Iraq's weapons of mass destruction and its links to terrorist groups. Thus, Japan's cooperation could be seen as a kind of non-combat form of collective self-defence. Since it has become clear that Iraq neither possessed weapons of mass destruction nor had close links to terrorists, there is no longer a defence basis for America's action in Iraq. The newer justification has become the promotion of democracy – making it, perhaps, a humanitarian intervention. This changes the nature of Japan's involvement completely. It cannot be classified under collective security since it is unauthorised by the United Nations. It is purely bilateral international cooperation, and shows the most likely direction of Japan's international activity if the LDP draft is accepted as the new Constitution of Japan. It seems clear that if the LDP's draft were currently in force, Japan's 'international cooperation' in Iraq would have involved direct participation in combat.

Even in terms of collective security and other forms of collaboration with the United Nations, whether constitutional revision is the best path for Japan's international cooperation needs to be seriously considered. Peacekeeping operations, which involve a force from outside entering into a situation, presume that the outside force can grasp the situation with sufficient accuracy to act effectively – that it can, for example, distinguish one party from the other (Tutsi from Hutu, Serb from Albanian, and so on). The experience that the United States had in Vietnam and is currently having in Iraq indicates the mess that an outside force can get into when it is not sufficiently able to distinguish friend from foe. Intervention also involves taking sides, and if the intervening force is seen as representing the United Nations or the 'international community' it runs the risk of creating long-term rifts in the world.

Japan's effective participation may not hinge on the removal of the peace clause. When the Japanese Self-Defense Force was preparing to go to Iraq, reports indicated that the Iraqis welcomed the Japanese Self-Defense Force precisely because of the peace Constitution. People understood that the Japanese were not coming to fight.[41] The Self-Defense Force does not appear to have maintained such a good relationship with the people, but first reactions indicate that the Self-Defense Force could have played a role that would be possible for no other military force. Rather than being a hindrance to its participation in peacekeeping, the peace Constitution may be an invaluable resource.

CONCLUSION

This chapter has focused on the issue of constitutional revision in Japan. However, the issues raised are relevant to all countries. The defence rationale described above remains widespread and goes fairly unquestioned. Can we really continue with this way of thinking? While the question of what to do about threats is an important one, there is another question equally important:

are we really going to do something that throughout the twentieth century led to enormous escalations in both the quantity and quality of arms, to the diversion of funding from uses necessary for human well-being to arms production, and, all too often, to open conflict? If one thinks of the difference in the weaponry that was used in the Boer War at the beginning of the twentieth century and the nuclear, chemical and biological weaponry that were available at the end, the question becomes clear. Can we really sustain, can we survive, another century of this kind of advancement?

We have seen throughout the Cold War and again in the period since the September 11 terrorist attack how prepossessing the kind of tension associated with arms threats and counter-threats can be. We have seen how that particular issue overwhelms most other issues. With the dire ecological problems the world faces, the continuing poverty of the Third World growing, refugee flows, urgent health issues, can we afford to allow tensions to emerge that will displace these issues as matters of concern?

Nevertheless, as long as there is even a possibility of a threat being real, can a country be asked to ignore it? If a country does not ignore it, how can it deal with the threat without falling into the security dilemma? At least since the end of the First World War, the need for a way of having an adequate defence without this defence constituting a threat to others has been recognised. The principle of collective security as promoted first by the League of Nations and later by the United Nations was seen as a means to achieve this. Foster Dulles, speaking of collective security, says, 'A by-product of that is that national forces are so combined with each other that no national force, alone, is a menace.'[42] However, this presupposes a certain parity among the different parties. When one particular country is a superpower with military strength vastly exceeding that of even the second most powerful country (indeed with 47 per cent of total global military spending[43]) then the equation is changed completely. The Cold War and the emergence of superpowers have undermined this basis for security. Nevertheless, the insight behind the idea of collective security remains valid – broad multilateral relationships rather than bilateral relationships with superpowers are likely to provide a more stable and equitable basis for security.

Pacifists have argued for disarmament as a means of reducing tension, but the experience of the interwar years has created such a distrust of disarmament that it is very unlikely that a great number of countries will accept this approach.

The discussion of this chapter however suggests that Japan has shown a way beyond the security dilemma. In spite of the fact that the country has a history of aggression towards its neighbours, and in spite of its high military spending, Japan is not seen as an immediate threat by its neighbours. Neighbouring countries are distrustful, but at least as long as Japan retains the peace clause in the Constitution, the degree of threat felt by neighbouring countries is qualified by the fact that Japan could not undertake any aggressive expansionism.

This suggests that the way forward could well begin by other countries also adopting a similar clause in their constitutions. At least in democracies with an independent judiciary where the rule of law can be effective, this would make a difference. It could be a feasible first step to reducing tension without creating qualms about vulnerability. Far from changing its Constitution, Japan could use its diplomatic influence to promote similar constitutional clauses around the globe.

NOTES

1. Note that Komeito does not take the same position as the LDP on the question of Article 9. The Komeito is in favour of an addition to the present Constitution to recognise the Self-Defense Force, but without removing the stipulations against possession of the means of war that exist in the current Constitution.
2. The distribution of seats in the lower house of the Diet after the September 11 election was: LDP 295, DPJ 113, Komeito 31, Communist Party 9, Social Democratic Party 7, other smaller parties 6, independents 19, for a total of 480. The LDP is somewhat weaker in the Upper House, with only 46 per cent of the seats. With its coalition partner, Komeito, it has 56 per cent, still not the two-thirds majority required for constitutional revision. The DPJ has 82 seats which gives very marginally a sufficient number of seats (33.8 per cent) to block constitutional change. Since the Communist Party and the Social Democratic Party, both opposed to constitutional reform, control 6 per cent of the seats, if the LDP seeks to have its draft passed by the upper house as it stands now it will have to compromise with the Democrats, whose proposals for constitutional revision focus much more on cooperation with the UN.
3. To become official, this draft will need the support of two-thirds of both the lower and upper house (the LDP draft, if accepted, will reduce this requirement to 50 percent for subsequent constitutional revisions), and then go to a popular vote where 50 percent of the vote is required.
4. The Constitution of Japan at jttp://list.room.ne.jp/~lawtext/1946C-English. html (sighted 6 September 2005); Liberal Democratic Party, *Shinkenpou Souan* [New Constitution Draft], at http://www.jimin.jp/jimin/shin_kenpou/shiryou/pdf/051028_a.pdf (sighted on 9 September 2005).
5. Asaho Mizushima, 'Kempouchousakai ha Kenpoudaikyuujou wo dou Atsukattaka' [How the Constitutional Review Committee Dealt with Article 9], *Houritsu Jihou* 10.77, September 2005, p. 50.
6. The Constitution of Japan.
7. The second paragraph specifies in a rather vague way that the Self Defense Army must carry out its responsibilities under the authority of the Diet, and the fourth paragraph requires that the structure and command of the Self Defense Army be determined by law.
8. Liberal Democratic Party, *Shinkenpou Souan*.
9. House of Representatives Constitution Review Committee, *Shuugiin Kenpou Chousakai Houkokusho* [House of Representatives Constitution Review Committee Report], April, 2005, p. 305, at http://www.shugiin.go.jp/itdb_kenpou. nsf/html/kenpou/houkoku.pdf/$File/houkoku.pdf (sighted on 12 September 2005). According to Kiyoaki Murata, in the process of writing the Constitution, the

phrase 'In order to accomplish the aim of the preceding paragraph...' was added by Prime Minister Ashida with the specific intent of restricting the meaning of the second paragraph to a relinquishment of the means of warfare as a means of 'settling international disputes', leaving open the possibility of possessing such means for the purposes of defence. Murata argues that both the English and the Japanese versions of the Constitution make this interpretation possible. This would make the Self-Defense Force consistent with the Constitution. Contrary to what Murata says, the English version does not allow that interpretation. However, there may be a slight difference in the English and Japanese versions, allowing at least the possibility of that interpretation from the Japanese text. See Kiyoaki Murata, 'Kenpou 9jou no Nazo: Makkasaa wa Nani wo Kangaete ita ka' [The Riddle of Article 9: What MacArthur had in Mind], in 'Seiron' Henshuubu, *Kenpou no Ronten* [Debated Issues of the Constitution], Sankei Shinbunsha, 2004, pp. 180–182.
10. Democratic Party of Japan Constitution Review Committee, *Minshutou Kenpou Teigen* [Democratic Party of Japan Constitution Proposal], 31 October, 2005, p. 2, at http://www.dpj.or.jp/faxnews/pdf/20051031181802.pdf (sighted on 12 September 2005).
11. Such recommendations were made, for example, in the committees of the two chambers of the Diet, see Mizushima, p. 50.
12. '*Kenpou ni Sensou houki wo*', *Motogaikoukan, Shuusen Chokugo ni Shushou he Shokan* ['Include Relinquishing War in the Constitution: Letter of a Former Diplomat to the Prime Minister'], *Asahi Shinbun*, 14 August 2005, available at http://www.asahi.com/national/update/0814/OSK200508130084.html (sighted on 31 August 2005).
13. Rebecca MacKinnon (CNN Tokyo Bureau Chief), 'Japan Feels N. Korea Long-term Threat', 2 September 2003, at http://edition.cnn.com/2003/WORLD/asiapcf/east/09/02/japan.defense (sighted on 3 September 2005).
14. Interpretations of the Constitution that do not recognise the constitutionality of the Self-Defense Force may give a broader listing of possible actions not recognised by the current Constitution, but at least when the Self-Defense Force and the right to self-defence is recognised as constitutional, pre-emptive strikes and exercising collective self-defence are the only two activities that are prohibited – that is, of course, in terms of defence. Participation in military activities of international cooperation will be discussed later.
15. 'Panel Backs "Flexible" Defenses, Arms Trade', *The Japan Times*, 5 October, 2004.
16. 126th Session of the Diet, 25 March, 1994, First Consulter Tomohisa Sakanaka, at http://kokkai.ndl.go.jp/SENTAKU/sangiin/126/1382/main.html (sighted on 7 September 2005).
17. See, for example Riichi Furugaki, 'Collective Self-defense for Japan', *CSIS Japan Watch,* May 2000, p. 1, at http://www.csis.org/media/csis/pubs/jw000501.pdf (sighted on 12 September 2005).
18. House of Councillors Constitution Review Committee, *Nihonkoku Kenpou ni Kansuru Chousa Houkokusho* [Report of Review on the Japanese Constitution], April 2005, p. 66, at http://www.sangiin.go.jp/japanese/kenpou/houkokusyo/pdf/honhoukoku.pdf (sighted on 15 September 2005). The report indicates that there were differences of opinion on whether this international cooperation should include the possibility of military action (since the two Diet committees represented the whole of the two respective chambers and not just particular political parties, differences of opinion are to be expected).

19. Liberal Democratic Party, *Shinkenpou Souan*.
20. Garrett L. McAinsh, 'Appeasement Policy', in Linus Pauling (ed.), *World Encyclopedia of Peace*, vol. 1, New York: Pergamon Press, 1986, p. 28.
21. MacGregor Duncan has shown that Munich itself was not a simple failure of appeasement – for Britain, it was a way of buying time to rearm and for Hitler, whose intention had been to take much more than just the Sudetenland, it was a failure, not an easy win that stimulated his greed. See Macgregor Duncan, *Munich: Reassessing the Diplomatic Value of Appeasement*, Woodrow Wilson School of Public and International Affairs, available at http://www.wws.princeton.edu/cases/papers/appeasement.html (sighted on 26 August 2005).
22. For a discussion of the significance and the dubiousness of the domino theory, see Alan Renouf, *The Frightened Country*, Melbourne: Macmillan, 1979, Ch 8.
23. Janeen Webb and Andrew Enstice, *Aliens and Savages: Fiction, Politics and Prejudice in Australia*, Sydney: HarperCollins Publishers, 1998, pp. 273–274.
24. Ibid., p. 136.
25. Ibid., pp. 143–144.
26. Fleetwood Chiddell, *Australia: White or Yellow*, London: William Heinemann, 1926. Chiddell does present some evidence of Japanese expansionist intent unrelated to Australia. Japan at the time did consider itself to be overpopulated, but sought to deal with this by increased opportunities for migration. Japan's expansionism was motivated by the desire to 'neutralise' the areas between itself and external threats (particularly Russia) as a means of protection and to gain access to resources. Population resettlement was a consideration, but a secondary one.
27. Ibid., p. 111.
28. Ibid., p. 117.
29. See James Joll, *The Origins of the First World War*, London: Longman, 1992, particularly Chapter 4 and Chapter 6.
30. Takashi Kitazume, 'Asian Security Symposium: Search for New Options Needed; Alliance lacks solidarity in handling North Korean nuclear crisis', *Japan Times Online*, at http://www.japantimes.co.jp/cgi-bin/getarticle.pl5?nn20050610d1.htm (sighted 19 September 2005).
31. 'China, Russia Start Joint Military Exercises', *China Daily*, at http://www.chinadaily.com.cn/english/doc/2005-08/18/content_470125.htm (sighted on 13 September 2005). See also *The Japan Times*, 19 August 2005.
32. Elizabeth Sköns, Wuyi Omitoogun, Catalina Perdomo and Petter Stålenheim, 'Military Expenditure', *SIPRI Yearbook 2005: Armaments, Disarmament and International Security*, Oxford: Oxford UP, 2005, p. 318.
33. CIA, *The World Factbook*, at http://www.odci.gov/cia/publications/factbook/index.html (sighted on 15 September 2005).
34. Tokyo (AFP), 'Japan Defense Shake-up Bound to Unsettle Asia: Experts', 5 October 2004, at www.spacewar.com/2004/041005074919.crngt2sb.html (sighted on 6 October 2004).
35. Warren I. Cohen, *The Cambridge History of American Foreign Relations, Vol. IV: America in the Age of Soviet Power, 1941–1991*, Cambridge: Cambridge UP, 1993, p. 3.
36. Renouf, *The Frightened Country*, p. 40.
37. Kyodo News International, 26 July, 2004, at http://www.findarticles.com/p/articles/mi_m0XPQ/is_2004_August_2/ai_n6268601 (sighted on 12 October 2005).

38. Colin Powell, 'June 10 Remarks at Asia Society Dinner in New York, 11 June 2002', at http://www.usembassyjakarta.org/powell7.html (sighted on 1 September 2005).
39. See, for example, Ralph A. Cossa and Brad Glosserman, *U.S.–Japan Defense Cooperation: Has Japan Become the Great Britain of Asia?*, Issues & Insights, Pacific Forum CSIS, 5(3), March 2005, pp. 19–20.
40. James Bowen, 'Japanese Military Aggression Exposes the Inadequacy of Australia's Defences', at http://www.users.bigpond.com/battleforaustralia/battaust/Austinvasion.html (sighted on 8 September 2005).
41. See *Asahi Shinbun*, Morning Edition, 20 January 2004, p. 38; Evening Edition, 9 February 2004, p. 18. See also *Chuunichi Shinbun*, 28 December, 2003, at http://www.chunichi.co.jp/iraq/031228T1411.html (sighted on 21 September 2005).
42. Dulles, State Department Press Release No. 168 of 1951, quoted in Renouf, *The Frightened Country*, p. 39.
43. Sköns et al., p. 319.

6. Can Japan Create a Basis for its Internationality?

Jiro Yamaguchi

Article 9 of the Constitution has been the most important norm in Japanese security policy for sixty years. The 'no war, no weapon' clause has created the image of a 'peace state' in both domestic and international society. However, since the end of the Cold War, the Japanese Constitution has been one of the country's most salient political issues. Both major parties, the Liberal Democratic Party and the Democratic Party, have proposed amending the Constitution in the near future. This chapter seeks to explain how constitutional politics has evolved since the Second World War and contemplates the fate of the Constitution. It seems likely that a new framework for Japanese security strategy will appear from debate on the Constitution. Since most Japanese were born after the Second World War, the old consensus around the idea of a 'peace state' (*heiwa kokka*) has dissipated, and given way to an active debate on amendment of the Constitution. The focus of this debate is of course Article 9. I do not argue here that Japan will return to a militarist state by amending Article 9, nor conversely that people will retain the pacifist ideal of Article 9. Various opinion polls indicate that the Japanese people still want to keep the 'spirit' of the 'peace Constitution' while hoping that Japan will play a more active role in international society. This chapter seeks to clarify different aspects of the debate about Article 9 and tries to explore what consensus can be formed in constitutional politics.

HISTORICAL BACKGROUND

The Japanese Constitution, which guarantees democratic political institutions and the protection of human rights, is typical for a modern democratic country. The first two chapters of the Constitution, however, are exceptional, and each is closely related to Japan's wartime defeat. Chapter 1, which deals with the status of the emperor, established partial continuity between the prewar and postwar state. In the postwar settlement, US leaders accepted the plea of the old guard that the emperor was indispensable for national integration even if deprived of political power, and sought to use the throne to keep Japan under US influence. Other countries in the allied forces, however, wanted to hold Hirohito responsible for the war and many Asian countries resented him as a symbol of invasion and colonial rule. As long as the United States wanted Japan to maintain the emperor system, it had to create a mechanism in the Constitution effectively to prevent Japan from becoming a military threat again. In order to sever postwar Japan completely from its prewar militarism, the American-written constitutional document renounced war and proscribed the maintenance of armed forces in chapter 2, Article 9.

Thus, the first two chapters of the Constitution are mutually dependent.[1] Chapter 2 was written to make chapter 1 acceptable overseas – particularly to those countries that had been invaded by Japan. If Japan had abolished the emperor system and truly become a democratic republic, it would not have needed Article 9 to regain the trust of international society. Without Article 9, the emperor's postwar status would have been unacceptable to Asian-Pacific countries. In this sense, Article 9 originated from a desire to preserve the emperor system in the postwar period.

Of course, not everyone welcomed the postwar Constitution. Political views on the Constitution can be divided into three distinct categories. First, pacifists, who formed a pro-Constitution group, interpreted Article 9 literally and strongly opposed rearmament. To use John Dower's phrase, they 'embraced defeat'[2] and attempted to safeguard the newly established peace and democratic reforms enacted by the American occupation. Paradoxically, they were largely socialists who took an anti-American posture during the Cold War. The second group comprised pragmatic conservative elites, who accepted the postwar Constitution, at least provisionally for the time being. They deployed Article 9 to resist American demands for rapid rearmament in order to avoid economically exhausting the country. They, too, 'embraced defeat' to some extent, because they considered the Pacific War a reckless venture by foolish military leaders. Prime Minister Ikeda Hayato (1960–1964) and politicians of his faction were examples of this type. Many of them were high-ranking civil servants of the Ministry of Finance or were otherwise involved in economic policy during the war. They negated the militarism of the 1930s and 1940s and hoped to rebuild Japan by economic development after the collapse caused by the war. They were ambivalent about the postwar Constitution. On the one hand, they were nationalistic enough to feel uncomfortable about the 'imposed' Constitution. On the other hand, they found Article 9 quite convenient to restrain military expansion and concentrate national resources on domestic economic development. The third group consisted of right-wing traditionalists, who felt humiliated by the postwar Constitution, and were intent on amending the Constitution, especially Article 9, at the earliest possible date.

Between 1945 and 1960, political conflict centred on the Constitution, with the emergence of the Cold War adding to the polarisation.[3] On the Left, political parties and trade unions mobilised popular opinion against rearmament and revision of Article 9. Employing slogans such as 'young men, don't take up arms again!' socialist leaders gained widespread public support for pacifism. On the right, conservatives were galvanised by changes in American policy towards Japan. As the Cold War intensified, the United States transformed Japan into a fortress on its Far East front. Japan was no longer a harmless democratic country but a junior partner of the United States in the conflict against the Soviet Union. When the Korean War erupted, Japanese leaders complied with US demands to create an armed force, but limited its size and military capability.

Once the occupation ended, conservatives advocated the elimination of Article 9 and the strengthening of the Self-Defense Force (SDF). The principal goal of the Socialist Party was to prevent the Constitution from being amended. It also advocated progressive social policies and demanded rapprochement with communist countries. Conservative forces united within the Liberal Democratic Party (LDP), which proclaimed its intention to craft a new Constitution written by Japanese to replace the one drafted by the Americans. The main pillar for the LDP was anti-communism. While the Socialists defended the postwar reforms in the late 1950s, the LDP sought to restore some of the elements of the prewar system.

This early constitutional dispute reached its apex in 1960 when the Kishi cabinet tried to amend the US–Japan Security Treaty and strengthen military cooperation between Japan and the United States. The Left feared that the treaty would lead Japan into war through its alliance with the United States. Prime Minister Nobusuke Kishi's aggressive posture enhanced these fears. Although Kishi managed to have the treaty approved by the Diet, he was obliged to resign as prime minister in the face of huge public protests. It was clear that most people were attached to the postwar regime and that constitutional revision was impossible.

The next prime minister, Ikeda Hayato, shifted the constitutional policies of the LDP. He virtually gave up on amending Article 9. Instead of elevating Japan's political status internationally, Ikeda concentrated on Japan's economic development.

During the 1960s, the LDP altered its interpretation of Article 9. The party claimed that Article 9 did not prohibit Japan from possessing the right of self-defence but did inhibit it from becoming a military power that could seek hegemony in the world. So long as the SDF did not go beyond defence, the force was deemed to be constitutional. The limited mission of the SDF was captured by a newly coined term, 'exclusively defensive defence' (*senshu bouei*). In this manner, an enduring postwar security framework was established in the 1960s. In order to distinguish the pro-constitutional sentiment in the progressive camp and the more *realpolitik* attitude among the ruling elites in the 1960s, I call the former pacifists and the latter pragmatists.[4]

In the postwar security framework constructed by the pragmatists, Article 9 and the security treaty were no longer contradictory. While Article 9 allowed Japan to maintain limited armed forces to deal with a small-scale invasion, the US–Japan Security Treaty complemented this defence. In this way, Article 9, the SDF, and the Security Treaty became mutually supportive.[5]

Conservative elites found Article 9 useful for pursuing an economically oriented statecraft. Article 9 served as an excuse to limit military spending and concentrate on economic growth. It also freed Japan from troublesome tasks such as contributing militarily to international conflicts. The pragmatists of the 1960s created the postwar security framework in the wake of the bitter confrontation between the pacifists and the traditionalists. In this sense, the postwar security framework affected a truce between these two groups. Traditionalists who pushed for full-scale rearmament, though, remained a minority throughout the Cold War period. The public came to accept the postwar security framework and strongly supported both Article 9 and the security treaty. Thus, the postwar security framework created a comfortable situation for Japanese policy makers. The United States, of course, was frustrated with the passive approach of the Japanese government to military commitments. However, the postwar security framework was so stable that all the United States could do was to urge the Japanese government to increase its financial support for US bases in Japan.

POST-COLD WAR EROSION OF SUPPORT FOR THE POSTWAR SECURITY FRAMEWORK

Japan, which had benefited more than any other country from the Cold War, was abruptly pushed out of its comfort zone when the long standoff between the United States and the Soviet Union ended. Japanese leaders were unclear about what security policy was best in the new environment. With the end of the Cold War, regional conflicts erupted one after another. Some of these conflicts including Iraq's invasion of Kuwait and ethnic cleansing in the Balkans, were regarded as clearcut confrontations between aggressors and victims. Issues such as peacekeeping and humanitarian intervention came to receive a great deal of attention internationally and Japan faced an entirely unfamiliar dilemma.[6] During the Cold War, Japan was generally able to take a relativist position vis-à-vis military conflicts, because the United States and the Soviet Union confronted each other (or fought proxy wars) in pursuit of their own national interest. Most Japanese people were convinced that non-involvement, based on Article 9, was a legitimate response to Cold War conflict. After the end of the Cold War, however, the Japanese government found it difficult to maintain such detachment. Article 9, which denied the use of Japanese military force to help settle international conflicts, seemed empty and meaningless when tyrants waged war and massacred civilians throughout the world. If Japan did not wish to contribute to international peace and justice, could it not be rightly accused of being selfish?[7]

Pacifist defenders of Article 9 faced a serious dilemma in the early 1990s. If they clung to their strict interpretation of Article 9, Japan could not contribute militarily to cooperative international missions even if these furthered international justice. Further complicating matters, the Socialist Party, had its first chance in forty years to push the LDP from power after a series of major scandals. The LDP's decline presented the socialists with a new window of opportunity, yet it also intensified their dilemma. So long as they stubbornly defended Article 9, they would be unable to participate in a coalition government. To resolve this dilemma, reformers within the Socialist Party proposed that the party recognise the legitimacy of the SDF and the Security Treaty, and promote the creation of a collective security system in East Asia. The new generation of baby-boomers in the Socialist Party had come from professional careers as lawyers and doctors before entering the political world in the early 1990s. They wanted to transform the Socialist Party from an ideological pacifist minority into a governing party. To this end, they thought it indispensable to take the pragmatists' approach to security issues. Their proposals, however, did not meet with party-wide consensus because many members continued to insist on a strict interpretation of Article 9. In particular, hardline leftists found a new identity in their pacifist ideology after the collapse of the Soviet Union. Grassroots organisations were still heavily influenced by this kind of dogmatic approach. The party was not able to settle on a policy change and would soon be overwhelmed by the rapidly changing political landscape.[8]

In the early 1990s, before the LDP momentarily lost power, the government began to expand the role of the SDF after recognising the limitations of Japan's contribution to the Gulf War. As Michael Seigel argues in the previous chapter, this constituted the beginning of the current wave of efforts to change the Constitution. In 1992, the Diet passed the International Peace Cooperation Law, allowing the SDF to participate in United Nations peacekeeping operations, and Japan dispatched troops to several countries (Cambodia, Mozambique, Congo, Angola, East Timor, and Golan Heights) in the 1990s. They engaged in humanitarian aid activities, including construction work, water supply, and medical care.

In the government's view, a more important task was to enhance US–Japanese security cooperation. The United States, for its part, sought to redefine the US–Japan Security Treaty in the 1990s, after the principal target of the alliance, the Soviet Union, collapsed. But as coalition cabinets rose and fell during the mid-1990s, Japan was unable to deal with the matter. A debate ensued about what security model was most appropriate, with some insisting that Japan should become a 'normal' state with fully fledged military forces and assume a more active political role in international affairs.[9] One party proposed that only civilian soft power be used to contribute to international society.[10]

This debate, however, was little more than a sideshow in the midst of political turmoil. The LDP recovered from its devastating experience during the time of non-LDP coalition government, regaining power after the 1996 general election. When it formed a coalition with the Japanese Socialist Party (JSP), it refrained from presenting a hawkish profile on security and historical issues. The LDP appeared to share the commitment to the peace Constitution as long as it needed the Socialist Party to regain power. In 1996, Hashimoto Ryutaro became prime minister and solidified his power by winning the election in October. It was then that a more earnest redefinition of the security treaty between Japan and the United States got under way. The Clinton administration, facing a number of security flashpoints around the world, would have been relieved to find a reliable counter-part in Japan.[11] The United States had long been pressing Japan to provide substantive support for the global deployment of US armed forces.

In the late 1990s, the Japanese government became far more responsive to US proposals for a redefinition of the alliance. The security treaty no longer simply guaranteed Japan's security but required Japan to support US global military strategy. The expectation now was that Japan would provide logistical support in accord with US wishes, thereby changing the *raison d'être* of the SDF. Its mission was no longer simply defence. It was now meant to operate globally even if it did not participate directly in armed conflict. In addition, the government had established domestic legal mechanisms to legitimise expansion of the SDF, including the so-called emergency laws.[12] After September 11, the United States attacked Afghanistan and Japan sent the SDF to the Indian Ocean to provide fuel and logistics. The SDF also dispatched a contingent to Iraq in support of the US occupation. Given that neither deployment was allowed under the existing legal framework of the SDF, the government and the LDP passed a provisional law to enable the SDF to be deployed far beyond Japanese territory. These policy changes make it clear that most mainstream conservative leaders had abandoned the postwar security framework and chosen instead to deepen Japan's commitment to American military strategy.

A significant change took place in the LDP in the late 1990s and early 2000s. Pragmatists either got old and retired from politics, or left the LDP during the process of party realignment in the 1990s. At the same time, sons and grandsons of the traditionalists, notably Abe Shinzo, came to play a more important role in the party. They were frustrated with the restrained posture that Japan had been taking on military issues. They wanted to make Japan a normal state with full-fledged military power. Pressure from the United States was an effective tool to break the legal framework that confined the SDF to self-defence. In addition, the abduction of Japanese citizens by North Korea provided a favourable climate for policy change towards greater military activism.

However, as indicated by the public's response to the deployment of the SDF to Iraq, there was no consensus on this policy shift. Public opinion was evenly divided on sending the troops to Iraq, although few politicians in the LDP opposed their deployment.

THE ENSUING CONSTITUTIONAL DEBATE

The Koizumi government argued that Japan could send troops to Iraq under Article 9. The Self-Defense Force, it was claimed, could go to safe regions to provide humanitarian aid. They could be sent to an active war zone because Article 9 prohibited the use of military force and denied the right of belligerency. The government insisted that the war in Iraq was over and that an incidental terrorist attack did not constitute an act of war.

For his part, Prime Minister Koizumi openly declared his wish to amend the Constitution in the near future. Both houses of the Diet established special committees for research on the Constitution, which submitted reports on amendment in 2005.[13]

The LDP was eager to enlist public support for revision. Kan Naoto, former chair of the Democratic Party, indicated his party's wish to submit a draft for a new Constitution by 2006. Once the most widely heard slogan was 'defend the Constitution'. Frequently heard phrases now included 'creating a new Constitution', 'supplementing the Constitution', and 'discussing the Constitution'. There appeared to be a growing consensus that Japan should have a new Constitution.[14]

The positions in the emerging constitutional debate coalesced around the same three groups that we have already discussed – pacifists, pragmatists, and traditionalists – except that now pacifists had almost disappeared from the political arena. As mentioned earlier, the Socialist Party drifted in the 1990s and was never able to find a new identity. When a neo-conservative party led by Ozawa Ichiro challenged the postwar security framework during the first North Korean nuclear crisis in 1994, the Socialist Party created a coalition government with the LDP to block Ozawa. But by doing so, the Socialist Party abandoned its strict interpretation of Article 9 and accepted the postwar security framework. As part of the pact with the LDP, the Chairman of the Socialist Party, Murayama Tomiichi, became prime minister, and the party officially recognised the legitimacy of the Self-Defense Force, exclusively for defence, and the US–Japan Security Treaty.

This change, however, was far from strategic. Murayama declared that the SDF was constitutional and that his party would firmly support the US–Japan Security Treaty. This abrupt conversion left many disillusioned. At the same time, it was not persuasive enough to attract independent voters. His conversion appeared to be an opportunistic excuse to justify the coalition with the LDP in 1996. The party split into hardline pacifists and pragmatists. The former remained in the party (which changed its name to the Social Democratic Party) and remained committed to their strict interpretation of the Constitution. The latter joined the Democratic Party. Therefore, the strength of the Social Democratic Party diminished with each election, and in the 2003 general election, it became a negligible minor party holding only six seats in the Lower House. It was barely able to maintain its seats in the 2005 Lower House election. The once popular socialist politician, Doi Takako, who embodied the pacifist position, took responsibility for the defeat in 2003 and resigned as the party's chairperson. The North Korean abduction incidents decisively undermined the credibility of the Social Democratic Party because it was known to have close ties with North Korea. In the eyes of many, the SDP could not be trusted to look after the security of Japanese people, and 'pacifist' came to mean 'unrealistic'.

The rapprochement between pacifists and pragmatists in 1994 did not significantly strengthen the pragmatist position. The majority of LDP politicians pretended to respect the spirit of the Constitution only in order to tame the Socialist Party. A number of traditionalists, notably former trade and industry minister Hiranuma Takeo, called themselves 'liberal' in negotiation with the Socialist Party when the two parties agreed to form a government. However, once the socialist party vacated the government benches, they returned to hawkish traditionalism and promoted the transformation of the security treaty. Having regained power, the LDP, especially after the late 1990s, tilted towards nationalism. Moderate conservative politicians, such as Miyazawa Kiichi who established the postwar security framework, had retired from the political stage. Another guardian of the postwar Constitution, Gotoda Masaharu, died in 2005. No successors emerged although a few pragmatists, such as Kato Koichi, were still to be found, but they were effectively marginalised by Koizumi. Conscious of the overwhelming power of the United States, prime ministerial candidates were reluctant to make US–Japan relations a big issue.

The traditionalists intent on amending the Constitution now dominate the debate. The right wing of the LDP succeeded in raising a new generation of politicians in the 1980s and 1990s. Many of these LDP traditionalists are sons or grandsons of 1940s and 1950s rightists. They wish to make Japan a prominent military actor and contest some of the democratic principles of the postwar Constitution.[15] They envisage a new Constitution that would define the emperor as head of state rather than a symbolic figure and a return to Japanese traditions and patriotic values (although this is not reflected in the new LDP draft proposal for a new Constitution). The traditionalists, who are also pro-American, take it for granted that Japan should follow the US lead in world affairs. They use pressure from the United States, for example Under Secretary of State Richard Armitage's 'requests' that Japan 'show the flag' and put its 'boots on the ground,' to mobilise public support for constitutional revision. On 21 July 2004, in a meeting with Nakagawa Hidenao, now chairman of the Policy Research Council, Armitage went so far as to demand that Japan revise Article 9 in order to deepen military cooperation with the United States.[16] Conservative politicians and senior officials of the Ministry of Foreign Affairs often visit Washington and meet high-ranking officials in the State and Defense Departments. Some of the Democrats have also joined the revisionists. In Washington in December 2005, Maehara Seiji, chair of the Democratic Party, proclaimed, in line with Armitage's demand, that Japan should amend Article 9 so that it could participate in collective defence. In this sense, the current movement for revision is based on a coalition between traditionalists and the United States.[17]

PROSPECTS FOR THE CONSTITUTION AND PRINCIPLES FOR JAPANESE NATIONAL STRATEGY

To understand the emerging pressure for constitutional amendment, it is necessary to consider the entire reform process since the early 1990s, from Hosokawa's political reforms to Hashimoto's administrative reforms and Koizumi's structural reforms.

The Japanese political system in its entirety was suffering from what might be called 'system fatigue,' as evidenced in a range of ills of increasing severity. From the early 1990s the Japanese economy stagnated for more than a decade with the government unable to implement effective policy for economic recovery. During this period of stagnation, stability and equality declined, and Japanese society became polarised. Unfortunately, the series of rapid reforms implemented during this period were not designed to address the pervasive structural problems underlying those ills. As a result, meaningful reform of the political system remains an unresolved and daunting task. By channelling the nation's political energies into superficial 'quick fixes,' advocates of reform ensured that the underlying problems would be with Japan for years to come.

The fact is that reform during this period was first and foremost the currency with which politicians and parties sought to buy the public's support, each trying to outbid the other. First, the electoral system, then the administrative apparatus, and now the Constitution have successively become the object of reformist zeal. From the mid-1990s, the ruling coalition held on to power not by carefully implementing reform but by waving the banner of reform as vigorously as it could, appearing busily occupied with systemic change. Large-scale reforms, including changes to the electoral system or the organisation of state ministries, are major issues for the politicians and bureaucrats affected and make for high political drama. They attract public notice and raise expectations that they will solve the nation's ills. (The politicians who direct these efforts become a magnet for the public's hopes for positive change.) Many Japanese were persuaded that the economic malaise and social disorder that had afflicted Japan would be solved once these systems were reformed, with little thought given to the need to audit the results or seriously grapple with enduring problems.

This was partly because the focus of reform kept constantly shifting.[18] In a flurry of reform in the 1990s, institutional change became an end in itself rather than the means to achieve substantial goals. Few in the political arena took the trouble to look closely at the policy content associated with the new political and administrative institutions.

To be sure, the electoral system and the administrative apparatus are important elements of the political system, but they have no direct bearing on the fundamental issues, namely, the clash of interests and the distribution of values in substantive economic policy. They are simply the internal rules that govern the activities of government 'professionals' – namely, politicians and bureaucrats. Unable to take on such substantive policy challenges as reducing the fiscal deficit, restructuring the social security system, or redesigning the country's economic structure, politicians constructed instead a shallow reform agenda divorced from the underlying social and economic realities, which helps to explain Koizumi's rapid political rise and his emphasis on structural reform.

Koizumi's prime ministership has overturned some of the most significant principles of post war Japanese politics. He has sent SDF troops to Iraq to support the American military operation and made frequent visits to the Yasukuni shrine as if intending to provoke China and Korea. Under his leadership, Japan became more closely entangled in US strategy, and more isolated in Asia. In domestic policy, Koizumi's structural reforms called into question accepted notions of equality and fairness in Japanese society. Under his leadership, efforts to amend the Constitution gained considerable impetus. The traditionalists ascribe all social ills to the Constitution. They argue that the law of the land has brought about a decline in morality and ethics and paralyzed the nation. Such criticism of postwar political values is closely related to their dissatisfaction with history education in postwar Japan. They insist that history textbooks overemphasise Japan's war crimes and that such education deprives children of pride and confidence in their society. Not surprisingly, the movement for constitutional change is closely related to history textbook revisionism. Placed in this context, excision of Article 9 amounts to justifying Japan's wartime and colonial past, which is bound to trouble Asian countries that still harbour fears of Japanese militarism.

CONCLUSION

Whether amendment of the Constitution is carried out or not is likely to depend on political developments after Koizumi's departure from the political stage. There are two possible scenarios. One is a continuation of the Koizumi line. If the next leader persists with Japan's deep involvement in US military strategy and difficult relations with East Asia, the nationalists will continue to agitate for constitutional change. But even if the Democratic Party were to join this project, the outcome would not be a foregone conclusion. A national referendum is necessary to amend the Constitution, and it is by no means certain that the electorate would agree to the amendment.

The other scenario is a modification of the Koizumi line. If a moderate leader such as Fukuda Yasuo or Tanigaki Sadakazu were to succeed after Koizumi, a greater effort would be made to improve relations with East Asia. If discussion on the Constitution proceeded in tandem with the easing of tensions in East Asia, a more constructive approach to Japanese security policy might be possible in the new circumstances.

Several problems would require close attention. If, in order to make a version of the second scenario feasible, the overall objective is to establish a sustainable East Asian region, then a number of preliminary tasks must be addressed.

The first task is to create a policy making framework that can develop national security policy on the basis of rational discussion. In the wake of recent political reforms, a two-party system based on broad consensus about the political and economic regime appears to be developing. Against this backdrop, debate on the Constitution should be handled in ways that do not disturb the international environment in East Asia. To this end, Japan should reaffirm at every opportunity the principle that Article 9 will be maintained even if the text of the Constitution is revised.

The second task is to resolve the dispute over the history issue. Japan should take the initiative in seeking a post-Second World War role, as Germany did in Western Europe. Japanese leaders should define the collapse of the Japanese Empire as the beginning of independence and autonomy in Asia. This point again relates to the Yasukuni issue. If the Koizumi line is modified by the next leader, Japan and other Asian countries may be able to develop a common understanding of the postwar period.

The third task is to share the experience of postwar Japan with neighbouring countries. Japan has had considerable success since the war in combining peace and prosperity with social stability. Now latecomers, notably China, are facing socio- economic and environmental pressures caused by rapid economic growth. Japan can, based on its own experience, provide, if not a model, at least useful advice on a range of relevant policy processes and mechanisms.

NOTES

1. Tetsuro Kato, *Shocho Tennnosei no Kigen (Origin of Emperor as Symbol)*, Heibonsha, 2005, pp. 217–226.
2. John W. Dower, *Embracing Defeat: Japan in the Wake of World War II*, New York: W. W. Norton & Company, 1999, pp. 225–253.
3. Masumi Ishikawa, *Sengo Seiji-shi (Postwar Political History)*, new edition, Tokyo: Iwanami Shoten, 2004.
4. Jiro Yamaguchi, *Sengo Seiji no Hokai (Collapse of Postwar Politics)*, Tokyo: Iwanami Shoten, 2004, pp. 3–9.
5. Jiro Yamaguchi, *Nihon Seiji no Saihensei to Higashi Ajia Kihan Chitujo no Sozo (Transformation of Japanese Politics and Creation of Norm of Order in East Asia)*, in Yasuaki Onuma (ed.), *Toa no Koso* (Vision of East Asia), Tokyo: Chikuma Shobo, 2000, pp.169–170.
6. Jiro Yamaguchi, 'The Gulf War and the Transformation of Japanese Constitutional Politics', *The Journal of Japanese Studies*, 18 (1), Winter 1992, 155–172.
7. Ozawa Ichiro, former secretary general of the LDP, for example, criticised the postwar pro-Constitution movement as selfish pacifism. See Ozawa Ichiro, *Nihon Kaizo Keikaku (Blue Print for Reform of Japan)*, Tokyo: Kodansha, 1993.
8. Jiro Yamaguchi, 'Tou Kaikaku no Seijigaku (Politics of Party Reform)' in Yamaguchi and Ishikawa (eds.), *Nihon Shakaito (Japanese Socialist Party)*, Tokyo: Nihon Keizai Hyoron Sha, 2003, pp. 130–139.
9. Ichiro, *Nihon Kaizo Keikaku*.
10. Masayoshi Takemura, *Chiisakutemo Kirari to Hikaru Kuni (Japan as Shining State Even if it is Small)*, Tokyo: Kobunsha, 1993.
11. Funabashi Yoichi, *Domei Hyoryu (Drift of Alliance)*, Tokyo: Iwanami, 1998.
12. Cf. Kenpo Saisei Foramu, *Yuji Hosei Hihan (Critique of the Emergency Law)*, Tokyo: Iwanami Shoten, 2003.
13. *Horitsu Jiho*, September 2005, special issue on the research committees on the Constitution of the Diet, provides the most convenient resources about these reports.
14. The latest opinion polls by the Mainichi Newspaper show that nearly 60% of the people agree that the Constitution needs to be amended while 34% disagree. Concerning Article 9, 62% oppose amendment while 30% agree to it. *Mainichi Shinbun*, October 5, 2005.
15. Some progressive citizens' groups have opened websites about the debate on the constitutional amendments in the Diet. They are useful to understand what the LDP Diet members are arguing in the committee. See http://members.jcom.home.ne.jp/web-kenpou/, and http://www.annie.ne.jp/~kenpou/index.html (sighted 18 November 2005).
16. *Asahi Shimbun (Evening)*, July 22, 2004.
17. Concerning proposals by conservative elites, see *Asuteion*, 62, 2005, special issue on 'Amendment of the Constitution from a forward-looking perspective'.
18. Yamaguchi, *Sengo Seiji no Hokai*, pp. 55–59.

7. Beyond the Japanese Constitutional Dilemmas*

Yoshikazu Sakamoto

THE ABANDONED PEOPLE AND THE RIGHT OF INDIVIDUAL SELF-DETERMINATION

The year 2005 was the sixtieth anniversary of the end of the Asia-Pacific War (1931–45). The phrase 'sixty years of the postwar' is widely used to mean 'sixty years since the end of the war' or 'these past sixty years'. However, the term 'postwar' itself is premised on a distinction between a 'pre-war' and a 'wartime'. Further, whereas in most of the victorious Allied nations the 'postwar' refers to the end of war, generally pointing to 'back to normality' or the restoration of continuous development, in Japan, perhaps more than in Germany, prior to the sixty years of postwar, there is the abysmal disjuncture between 'postwar', on the one hand, and 'pre-war' and 'wartime', on the other. For many Japanese people, it is this experience of disjuncture that is the starting point of 'postwar'.

Understandings of this disjuncture are etched into the diverse biographies of each individual. Although all these understandings cannot be lumped together and conceptualised in any simplistic, generalised way, they contain one important major difference: that is, the difference between the generation that lived through the war (or died during it) who more or less consciously viewed the war from some sort of social science perspective, on the one hand, and the slightly younger generation that was not baptised into social science, on the other. The former were those who, for example, had been exposed to the perspective of Marxism or liberalism, although these foreign ideologies began to be officially banned under the militarist regime as of the 1930s.

There are more than a few among the generation prior to mine who were capable of viewing the Emperor from an intellectual, if not critical, perspective.

---

* This article was originally published in the September 2005 issue of the monthly journal Sekai (The World). It was slightly abbreviated and translated for JapanFocus.org and Z-Net by Vanessa B. Ward, Victoria University of Wellington, New Zealand, and was later revised and updated by the author for inclusion in this book.

For those of my generation, (I was born in 1927) however, the Emperor was an object of worship as the living god. At least it was self-evident that the Emperor *should be* an object of worship. For instance, although I was not a so-called 'militarist youth' and had some personal doubts about the divinity of the Emperor, I was convinced that I *should* believe in the Emperor. This generation was deeply inculcated with the belief that there was something in Japanese tradition worth defending to the death.

There is a considerable gap between these two generations or, more accurately, these two mindsets. And letters such as those contained in *Kike wadatsumi no koe* (*Listen to the Voices from the Sea: Writings of the Fallen Japanese Students*) overflow with the agony of a soul that is ripped apart by these two mindsets. In this regard, people with the latter mindset who had no way of seeing things through the lens of social scientific analysis were probably in a position to die less painfully thanks to intellectual euthanasia.

For this latter generation, the break caused by the end of the war made them acutely aware of two things. The first was the experience of the *abandonment of people*. Many of them were to reach the age of conscription in the autumn of 1945, readying themselves for the imminent decisive battle for the homeland. They resolved to blow themselves up in front of the enemy's tanks and die an honourable death. They had convinced themselves that this was the only meaningful action left for them to take.

However, with the end of the war, they came to realise that, in reality, to die in this way would be nothing but a meaningless sacrifice. After the war, there was in any case a time when the state did not provide even the minimum rations needed to sustain the starving masses, and many of them had to cultivate a vacant plot and somehow eke out an existence as unskilled farmers.

Thus, the state that had prosecuted the war abandoned the people in the postwar just as it had in wartime. People of my age had believed, or thought they believed, that their very raison d'être was to go to the front in order to defend the country and protect the family. But with the state's betrayal and collapse, they fell into a state of aimlessness that was then described as *kyodatsu* (exhaustion and despair). At this time, though still lacking detailed knowledge, they had begun to suspect that what the Imperial Headquarters had called the 'honourable death to the last man' in the islands of the Pacific, including Okinawa, must have been the massive abandonment of soldiers and people on those islands. In fact, many of them witnessed the countless abandoned people who had been burnt out of their homes in the air raids. To give but one example, a hundred thousand citizens were killed overnight in Tokyo on 10 March 1945. Out of this was born a searing distrust for state authority and the ruling class that deceived the people through the manipulation of false myths.

Another conclusion drawn from the experience of those days was that it was not for the state but for the individual to decide how to live and how to die, that this was intrinsically a matter of *individual self-determination*. In the second half of 1945, radio programmes and newspapers began disclosing official lies about the historical truth of the war, which further strengthened people's conviction about their right to self-determination. They shared a feeling close to hatred, rejecting the state authority that had so unscrupulously sacrificed its people.

This was the *postwar starting point* of my generation. At the time this experience was shared by many who had sustained injuries beyond description. Though my experience was far less agonising and not worthy of particular mention, I have touched upon it here for reasons that will become clear.

The new Constitution was proclaimed barely one year after the war. This lent language in the form of legal norms to people's raw experience which was the point of departure for their life in the postwar era. In other words, denunciation of the state's wartime abandonment of its people came to be articulated as 'pacifism', and the people's right of individual self-determination as 'democracy'.

This was an impressive conceptualisation. In reality, however, the Constitution was not the starting point of the 'postwar'. On the contrary, the terms of the Constitution confirmed and reinforced their postwar starting point. As a set of rules by which the people could make state power accountable, the Constitution was, of course, of paramount importance. Yet, the *start of the postwar* not only preceded the Constitution in time, but it was also more fundamental as a philosophy and as an existential experience that breathed life into the Constitution.

Therefore, I myself have hardly ever used the phrase 'defend the Constitution'. Rather, as I pointed out in 1960, unlike the pacifism that emerged in the West, which was characterised by intense conflict with the dominant social and political system, Japan's constitutional protection movement was problematic in so far as it tended to depend on the Constitution which professes to represent the principles embodied in the dominant system.[1]

With the sixtieth anniversary of the postwar now behind us, it is timely to reflect on developments since from a critical perspective anchored in the immediate postwar experience just outlined.

THE PROBLEM OF THE DOUBLE STANDARD AND THOUGHT SUSPENSION

In the early postwar period up to 1947, occupation policy, the Constitution and people's existential reality coincided. For those who had been abandoned and discriminated against, especially workers, peasants and women (as well as Korean and other non-Japanese residents), defeat and occupation meant liberation.

However, from 1948, the intensifying Cold War spread to Japan and the phrase 'make Japan a bulwark against Communism' began to be used publicly by the occupation authorities. Instead of democratisation and demilitarisation, the tightening of anti-Communist controls and economic reconstruction came to the fore. Occupation policy started to take what was widely called a 'reverse course', the logical extension of which was the formation of the US–Japan security system. Thus intense conflict emerged between occupation policy, on the one hand, and the Constitution and the postwar starting point, on the other. In the early 1950s this conflict centred largely on the issue of the peace treaty.

Broad resistance to the 'reverse course' and the US–Japan security system took the form of a movement committed to peace and non-alignment in opposition to rearmament and US military bases. A spontaneous mass movement arose aimed at building, through its autonomous struggle from below, a peace-oriented democracy rooted in Japanese soil, opposed to the demilitarisation and democratisation through occupation, initiated by the United States from above. The convoluted process by which American ideology in the early occupation period was indigenised through resistance to later American policy in practice was an extremely important factor in the consolidation of Japan's postwar reform.

The movement against the 1960 Security Treaty combined opposition to the US–Japan military alliance and protest, grounded in the deep sense of crisis, against the anti-democratic stance taken by the Kishi Nobusuke administration. This was the period when the growth and mutual reinforcement of constitutional pacifism and democracy in Japan reached their peak.

From the 1960s to the 1970s and into the 1980s, while East–West peaceful co-existence was somehow strengthened internationally, Japan experienced a high rate of domestic economic growth. While tensions eased abroad (détente), the political tensions at home, which had polarised conservatives and progressives, also eased as economic conditions improved.

Two strands of experience underpinned these developments. The first was the initial postwar existential experience. This was the root of postwar pacifism. But the number of people who shared this experience gradually declined, or memory of it weakened, and inevitably their influence diminished. As a result, even though the movement to defend the Constitution based on this experience slowed the drift towards conservative constitutional revision, it gradually became harder to sustain.

Moreover, this pacifism was aimed at rebuilding and developing Japan by non-military means; but non-military development was equated with economic development. Prime Minister Yoshida Shigeru was the first of many to speak of 'putting public welfare before military affairs'. But insistence on prioritising public welfare was for all practical purposes merged into prioritising economic growth. In this sense, constitutional pacifism, precisely because it reinforced the ideology of economic growth which provided a rationale for becoming a great economic power, tended to lose its effectiveness as a viable source of policy alternatives. In this respect, too, it became difficult for it to function as anything other than a passive brake on gradual rearmament.

On the other hand, the postwar generation, having no direct knowledge of the catastrophic disjuncture of the immediate postwar, went through the unprecedented experience of high-speed growth. High rates of economic growth came to be viewed as the uninterrupted process by which life would continuously get better over time. As a consequence, this generation was a stranger to the idea that at some point in the future a collapse or rupture in history, such as war, might occur. Awareness of the unanticipated but possible breakdown of history was bound to diminish. There was by contrast a general satisfaction with the maintenance of the status quo, that guaranteed individuals' private interests. A state of affairs emerged in which the idea of constitutional protection amounted to little more than passive non-support for constitutional revision.

This passive brake and passive non-support for substantive revision of the Constitution continued into the 1970s and 1980s, and the severe tension between Article 9 of the Constitution and reality was thereby relieved. This situation eventually gave way to support for so-called 'constitutional revision through interpretation', that is *de facto* amendment. Within this, there emerged a double-standard regarding Article 9 and, in a large part of the population, what can be described as a suspension of thought to avoid having carefully to scrutinise the constitutional dilemmas.

First, Article 9 of the Constitution was originally intended to mean 'non armament'; but before long an attitude supportive of both the Constitution *and* the Self-Defense Forces became widespread.

In an opinion poll conducted by the *Asahi* newspaper three months after the outbreak of the Korean War in June 1950, 54 per cent of respondents endorsed the 'creation of an army', while 28 per cent opposed it. It is likely that this response related to the shock of the Korean War; but regardless of its motivation, it was far removed from the principles of Article 9.

An *Asahi* opinion poll conducted immediately following the conclusion of the San Francisco Peace Treaty in September 1951 found that 71 per cent of respondents favoured the formation of an army. At the time, the view that 'when Japan becomes independent it will be only proper for it to possess an army' had gained currency, which probably explains this result.

However, when the Hatoyama Ichiro Cabinet was formed in 1955 and set forth its platform for constitutional revision and Japan's independent Constitution making, the proportion of those opposed began to increase. An *Asahi* opinion poll showed 42 per cent of respondents were opposed to the revision of Article 9, and 37 per cent in favour – suggesting an increase in the number of people who perceived the emergence of an administration seriously intent on changing the Constitution. As high economic growth accelerated, an *Asahi* opinion poll conducted in August 1962 (when the Ikeda Hayato Cabinet was in office) found that those 'opposed to constitutional revision to permit an army' constituted 61 per cent, compared to 26 per cent in favour. In other words, the idea of constitutional protection once again enjoyed majority support.

The ensuing trend would prove problematic. Sato Eisaku formed a cabinet in autumn 1964. An *Asahi* poll conducted at the end of 1968 showed that 64 per cent of respondents were opposed to constitutional revision and 19 per cent in favour. However, at the same time, 64 per cent thought that military force was necessary. Moreover, 19 per cent indicated that 'the Self-Defense Forces should be strengthened', 55 per cent that 'the present force level is acceptable', representing a total of 74 per cent. Up to 40 per cent of respondents thought, 'the Self-Defense Forces are not unconstitutional' and only 17 per cent thought they were unconstitutional. In other words, the idea that the Constitution and the Self-Defense Forces were compatible began to be widely accepted – a position that continued to gain support steadily thereafter.

When debate over Article 9 of the Constitution emerged in the 1950s, the cardinal point of contention was whether or not the Self-Defense Forces were unconstitutional. Most constitutional lawyers, including academics, stressed the unconstitutionality of the Self-Defense Forces. Today, however, there are few professionals for whom the constitutionality of the Self-Defense Forces constitutes the primary focus of their opposition to constitutional revision. This intellectual ambiguity is probably a reflection of the changes in public opinion indicated above. In addition, the focus of recent argument for upholding the Constitution is no longer opposition to the Self-Defense Forces as such, but opposition to Japan becoming a country that can wage war, particularly abroad.

Moreover, although it is sometimes asserted that Article 9 of the Constitution is something that Japan can be proud of and that the rest of the world should emulate, not a few foreigners have responded to this by raising questions about the relationship between Article 9 and Japan's military expenditure, now the fourth largest in the world after the United States, Britain and France. They question the cogency of this justification for Article 9 in the absence of large-scale reduction of Japan's military arsenal. It is up to the Japanese nation to develop a clear and credible answer to this criticism.

A second and related problem pertains to the relationship between Article 9 and the Security Treaty. In 1959, the Tokyo District Court's '*Date* Judgement' declared that the stationing in Japan of American armed forces in accordance with the Security Treaty was unconstitutional in the light of Article 9. Then, in January 1960, the 'year of *Ampo* (the US–Japan Security Treaty)', the most popular response (out of various options available) to the question 'which is the best way to maintain Japan's security' was 'for Japan to be a non-aligned country' (35 per cent). The next highest preference was 'to depend upon the

UN' (24 per cent), making for a combined total of 59 per cent. Dependence 'upon the United States' attracted a mere 14 per cent of respondents.

However, as the era of high growth continued, this pattern changed. Ten years later (June 1970) when the security pact became legally terminable with one year's notice and the extension of the Treaty was being debated, 37 per cent of those surveyed responded to the question of whether or not to extend the Treaty by agreeing that 'Japan benefits from the Security Treaty', while 14 per cent disagreed. In the same *Asahi* poll, 55 per cent were opposed to revision of the Constitution, while 27 per cent were in favour, a likely reflection of the supportive climate for both the Security Treaty *and* the Constitution.

Third, the worldwide abolition of nuclear weapons was an aspiration of utmost importance for postwar Japan. In particular, anti-nuclear public sentiment drew strong support from the poignant appeals of Hiroshima and Nagasaki atomic bomb survivors. Reflecting this, the government *did* repeatedly advocate the abolition of nuclear weapons at the United Nations, invoking Japan's status as 'the only country on which atomic bombs have been used'. Yet, Japan also accepted the nuclear umbrella of the United States. This was best exemplified by Prime Minister Sato Eisaku who publicly declared in the Diet in 1968 that his government would preserve 'the three non-nuclear principles (not to possess, not to manufacture, not to introduce)', for which he was later awarded the Nobel Peace Prize. Significantly, his statement in the Diet was followed by the observation that 'we will preserve the three non-nuclear principles but rely on the power of America's nuclear deterrent'.

In 1975, the proportion of those who thought that 'the nuclear umbrella is necessary' gradually increased to close to 30 per cent, and in 1985, to 34 per cent. Opposition to nuclear visits, namely to the entry into Japanese ports of US nuclear-powered aircraft carriers and submarines continued; but as a result of the US–Soviet détente, questions about the nuclear umbrella gradually fell away even from media attention.

When India and Pakistan conducted nuclear tests in 1998, Japan expressed its opposition by imposing economic sanctions. India countered by reminding Japan that it was under America's nuclear umbrella. India, for its part, was not protected by such an umbrella, and therefore had the right to possess its own nuclear shield. While the Japanese government opposed nuclear proliferation, it had no effective counter to India's nuclear umbrella argument. Public opinion was yet to develop an articulate response on this question.

Fourth, since the time of the Peace Treaty, and again following the 1960 Security Treaty, opposition to US military bases gained in strength. However, although opposition to military bases on the mainland undoubtedly yielded some results, the concentration of bases on Okinawa came to be tacitly accepted. Underlying this double-standard is the ongoing discriminatory mentality that treats Okinawa as abandoned people, just as Okinawa was sacrificed during the Pacific War.

If people wish to defend the Constitution and to take steps towards the removal of US bases and the nuclear umbrella, they are required to address more seriously the task of devising a concrete alternative to government policy which persistently constructs a hypothetical enemy in East Asia. The aim must be to reduce tensions and armaments in the region, with a view to building an East Asian security community. Preservation of the Constitution is of course important, but defence of the Constitution alone is not enough.

Fifth, according to the Japanese government, 'UN-centrism', along with cooperation with the United States and friendship with Asia, has been presented as one of the three official pillars of Japan's postwar foreign policy. But what is Japan's real stance vis-à-vis the United Nations?

Immediately before the Gulf War, the PKO (UN Peacekeeping Operations) Bill was put before the Diet in 1991. In the end, while its status remained controversial, a contingent of the Self-Defense Forces was sent to Cambodia as part of the peacekeeping operation. At the time, 141 Socialist Party members of the House of Representatives announced their intention to resign if the Bill passed. Yet, though the Self-Defense Forces participated in the operation, they stayed on as Diet members. In other words, participation by the Self-Defense Forces in peacekeeping was somehow reconciled with Article 9.

Later, it became apparent that what the Japanese government meant by the term 'international contribution' was not so much cooperation with the United Nations as with the United States. Japan was quick to support America's Iraq War, although it did not have the approval of the Security Council. In contrast, even without Article 9, France and Germany refused to take part in the war. Subsequently, Japan committed much energy to gathering support for its bid for a permanent seat on the Security Council. Many of Japan's neighbours, however, suspected that the real motivation was not so much 'UN-centrism' as Japan's aspirations for great power status.

ON WHAT BASIS: 'THE CONSTITUTION' OR 'THE START OF THE POSTWAR'?

It follows, then, that Japanese pacifism based on the Constitution contains a double-standard. The actual state of the Constitution may be described as one of thought suspension whereby this contradiction, rather than being squarely faced, is left in a state of ambiguity.

This double-standard reflects more than the manifest political conflict between a conservative administration, on the one hand, and the socialist opposition parties or the constitutional protection movement, on the other. Rather the double-standard implicit in Constitution *and* Self-Defense Forces, Constitution *and* the US–Japan Security Treaty, and anti-nuclearism *and* nuclear umbrella has permeated the consciousness of much of the population. It is not accurate to describe this gap as one between professed and real intention. There are many for whom *both* standards represent real intention. Here, we are faced with a profound dilemma, which helps to explain the tendency to avoid thinking about it. Yet, precisely because it is not merely professed but also real intention, constitutional pacifism continues to this very day to carry considerable internalised potential.[2]

The problem is therefore not the Constitution *per se*. The gap between the prescribed standard and reality is not itself unusual. Given that the Constitution has been affected by the double-standard, the greatest difficulty arises from the fact that the call to defend the Constitution has often been made without any positive, concrete program on how to change the current actual situation and so overcome this double-standard. When it comes, for example, to Japan's security, if both the Self-Defense Forces and the US–Japan Security Treaty are unconstitutional and unacceptable, there must be clear and careful consideration of alternative options. To leave the problem unresolved and avoid thinking about it in effect amounts to acceptance of the double-standard by which the Self-Defense Forces and the US–Japan Security Treaty exist in tandem.

Conscious of the fact that the argument for unarmed neutrality advocated by supporters of constitutional protection contains an element of vulnerability, I was inspired to write an essay the year before the 1960 revision of the Security Treaty.[3] The proposal was that the Self-Defense Forces be placed under UN command and transformed into a UN police force stationed in Japan. If necessary, part of the force could be authorised to participate in UN peacekeeping operations. It was followed in 1982 by a further proposal involving the UN to a lesser degree.[4] It outlined what I called a 'three-layered defence' plan whereby the Self-Defense Forces would be reorganised into a coastal, air and territorial defence force for armed operations solely within Japanese territorial waters and air space. Its functions would be limited to providing a barrier against attack ('barriers' do not attack). In addition, a UN standby force would be constituted through voluntary enlistment of individuals and participation in UN peacekeeping operations. Further, programs for civilian non-violent resistance would be prepared.

In principle these proposals are based on the recognition of the right of self-defence, which is a corollary of the right to self-determination. The right to decide one's way of life (and death) naturally includes the right to resist in the event of unlawful aggression. This is a natural right that takes precedence over the Constitution or any positive law. What was suggested above is an attempt to institutionalise the combination of the three levels of the citizen's right to self-defence. These proposals may not be the best alternative. What is worrisome in the constitutional pacifist discourse is the fact that there has been too little debate on this issue.[5]

More important than the appropriateness of various concrete suggestions for alternative security systems are the three principles underlying the argument outlined above. First, if one is to defend one's own right to self-determination and self-defence, one must take care not to infringe the rights of others to self-determination and self-defence. This means not posing a threat to other countries, not being in any sense aggressive or offensive, and not triggering an arms race. It is worth noting in this context that nuclear weapons are inherently aggressive since they are never intended for use within one's own territory but only against enemy countries; and missile defences which will ultimately aim for the earliest possible assured destruction of enemy missiles will have the same capability as a missile offence targeted on an enemy military base.

Second, the defence system envisaged here should contribute not to single state-oriented security, but to a more peaceful world order through the promotion of arms control and disarmament. That is why this author has argued for some time that for Japan a key objective must be to cooperate with and participate in UN peacekeeping operations aimed at ensuring a cease-fire based on the consent of the parties in conflict and at facilitating and promoting their coexistence in peace.

Third, defence organisations should avoid actions or strategies that produce abandoned people, particularly at home, and should therefore, as a matter of principle, abolish ground combat units likely to turn Japanese soil into a battlefield. In this context, there is a serious problem in the 'National Protection Law (2004)' that ignores the danger of the abandonment of non-combatants resident in these small islands.

Having advocated the idea of constitutional protection and unarmed neutrality without probing this sort of defence scheme and its principles, the Socialist Party Prime Minister Murayama Tomiichi, after forming his coalition cabinet in 1994, abruptly switched to support for the Self-Defense Forces and the US–Japan Security Treaty. It was no accident that the rationale behind this change remained unclear to the end. Put another way, envisioning alternative policy options is critical to overcoming the double-standard.

By contrast, the incumbent conservative forces, in a final acknowledgement of the double-standard, have called for constitutional revision, by which they mean the return to 'a normal state'. Viewed against this backdrop, there is probably a limit to how much resistance can be expected to this sort of constitutional revisionism from the predominantly status quo-oriented constitutional protection movements, which have thus far tended to shy away from directly confronting the problem of the double-standard.

Without articulating a coherent solution to this problem, there can be no effective counter to the conservative Liberal Democrat strategy which is designed to entrench the revisionist mood among both media and public. This is why it is more important than ever to bring back to life what I define as the 'starting point of the postwar'. This starting point requires the development of a practical, step-by-step, persistent program to change the system of politics, economy, society and education, and so attend to the needs of people who have been the subject of discrimination and marginalisation. The aim must be to maximise individual self-determination. What needs to change *first* is not the Constitution but contemporary realities. In this sense, the current imperative is to *activate* the Constitution, not merely to preserve it.

The starting point of the postwar is not what took place sixty years ago; it is the act of probing thoroughly the ways of the Japanese state and charting a new direction for the future. It is the ever present point of departure, including that of our times.

As stated at the outset, the Constitution was not the starting point of the postwar. For the people of Japan, the present task is not to defend the Constitution on the basis of current provisions. It is to interpret the postwar history of the Constitution and to envisage its future on the basis of the starting point that precedes and breathes life into the Constitution, and in the light of the postwar existential experience of the people.

INSENSITIVITY TO ASIA'S DEMOCRATISATION

These problems have implications not only for the Japanese; they also affect how Japan responds to international voices.

Relevant here is the distrust and anger that Asian people feel towards Japan as it regresses to state nationalism and seeks to become 'a normal country'. Their misgivings find expression in two questions: what is Japan's attitude to its war responsibility? And, how does it understand its history?

At the start of the postwar, there was a deep and widespread popular sentiment that the responsibility of the Japanese leadership in causing the war and sacrificing millions of abandoned people should be rigorously addressed. This responsibility was conceived mainly in relation to Japan's domestic context.

The sense of responsibility for people other than Japanese was articulated not by the Japanese public but by the Tokyo International Military Tribunal. After the conclusion of the Peace Treaty, Japan did pay reparations to such countries as Indonesia and the Philippines in response to their claims. However, these reparations were made principally to states, not directly to the people who had suffered, and in fact served to support the oligarchic or dictatorial regimes prevailing at the time. While calling them 'reparations', Japan used its contributions to secure its markets in Southeast Asia.[6] In the case of South Korea in 1965, Japan paid the military regime of Park Chung Hee five hundred million dollars in grants and loans in what was termed 'economic cooperation'.

Following the end of the Cold War and the concomitant advance of democratisation in a number of Asian countries, the question of what to do about those Asian people who had been ignored and abandoned by Japan was taken up by victims of Japanese militarism, who had hitherto been silenced by dictatorial regimes. At issue here was compensation for, among others, the 'comfort women' and the victims of forced labour.

The response of Japan's conservative administration and a considerable section of the media was often insensitive to the voices of Asia's abandoned people. How can we explain this insensitivity? Even when the 'comfort women' continued weekly demonstrations over several years in Seoul and brought court cases in Japan, few seemed able to share their suffering. In contrast, a nationwide outcry has been raised against the abduction of a number of Japanese citizens by the North Korean intelligence agencies. The abduction is no doubt a criminal act. But the protest seems disproportionate given the disregard for the equally criminal abduction of hundreds of thousands of Koreans and Chinese by the Japanese militarist authorities. The question needs asking: are the Japanese indignant because of the humanity or nationality of the abductees?

The related question arises: does a culture exist in Japan that recognises universal norms, rules, or laws beyond the state by which individual human conscience is bound? The idea of universal norms akin to natural law in the West is barely evident in the Japanese tradition. At the core of Japan's traditional political ethos was loyalty to the emperor, the lord, the head of the family, and the kinship group. This explains perhaps why there is no culture beyond that of the state to support a sense of responsibility towards individuals and 'others' whom the Japanese state had turned into abandoned people. Without dwelling on the comparison with postwar Germany, Japan must acknowledge this as its problem.

A further difficulty is Japan's inability to recognise the renewed emphasis in much of Asia on Japan's historical responsibility as a trend connected with Asia's democratisation. The gap, for example, between activists in the South Korean democratisation movement who subsequently came to power and the Japanese conservative government is hard to bridge when it comes to the issue of historical responsibility for colonial rule and war.

Japanese amnesia when it comes to the feelings of the victimised Asian peoples is strikingly demonstrated by Prime Minister Koizumi Junichiro's audacious insistence that his annual visit to the Yasukuni shrine is no cause for official Korean and Chinese criticism. This, despite the fact that the fourteen principal war criminals are enshrined there alongside the Japanese war dead. His act has deepened distrust of Japan in the minds of neighbours and even in the West, and contributed to Japan's international moral isolation.[7]

In Japan, there are those who view objections to Japanese historical amnesia as evidence of Korean extreme nationalism and 'anti-Japanese education'. This perception is not well founded. As part of its effort to advance democratisation, the Roh Moo Hyun administration attempted to cleanse its own national history. It closely examined what is called 'pro-Japanese unpatriotic conduct', but it also scrutinised the actions of its own dictatorial administration and military regime. Criticism of Japan has emerged as part of the investigation of the wrongdoings and mistakes committed by Koreans, including the pro-Japanese collaborators. Postwar Japan has not engaged in comparable self-examination of its war responsibility, and finds it difficult therefore to understand the meaning of South Korea's behaviour. The Japanese have a tendency to read the issue in terms of 'Korean nationalism', Korea's 'anti-Japaneseness' and the barren territorial dispute over 'Takeshima' (Dokdo) islets, with little empathy for South Korea's autonomous, often agonising, efforts to democratise itself.

In the case of China, some aspects of the anti-Japanese demonstrations that occurred in the spring of 2005 remain unclear, but the evidence suggests that these were not demonstrations orchestrated by the government. It may well be that this was the first time since the formation of the People's Republic of China in 1949 that spontaneous protests, not mobilised by the government, occurred across different regions on such a wide scale.

As a sign of China's future direction, these demonstrations are extremely significant. The violence that occurred was undoubtedly regrettable, but when Japan called on China to take responsibility for the violence of the anti-Japanese demonstrations, the Chinese government moved to suppress the demonstrations, including non-violent protests. Japanese companies were thus able to continue with business as usual. Put simply, the Japanese became the beneficiaries of the Chinese government's sweeping oppressive actions. By contrast, at the time of the 1989 Tiananmen incident, many Japanese had expressed outrage at what they considered 'the injustice of cracking down on the student protests'. Now, however, they were calling on the Chinese government to suppress the demonstrations. When Japanese who present themselves as 'liberal democrats' critical of China's one-party rule are confronted with the 'anti-Japanese' character of the Chinese popular protest, they seem prepared to nip democratisation in the bud.

The question here is how seriously Japan should take the issue of democratisation in Asia – an issue which is not unconnected with how Japan approaches the task of its own continued democratisation, which remains very much an unfinished project.

To summarise, there is, if anything, a growing tendency to forget and to neglect Japan's historical role in invading and colonising Asia, a role that turned victims into abandoned people, and deprived them of the right of self-determination. This is but a symptom of a deeper ailment, namely postwar Japan's own lack of self-scrutiny and the shallowness of its democratic self-transformation.

EPILOGUE

The US occupation authorities drafted Japan's Constitution, and built a system designed to reflect the will of the Japanese people. Notwithstanding its espousal of democratic principles, the United States often ignores the UN Charter and by virtue of its unilateralist tendencies often thwarts the institutionalisation of a multilateralist world order. In other words, it is turning its back on institutions that enshrine a consensus based upon the right of the self-determination of peoples. In this sense, we are witnessing what may be termed 'America's global occupation' which far exceeds in scale America's occupation of Japan. Our task in the twenty-first century is to strive for democratisation on a global scale in order to give effect to the right of self-determination, particularly for marginalised and abandoned people anywhere in the world. This is not an easy task. But it is precisely the 'starting point of the postwar', which remains very much with us today.

NOTES

1. I have outlined this misgiving in 'The Psychology and Theory of the Peace Movement', *Sekai* (August 1962), reprinted in *Sakamoto Yoshikazu Shu* (Selected Works), Tokyo: Iwanami Shoten, 2004, vol. 3, pp. 241–245.
2. It is noteworthy that, according to a recent *Asahi* opinion poll, to the question, 'do you find any need for revision of the Constitution?', 55% of the respondents answered 'yes' and 32% 'no'. But of those who replied 'yes', only 9% did so 'because Article 9 is questionable', and the largest number, 38%, did so 'because new rights and institutions must be incorporated in the Constitution', presumably referring to 'the right to environmental protection' and 'the right to privacy protection' that have been advanced by some parties and media. Although 62% of respondents favoured the stipulation of the Self-Defense Forces in the Constitution, 64% of those who are for the stipulation preferred the addition of an amendment without changing the present provisions of Article 9, and 54% were against turning the Self-Defense Forces into an 'Army'. *The Asahi Shinbun*, 3 May 2006.
3. 'Churitsu Nihon no Boei Koso' (Ideas for Defending a Neutralist Japan), *Sekai* (August 1959); *Sakamoto Yoshikazu Shu*, vol. 3, pp. 116–129.
4. 'Nihon no gunjika ni kawaru mono' (An Alternative to the Militarisation of Japan) in *Gunshuku no seijigaku* (The Politics of Disarmament), Tokyo: Iwanami Shoten, 1982, pp. 149–162, reprinted in *Sakamoto Yoshikazu Shu*, 2004, vol. 4, pp. 191–203.
5. A recent rare exception is Koseki Shoichi, Maeda Tetsuo, Yamaguchi Jiro and Wada Haruki; 'Kenpo 9 jo iji no moto de, ikanaru anzen hosho ga kano ka' (What Sort of National Security System is Possible Under Article 9 of the Constitution?), *Sekai* (June 2005), pp. 92–109.
6. See, for instance, William S. Borden, *The Pacific Alliance: United States Foreign Policy and Japanese Trade Recovery, 1947–1955*, Madison: University of Wisconsin Press, 1984, pp. 203–204.
7. According to a recent *Asahi* opinion poll, 53% of the respondents 'know that the Tokyo International Military Tribunal existed but do not know what it did', and 17% 'do not know it existed'. In other words, 70% have no knowledge of or interest in the war crimes trial – a feature particularly notable among the younger generations. This provides a backdrop to Koizumi's insensitivity. At the same time, however, to the question, 'do you think that the Japanese have made full efforts to investigate and clarify for themselves why Japan

waged the war that ended about 60 years ago?', 18% replied 'yes', but 69% replied 'not enough'. Public opinion at present is, it seems, characterised by a degree of ambiguity and ambivalence, reflecting the double-standard, *Asahi Shinbun,* 2 May 2006.

A NOTE ON SOURCES

On the postwar experience of historical disjuncture see: John W. Dower, *Embracing Defeat: Japan in the Wake of World War II,* New York: W.W. Norton & Co./The New Press, 1999; and Mari Yamamoto, *Grassroots Pacifism in Post-War Japan: The Rebirth of A Nation,* London: Routledge Curzon, 2004.

On the Constitution (Article 9) and rearmament, in defence of constitutional pacifism see: Naoki Kobayashi, *Heiwa Kenpo to Kyousei 60nen* (a Sixty Year Symbiosis with the Pacifist Constitution), Tokyo: Jigakusha Shuppan, 2006; Tadakazu Fukase, *Senso Hoki to Heiwateki Seizonken* (Renunciation of War and the Right to Live in Peace), Tokyo: Iwanami Shoten, 1987; Asaho Mizushima, *Buryoku Naki Heiwa* (Peace without Force), Tokyo: Iwanami Shoten, 1997; Masao Kunihiro and Charles M. Overby, *Chikyu Kenpo Dai 9 jo* (Article 9 as a World Constitution), Tokyo: Kodansha International, 1997 – the authors characterise Article 9 as a model to be emulated globally.

On analysis of the political context see: Masahide Ohta, *Minikui Nihonjin: Nihon no Okinawa Ishiki* (Ugly Japanese: The Japanese View of Okinawa), Tokyo: Iwanami Shoten, new edition, 2005; Michael Schaller, *The American Occupation of Japan: The Origins of the Cold War in Asia,* New York: Oxford University Press, 1985; Robert E. Ward and Sakamoto Yoshikazu (eds), *Democratizing Japan: The Allied Occupation,* Honolulu: University of Hawaii Press, 1987 (Japanese edition: *Nihon senryo no kenkyu,* Tokyo: University of Tokyo Press, 1987).

On views of the Liberal Democratic Party's leaders see: Yasuhiro Nakasone and Miyazawa Kiichi, *Tairon – Kaiken/Goken* (Debate on the Constitution – Revise or Uphold?), Tokyo: Asahi Shinbunsha, 1997 – both authors are former prime ministers but take an opposite position on the issue of the revision of Article 9; Ichiro Ozawa, *Nihon Kaizo Keikaku* (a Blueprint for Reforming Japan), Tokyo: Kodansha, 1993 – the author is now the head of the opposition party, the Democratic Party; Ozawa has a unique idea to make Japan a 'normal country'.

On Japan's war responsibility to Asian peoples see: Shinichi Arai, *Senso Sekinin* (War Responsibility), Tokyo: Iwanami Shoten, 1995; and Tetsuya Takahashi, *Sengo Sekinin Ron* (On the Postwar Responsibility), Tokyo: Kodansha, 1999.

PART III

Japan and Australia: A More Constructive Role for Middle Powers

8. Japan, Australia and the UN Disarmament Agenda

Michael Hamel-Green

Japan, as the first country to experience nuclear attack and its radioactive aftermath, and Australia, which experienced the radioactive fallout from French atmospheric testing in the Pacific from 1966 to 1974, have both been important and active contributors to UN strategies and approaches to nuclear arms control and disarmament. Japan has been conspicuous in promoting peace and disarmament education, and in advancing annual UN resolutions calling for 'a path to the total elimination of nuclear weapons'. Australia has been instrumental in establishing a nuclear-weapon-free zone in its own South Pacific region, and cosponsoring the 1996 Comprehensive Test Ban Treaty initiated through a UN General Assembly (UNGA) resolution.

However, both countries are under pressure to modify their disarmament and non-proliferation policies in response to a number of proliferation trends and developments. The existing five 'official' nuclear weapon states on the Security Council (United States, United Kingdom, Russia, China and France) have now been joined by four other declared or undeclared nuclear weapon states (Israel, Pakistan, India and North Korea). Previous commitments not to use or threaten to use nuclear weapons are rapidly eroding amongst the major nuclear powers. The recent round of international non-proliferation talks at the 2005 Non Proliferation Treaty (NPT) Review Conference failed to achieve any agreed outcome, mainly due to blocking manoeuvres of the nuclear powers. Two of the major nuclear powers, especially America under the George W. Bush administration and Britain under the Blair government, appear to be favouring military or pre-emptive approaches to dealing with proliferation rather than diplomatic and arms control approaches. Finally, there continue to be a number of regional conflicts – in the Middle East, the Korean Peninsula, Taiwan, and Kashmir – where the presence of nuclear-armed states could turn a regional crisis into a nuclear holocaust, with devastating effects both regionally and globally.

In this worrying context, middle powers such as Japan and Australia have a critical role to play in mobilising the international community through the

UN and other fora to avert a new and potentially catastrophic nuclear race. As Allan Patience (see Chapter 9) notes, middle powers may not have the same impact on the international stage as the major powers but can exert significant influence through 'niche diplomacy' in regional and multilateral fora.

This chapter seeks to examine whether Japan and Australia are sustaining their previous arms control and disarmament commitments in the current arms control context, and to what extent their policies have been influenced or weakened by their respective bilateral security relationships with the United States. The chapter will look at key aspects of Japanese and Australian policies and voting at the UN over the period from 2000 to 2005, from the last year of the US Clinton administration and during the ensuing Bush administration up to mid-2005.

It will do this in a thematic way by taking some of the key areas of the current UN disarmament and non-proliferation agenda, and examining how Japan and Australia are responding to this agenda, particularly in areas where they may be in tension with their bilateral security partner, the United States.

UN DISARMAMENT AND NON-PROLIFERATION AGENDA

The current UN disarmament and non-proliferation agenda centres primarily on the historic international consensus that was achieved at the 2000 NPT Review conference. The Final Report of this conference, agreed to by both the nuclear and non-nuclear states, called for thirteen 'practical steps' towards disarmament and non-proliferation, as well as a number of other measures.[1]

These steps included such measures as: early ratification of the Comprehensive Test Ban Treaty (CTBT); a Fissile Material Cut-off Treaty (FMCT); commitment to the irreversibility principle; unequivocal nuclear weapon state (NWS) undertakings to work towards total elimination of nuclear arsenals; reducing operational readiness of nuclear weapons; and commitments to a diminishing role of nuclear weapons in security policies. The 2000 NPT Review conference further called for legally binding security guarantees to non-nuclear NPT and nuclear-weapon-free zone (NWFZ) members, and establishment of additional NWFZ zones as a matter of priority, particularly in the Middle East and Central Asia.

US Policy in Relation to UN Agenda

The United States, under the Clinton administration, supported this agenda at the 2000 NPT Conference, and was the first country to sign the CTBT treaty. However, even under the Clinton administration, it also became the first country to refuse to ratify the treaty when a Republican-controlled Congress voted against ratification; and was the country most likely to vote against or abstain from disarmament resolutions advanced by overwhelming majorities of UN members at the General Assembly, resolutions the US opposed or refused to support included on proposals for non-use security assurances to non-nuclear states, Southern Hemisphere NWFZ initiatives, prevention of an arms race in Outer Space, commissioning of a UN experts' study on missile proliferation, non-first-use undertakings, multilateral talks on a nuclear weapons elimination convention, environmental protection in drafting arms control agreements, and withdrawal of reservations on the Geneva Protocols against chemical and biological warfare. In total, of 50 arms control and disarmament resolutions widely supported and endorsed at the UNGA in 2000, the last year of the Clinton administration, the United States rejected or refused to support 28 per cent, the highest proportion for any country in the world (see Table 8.1).[2]

Circumscribed and selective as the US disarmament policies at the UN were under the Clinton administration, US arms control policies weakened dramatically under the ensuing Bush administration, which adopted a new 'triad' of responses in its 2001 Nuclear Posture Review (NPR).[3] The review called for a combination of non-nuclear and nuclear forces, active and passive defences, including ballistic missile defences, and research and development to develop, build and maintain offensive forces and defensive systems. In relation to nuclear weapons, it spoke of the need to retain nuclear forces 'for the foreseeable future', apparently reneging on the 2000 NPT commitment to work towards elimination. In accordance with this posture, the US abrogated the 1972 ABM Treaty, widely regarded as a cornerstone in maintaining nuclear stability by ensuring that strategic deterrence is ensured and that incentives to proliferate are reduced. In terms of nuclear testing, the United States has not only continued to refuse to ratify the CTBT but has moved to shorten periods to prepare for nuclear testing, started researching a high yield 'nuclear earth penetrator', and increased its spending on nuclear forces to a total of $40 billion annually, 50 per cent higher than during the height of the Cold War in adjusted-for-inflation costs. While the United States and Russia did negotiate a new bilateral Strategic Offensive Reductions Treaty (SORT) involving a reduction in their *deployed* number of strategic nuclear warheads to a total of 1,700–2,200 each by 2012, the treaty does not involve adequate verification nor the actual destruction of the warheads, which can be stored and potentially redeployed; nor does it prevent the deployment of tactical nuclear weapons. In the latter case, the United States continues to deploy over 400 tactical weapons in European countries in violation of the NPT prohibition of NWS deployment or transfer of nuclear weapons to the territory of non-nuclear states.

At the 2004 UN General Assembly (UNGA), the United States rejected or refused to support 36 per cent of the 56 disarmament and arms control resolutions supported by overwhelming majorities of UN member-states (see Table 8.2).[4] Not only did it reject or not support similar resolutions to those

Table 8.1 2000 UN GA-endorsed disarmament resolutions: negative

					P5		
UNGA 2000		F[1]	N[2]	A[3]	US	UK	FRA
55/29	Role of science in security and disarmament	97	46	21	N	N	N
55/33N	Reducing nuclear danger	110	45	14	N	N	N
55/34G	Convention on non nuclear use	109	43	16	N	N	N
55/31	Non use guarantee	110	0	54	A	A	A
55/33A	Missiles	97	0	65	A	A	A
55/33B	ABM Treaty preservation	88	5	66	N	A	-
55/33X	ICJ Ruling on NWs and negotiations	162	4	1	N	N	N
55/36	Nuclear prolif. in Middle East	157	3	8	N	-	-
55/33I	NWFZ in Southern Hemisphere	159	4	5	N	A	N
55/33C	Nuclear-weapons-free world	154	3	8	-	-	A
55/33K	Environmental norms in arms control	165	0	4	A	A	A
55/33R	Path to elimination	155	1	12	-	-	A
55/33T	Nuclear disarmament	109	39	20	N	N	A
55/33D	Review of NPT	163	1	3	-	-	-
55/33P	Conventional arms control at regional level	163	1	1	-	-	-
55/33V	Landmines ban	143	0	22	A	-	-
55/41	CTBT	161	0	6	-	-	-
55/32	Arms race in outer space	163	0	3	A	-	-
55/33U	Transparency in armaments	149	0	16	-	-	-
55/33J	1925 Geneva Protocol	163	0	5	A	-	-
Total negative					8	5	6
Total abstentions					6	5	5
Total supported					36	40	39
Total unsupported					14	10	11
Per cent unsupported					28	20	22

[1] F = for
[2] N = against
[3] A = abstain

votes and abstentions by nuclear and selected non-nuclear states

P5		Other Nuclear			Japan and Australia		New Agenda Coalition			
CHINA	RUS	ISR	INDIA	PAK	JP	AUS	SWE	NZ	MEX	BZ
-	A	N	-	-	A	N	N	N	-	A
A	N	-	-	-	A	N	N	N	-	A
A	A	-	-	-	A	N	N	N	-	-
-	A	A	-	-	-	A	A	A	-	-
-	-	A	-	-	A	A	A	A	-	A
-	-	N	-	-	A	A	A	A	-	A
-	N	N	-	-	A	A	-	-	-	-
-	-	N	A	-	-	A	-	-	-	-
-	A	A	A	A	-	-	-	-	-	-
-	A	N	N	N	-	-	-	-	-	-
-	-	-	-	-	-	-	-	-	-	-
A	A	-	N	A	-	-	-	-	-	-
-	A	N	A	A	A	N	A	-	-	-
-	-	A	N	A	-	-	-	-	-	-
-	-	-	N	-	-	-	-	-	-	-
A	A	-	A	-	-	-	-	-	-	-
-	-	-	A	-	-	-	-	-	-	-
-	-	A	-	-	-	-	-	-	-	-
A	-	-	-	A	-	-	-	-	A	-
-	-	-	-	-	-	-	-	-	-	-
0	2	6	4	1	0	4	3	3	0	0
5	8	5	5	6	7	5	4	3	1	4
45	40	39	41	43	43	41	43	44	49	46
5	10	11	9	7	7	9	7	6	1	4
10	20	22	18	14	14	18	14	12	2	8

Table 8.2 2004 UN GA-endorsed disarmament resolutions: negative votes

					P5		
UNGA 2004		F[1]	N[2]	A[3]	US	UK	FRA
59/62	Role of science	106	48	21	N	N	N
59/77	Nuclear disarmament	117	43	21	N	N	N
59/79	Reducing nuclear danger	116	46	18	N	N	N
59/102	Convention on non n-use	125	48	12	N	N	N
59/64	Non-use guarantee	118	0	63	A	A	A
59/67	Missiles	119	4	60	N	A	A
59/69	Multilateralism	125	9	49	N	N	A
59/75	Acceleration disarmament	151	6	24	N	N	N
59/83	ICJ	132	29	24	N	N	N
59/106	Non-proliferation in Middle East	170	5	9	N	-	-
59/514	UN conference on elimination	138	5	38	N	N	N
59/76	Path to total elimination	165	3	16	N	-	-
59/91	Hague Code	161	2	15	-	-	-
59/83	NWFZ in Southern Hemisphere	171	4	8	N	N	N
59/68	Environmental norms	175	2	3	N	A	A
59/78	Disarmament and development	180	2	2	N	-	-
59/84	Landmine ban	157	0	22	A	-	-
59/109	CTBT	177	2	4	N	-	-
59/65	Arms race in outer space	178	0	4	A	-	-
59/70	1925 Geneva Protocol	179	0	5	A	-	-
59/81	Fissile material cut-off treaty	179	2	2	N	A	-
Total negative					16	9	8
Total abstentions					4	4	5
Total supported					36	43	43
Total unsupported					20	13	13
Per cent unsupported					36	23	23

[1] F = for
[2] N = against
[3] A = abstain

Japan, Australia and the UN disarmament agenda 129

and abstentions by nuclear and selected non-nuclear states

P5		Other Nuclear			Japan and Australia		New Agenda Coalition			
CHINA	RUS	ISR	INDIA	PAK	JP	AUS	SWE	NZ	MEX	BZ
-	A	N	-	-	A	N	N	N	-	-
-	A	N	A	A	A	N	A	-	-	-
A	A	A	-	-	A	N	N	N	-	-
-	A	N	-	-	A	N	N	N	-	-
-	A	A	-	-	-	A	A	A	-	A
-	-	N	-	-	A	A	A	-	-	-
-	-	N	-	-	A	A	A	A	-	-
-	-	N	A	-	-	A	-	-	-	-
-	N	N	-	-	A	A	-	-	-	-
-	-	N	A	-	-	A	-	-	-	-
-	A	A	-	-	-	A	-	-	-	-
A	-	A	N	A	-	-	A	A	A	A
-	-	-	A	A	-	-	-	-	A	A
-	A	A	A	A	-	-	-	-	-	-
-	-	A	-	-	-	-	-	-	-	-
-	-	A	-	-	-	-	-	-	-	-
A	A	A	A	A	-	-	-	-	-	-
-	-	-	-	-	-	-	-	-	-	-
-	-	-	-	-	-	-	-	-	-	-
-	-	-	-	-	-	-	-	-	-	-
-	-	-	-	-	-	-	-	-	-	-
0	1	8	1	0	0	4	3	3	0	0
3	8	11	7	5	7	7	5	3	2	3
53	47	37	48	51	49	45	48	50	54	53
3	9	19	8	5	7	11	8	6	2	3
5	16	34	14	9	13	20	14	11	4	5

that were unsupported by the Clinton administration as discussed above, but it reversed the previous US support for the Japan-sponsored 'Path to Nuclear Disarmament' resolution, which embodied many of the 13 steps supported by the international community in the 2000 NPT Review Final Report, including the need for early CTBT ratification, the need for irreversibility in arms control measures, reducing tactical nuclear weapons, and a diminishing role of nuclear weapons in security policies. Other UNGA resolutions rejected by the United States included: multilateralism in disarmament and non-proliferation; FMCT negotiations; early CTBT entry into force; continuation of a moratorium on nuclear testing; and a proposed UN conference 'to identify ways of eliminating nuclear dangers in the context of nuclear disarmament'.

However, the divergence between the respective US and UN disarmament agendas was most dramatically revealed in the May 2005 NPT Review Conference, where, in concert with several other nuclear powers, the Bush administration ensured the failure of the conference by refusing to endorse any substantive new disarmament initiatives, and by insisting that there be no direct reference to the previously agreed thirteen steps embodied in the 2000 NPT Final Report. The extent of US hostility to the UN disarmament and arms control was highlighted in the US delegation's list of amendments[5] to the notable efforts of the Swedish Conference Chairman and New Zealand Chairman to Subsidiary Body I to achieve consensus through their respective chairman working papers.[6]

The US list of amendments included:

- Deleting a call for NWS to 'refrain from nuclear sharing for military purposes under any kind of security arrangements'. Presumably this was to allow the United States to continue to deploy nuclear weapons in European countries under NATO arrangements, despite this being in breach of Article I of the NPT prohibiting 'transfer of nuclear weapons' to non-nuclear states.
- Deleting the chairman's proposition in the context of concern over non-state actors acquiring nuclear weapons that the 'most effective way to address this concern is the total elimination of nuclear weapons'.
- Deleting a paragraph referring to the 'principles of irreversibility, transparency, verifiability and undiminished security for all'.
- Deleting reference to an 'unequivocal undertaking by the nuclear weapon States to accomplish the total elimination of their nuclear arsenals'.
- Deleting a call for 'more intensified progress by the nuclear-weapon States in reducing or continuing to reduce their non-strategic and strategic nuclear arsenals'.
- Deleting a call in paragraph 7 for NWS to restrict the deployment and operational readiness of nuclear weapons.
- Deleting a call in paragraph 8 for nuclear weapon states to 'forego any efforts to research and develop new types of nuclear weapons'.

- Deleting reference to early entry into force of the CTBT.
- Deleting reference to 'further steps to assure non-nuclear-weapon States ... against the use or threat of use of nuclear weapons'.
- Deleting reference to legally binding security assurances in time for endorsement at the 2010 NPT Review Conference.

In summary, the United States rejected almost all of the key aspects of the UN 2000 NPT Review Conference Final Report agreements on such matters as commitments to total elimination of nuclear weapons, the irreversibility principle, reducing tactical nuclear weapons, de-alerting, preventing development of new nuclear weapons, non-use security guarantees, and transparency. As such, the United States seemed prepared to risk the whole underlying 'bargain' on which the whole NPT regime rests: non-nuclear states foregoing nuclear weapons in return for NWS moving towards nuclear disarmament.

Since the NPT Review Conference operates on a strict consensus basis, the United States was successful in ensuring that none of the proposed principles or recommendations above were included as formal recommendations of the 2005 NPT conference, although the Swedish Chairman was successful in having an asterisk included in the final report that referred to the fact that the review 'will be conducted in the light of the decisions and resolutions of previous conferences'.[7]

AUSTRALIAN AND JAPANESE DISARMAMENT AND NON-PROLIFERATION POLICIES AT THE UN

Despite being closely allied with the United States through their bilateral security relationships, Australia and Japan have continued to support the UN agenda on disarmament and non-proliferation in many key areas, at least in terms of voting decisions and declaratory positions in UN fora. Their close relationship with the United States has not led to an indiscriminate alignment at the UN with the new Bush administration positions on arms control and disarmament. This is evident from the speeches, working papers and official statements of Australian and Japanese representatives at the 2005 NPT Review Conference, and from their respective voting decisions on key arms control and disarmament resolutions at the 2004 UN General Assembly.

At the 2000 UNGA, in the last year of the Clinton administration, Australia opposed or abstained from 18 per cent of the 50 arms control resolutions, while Japan abstained from 14 per cent (see Table 8.1).[8] By comparison, at the 2004 UNGA, where the Bush administration opposed 36 per cent of arms control and disarmament resolutions, Australia opposed or abstained from 20 per cent of the 56 widely supported resolutions, while Japan abstained from 13 per cent. In at least nine resolutions opposed or not supported by the Bush administration, Japan and Australia voted with the majority of UN members. Japan was slightly more willing than Australia to vote differently from America, supporting a further four widely supported arms control resolutions that were opposed or not supported by the United States and Australia.

Widely supported UN resolutions on which both Australia and Japan differed from America included: their continuing support for the Japanese-sponsored 'Path to the Total Elimination of Nuclear Weapons; environment protection in arms control agreements; disarmament and development; early ratification of the CTBT; preventing an arms race in Outer Space; support for Southern Hemisphere NWFZ initiatives; reaffirmation of the 1925 CBW Geneva Protocols; and negotiations on a fissile material cut-off treaty.

Focussing more closely on specific aspects of the UN Disarmament and Non-proliferation agenda, there is much commonality in the approaches of Japan and Australia. Indeed both countries submitted a joint working paper on strengthening the NPT at the 2005 Review Conference, including such measures as universalising the NPT, further nuclear arsenal reductions, reducing the operational status of nuclear weapons, and immediate FMCT negotiations.[9]

Australia[10] and Japan[11] were also active in advancing working papers on a range of other arms control measures, including NWFZ initiatives in Central Asia and the Middle East, strengthening the safeguards regime, and, in the case of Japan, reducing tactical nuclear weapons and universalising controls over missile proliferation.

Due to the overall failure of the 2005 Review Conference to reach consensus agreement on final recommendations, none of the Australian or Japanese proposals were incorporated in the Final Report,[12] but their submissions did confirm the two countries' commitment to pursuing at least some arms control and disarmament positions at variance with the stance of their US security partner.

Inconsistencies and Weakening Commitments

While Australia and Japan have retained many of their core commitments to the UN disarmament and non-proliferation agenda despite the Bush administration's lack of support or even opposition to many aspects of this agenda, and have demonstrated a willingness to actively pursue key elements of the UN agenda in recent and forthcoming UN fora, there is also evidence to suggest a weakening, even inconsistency, in some of their arms control and non-proliferation approaches and practices. In some instances, this is very obviously related to their security relationship with the United States, and wish to retain (or fear of losing) both US conventional and nuclear forces as an element in their own security posture. These areas of weakness or inconsistency may be assessed in a number of areas, including commitment to multilateral approaches, test bans, nuclear weapon reductions, non-use security guarantees, nuclear-weapon-free zone establishment, disarmament coalition building, and UN negotiation processes.

Multilateralism

Both Japan and Australia have regularly voted against the Malaysia-sponsored UN resolution on promotion of multilateralism in disarmament and non-proliferation. The 2004 resolution was supported by 125 states, with 9 opposed and 49 abstentions.[13] The resolution enjoins states to 'refrain from resorting or threatening to resort to unilateral actions or directing unverified non-compliance accusations against one another to resolve their concerns'. The failure of Japan and Australia to support the resolution reflected their own respective willingness to be part of the US-led unilateral non-proliferation military action in Iraq outside UN multilateral frameworks, and, indeed, their own perceived security dependence on the United States in the context of their alliances with the United States.

Both Australia and Japan have also become active participants in the US-led, John Bolton-designed, Proliferation Security Initiative (PSI), aimed at preventing the proliferation of WMD and their delivery systems at sea, on ground or in the air, using national military interception capabilities of the 11 participating states.[14] This initiative, like the Iraq venture, is outside the multilateral framework of the UN Security Council, and therefore risks the possibility of further unilateral action based on unverified intelligence information. It is not surprising, as the Australian deputy secretary of the Department of Foreign Affairs has noted, that 'the PSI enjoys only modest expressed support in the Asia-Pacific region where it is sometimes perceived as a self-interested coalition working beyond, or at the margins, of international law'.[15] Coupled with statements by the Australian prime minister indicating that he would contemplate Australian pre-emptive action overseas in cases of terrorist threats to Australia, the PSI could well be interpreted as having potentially adverse or even hostile implications for many Asia-Pacific countries.

In the case of both the Iraq intervention and the PSI, both Japan and Australia appear to be at odds with their declaratory general support for multilateral approaches in documents such as the UN Millennium Declaration, and to be undertaking military or pre-emptive actions that could well prove counter-productive both in the sense of increasing the motivation and determination of some state and non-state actors to acquire weapons of mass destruction and in the sense of undermining the conditions for successful confidence-building and negotiations on proliferation problems.

Nuclear Testing

While both Japan and Australia have been very vigorous in supporting and helping implement the verification machinery for the CTBT, and in diplomatic initiatives to secure an early ratification into force, they have been somewhat selective in their public appeals to the major holdout states. They have been appealing to India, Pakistan and Israel to observe a moratorium and join the CTBT but have been relatively quiet in appealing to the United States to do likewise, despite the US refusal to ratify the CTBT and its preliminary steps to resume testing of certain types of nuclear weapons. Japan has argued that it has urged the United States to ratify the CTBT at recent conferences of the US–Japan Commission on Arms Control, Disarmament, Proliferation and Verification in 2003–2004,[16] but these representations have not been in the public arena, and exert little pressure on the United States in terms of wider constituencies of the international community.

Nuclear Weapon Reductions

Japan and Australia are formally committed through their support of the 2000 NPT Review 13 steps to seeking unequivocal undertakings by NWS to accomplish the total elimination of their nuclear arsenals, the principle of irreversibility, and seeking further reductions in both strategic and tactical nuclear weapons. Both have praised the 2002 SORT agreement between the United States and Russia while at the same time urging both states to 'implement fully' the treaty and hold further consultations.[17] However, neither Japan nor Australia have publicly expressed concern about how the treaty breaches the principle of irreversibility in not actually destroying the non-deployed weapons, thereby permitting the parties to redeploy the weapons at some future date.

Further, both countries have supported and cooperated with the US missile defence (MD) program, with Japan even deciding in 2003 to purchase an initial MD system.[18] While such systems are presented as being 'defensive' and while it is understandable that Japan should seek to protect itself from potential North Korean missile attack, there is again the problem that such systems could actually be counter-productive in provoking an increase in nuclear weapons on the part of adversaries seeking to overwhelm the MD system and preserve their own deterrent capabilities. Since such systems are as yet unproven, it would be even more ironical if renewed nuclear arms races and proliferation were triggered by the mere perception of the supposed effectiveness of a MD system.

In the case of Australia, a further inconsistency is its unwillingness to support the Swedish/New Agenda Group resolution at the 2004 UNGA on accelerating the implementation of nuclear disarmament commitments.[19] One can only assume that the resolution's call for nuclear weapon states 'not to develop new types of nuclear weapons' was worded too strongly for Australia's taste, given the announced intentions of its security ally, the United States, to develop new earth-penetrating nuclear weapons.

Non-Use Security Guarantees

The 2000 NPT Review Final Document noted that 'legally binding security assurances by the five nuclear weapon states to the non-nuclear-weapon states . . . strengthen the nonproliferation regime'.[20] At present, the five nuclear weapon states have only agreed to the 1995 Security Council Resolution 984, which takes note of earlier unilateral statements by the nuclear powers undertaking not to use nuclear weapons against non-nuclear weapon states who are members of the NPT, but with important reservations that would allow them to use weapons in cases where any attack was made in alliance with a nuclear weapon-state.[21] The 2002 US NPR identified 'contingencies for which the United States must be prepared' to respond with nuclear strike capabilities, including against North Korea, Iran, Iraq, Libya and Syria, and in 2003 President Bush signed National Security Directive 17, which referred to the United States reserving the right to 'respond with overwhelming force – including through resort to all of our options – to the use of weapons of mass destruction against the United States, our forces abroad, and friends and allies'.[22] This certainly implies a willingness to use nuclear weapons in cases where American or allied forces were faced with chemical or biological attacks. The failure of the nuclear weapon states (with the exception of China) to make unconditional nuclear non-use or threat of use guarantees to non-nuclear members of the NPT can only serve to undermine the treaty and the whole non-proliferation regime which it seeks to establish and maintain. Indeed, the failure to provide such a guarantee may have been a major factor in the decision of North Korea to withdraw from the treaty, and the question of security assurances is a key concern of North Korea in the current Six-Party talks. The United States and other Western nuclear powers are legitimately and justifiably concerned about whether certain NPT members, such as Iran, are complying with the NPT and associated IAEA safeguards, but neglect to consider the role of their own nuclear sabre-rattling, and refusal to offer binding safeguards in creating the incentives for non-nuclear NPT members to develop covert weapons programmes in violation of NPT provision (not to mention, more prosaically, their failure to adequately fund and resource IAEA inspection systems).

Despite their endorsement of the 2000 NPT Final Report judgement that non-use assurances would 'strengthen the nonproliferation regime', and despite their declaratory support for non-proliferation objectives and reducing the role of nuclear weapons in security postures, both Japan and Australia have been very ambivalent in their attitudes to negative security measures. Neither country included such measures in their jointly sponsored 'Path to Nuclear Elimination' resolution at the 2004 UNGA,[23] and neither supported the NAM resolution on nuclear disarmament (59/77) which does include such a measure.[24]

NUCLEAR-WEAPON-FREE ZONE (NWFZ) ESTABLISHMENT

NWFZs are a measure that allows regional groupings to impose bans on nuclear weapon acquisition and stationing to prevent or reverse proliferation within their own region, and to secure binding non-use or threat of use guarantees from the nuclear weapon states. Nuclear Free Zone treaties are now in place for almost the whole of the Southern Hemisphere and adjoining regions, including Latin America (1967), South Pacific (1985), Southeast Asia (1996), and Africa (1996 signed but not yet ratified). A further Central Asian NWFZ treaty has been negotiated and is expected to be signed soon. While nuclear weapon states seem unprepared to give binding non-use or threat of use guarantees to non-nuclear states, the United States, United Kingdom, Russia and China have all indicated their willingness to give such guarantees to NWFZ parties, and, indeed have done so for parties to the Latin America NWFZ, and, with the exception of the United States, for the South Pacific NWFZ as well. The United Kingdom, indeed, argued at the 2004 NPT Prep Com that 'the way forward on negative security assurances would be through NFWZs', while the United States indicated at the 2000 NPT review conference that it would continue to offer such assurances through treaty-based NWFZs.[25]

Both Australia and Japan have voiced strong declaratory support for NWFZs and endorsed the 2000 NPT Final Report, which reaffirmed the 'important role' that the establishment of new NWFZs played in extending negative security assurances, strengthening the non-proliferation regime, and contributing to nuclear disarmament.

Australia, for its part, took a lead role in negotiating and successfully establishing the SPNFZ in the mid 1980s which now has guarantees from all the nuclear weapon powers except the United States, and will ensure that there is no resumption of testing in the South Pacific region (France having continued to test right up until 1996).[26] The Australian DFAT website notes that 'Australia has been a long-standing supporter of the creation of nuclear weapon free zones as a means of enhancing regional security and reinforcing the global nonproliferation regime'.[27] Further, in a report that Australia submitted to the 2005 NPT Review Conference, Australia linked 'further progress on nuclear weapon-free zones' to the NPT Article VI goal of nuclear disarmament.[28]

Japan, similarly, has stressed its strong support for NWFZ. At the 2004 UNGA, Japan, like Australia, supported the SHWFZ, CANWFZ, Mongolian and Middle Eastern NWFZ resolutions. Japan has also actively contributed to the negotiations on the Central Asian NWFZ, hosting two treaty-drafting conferences at Sapporo, Japan, in October 1999 and April 2000.[29]

Despite the impressive record of Australia and Japan in both declaratory and active support for NWFZ initiatives, there are some surprising inconsistencies in their respective approaches.

Australia, despite its vote in favour of the Nuclear-Weapon-free Southern Hemisphere 2004 UNGA resolution sponsored by Brazil, Mexico, New Zealand and a number of other members of existing NWFZ zones, refused to attend the Mexico-hosted April 2005 Tlatelolco Conference of States Parties and Signatories to Treaties that Establish Nuclear-Weapon Free Zones, attended by some 36 NWFZ countries. Ostensibly, Australia refused to attend because the Nuclear Weapon States were not officially invited to attend the conference, although they were indeed invited to attend as observers.[30] The Conference reached consensus on a number of measures to strengthen coordination mechanisms between NWFZs, including periodic meetings and information exchange, and was a forum for new groupings, such as the Central Asian NWFZ countries, to gain support for their initiative.[31] The Australian boycott of the proceedings suggested that despite its declaratory stance in support of NWFZs, and participation in its own regional NWFZ arrangement, it is not as serious as it might be in working with other countries to ensure the effectiveness of such zones, and in cooperating internationally to extend the zones and gain recognition and security guarantees for them from the nuclear powers. As in the case of other inconsistencies in the Australian arms control and non-proliferation stance, this is probably related to its sensitivities concerning its nuclear alliance partner, the United States, which voted against the 2004 UNGA SHNWFZ resolution.

Japan, for its part, did attend the Mexico NWFZ conference, and displayed a greater willingness than Australia to differ with America on this initiative. However, Japan has its own blind spot when it comes to NWFZs. It seems to support them everywhere in the world except in its own neighbourhood, Northeast Asia. Understandably, it is concerned that North Korea is developing nuclear weapons and has demonstrated missile delivery capabilities of being able to target Japan itself. It is also part of the current Six-Party talks with North Korea aimed at ending the nuclear crisis and de-nuclearising the Korean Peninsula. However, despite a number of NGO proposals on establishing a NWFZ to cover the whole region (the two Koreas and Japan), Japan has studiously avoiding embracing the zone concept for itself. From a security point of view, and in particularly in a context where Japan (unlike Germany) has not fully reconciled with its neighbours on Second World War issues, it would be unsurprising if both North and South Korea were not concerned about agreeing to de-nuclearise without Japan also agreeing to be part of a binding regional de-nuclearisation agreement. This is particularly the case when Japan has the advanced technology, large plutonium stockpiles, and missile capabilities to be able to develop a nuclear weapons capability within a short space of time, possibly even months. As one Japanese NGO has argued, the Six-Party talks present a historic opportunity to develop a regional NWFZ in Northeast Asia in a negotiating context that would include both the regional states and the three adjoining nuclear weapon powers (United States, Russia and China) who could effectively guarantee the zone and offer it the necessary positive and negative security assurances.[32] Despite this historic opportunity, Japan appears to want its nuclear cake and eat it too: insisting that the Korean Peninsula be denuclearised yet retaining the options of developing its own nuclear weapons and making use of the US nuclear umbrella. While it insists on retaining these options, there is obviously going to be an adverse effect on proliferation within the Northeast Asian region, with North Korea, and even conceivably South Korea, seeking to counter Japanese nuclear capabilities.

Disarmament Coalition-building

In a context where the nuclear 'haves' are resisting further measures to achieve nuclear elimination as required under the NPT Article VI, there is an obvious need to develop new and broader coalitions at the UN to lobby for and pursue this goal. One group of concerned countries, the New Agenda Coalition, have already launched this process. The group includes Sweden, Brazil, Egypt, Ireland, South Africa, and New Zealand, and has already been successful in gaining broader endorsement of key disarmament measures and initiatives at the UN, particularly at the 2000 NPT Review Conference. There seems sufficient commonality in the declaratory positions of Australia and Japan compared to the members of this group to warrant both countries aligning and cooperating with the NAC and making it an even more effective forum for pursuing disarmament and non-proliferation objectives in UN fora. However, both Australia and Japan have not joined this coalition, and Australia, as discussed above, has even declined to work cooperatively with members of other NWFZs. Again, it may well be sensitivity to how their US security partner might view such coalitions that has constrained both Australia and Japan; yet international progress on disarmament and non-proliferation may well depend on such coalitions, as was evidenced in the case of the 1997 Ottawa Convention on banning landmines.

UN Negotiation Processes

While both Japan and Australia have supported Canadian and other members' moves to break the deadlock in the UN Conference on Disarmament by establishing an ad hoc committee to begin negotiations on a fissile materials control treaty, Australia (but not Japan) has refused to support a Mexican resolution at the 2004 UNGA to hold a conference 'to identify ways of eliminating nuclear dangers in the context of nuclear disarmament'.[33] At a time of further proliferation, particularly in South Asia, the Middle East and Northeast Asia, it seems self-defeating to close off new possibilities for UN members to begin analysing and looking for means to avert new nuclear proliferation dangers. The refusal to support this motion is consistent with the current Australian Foreign Minister Alexander Downer's dismissal of the 1996 Canberra Commission on the Elimination of Nuclear Weapons, as a 'talk-fest' that was not an 'effective counterproliferation outcome' compared to the 'practical steps' that Australia was now taking in the form of the Proliferation Security Initiative, ballistic missile defence, and global counter-proliferation architecture initiatives.[34] It remains to be seen whether these coercive and military measures do in fact reduce rather than provoke further proliferation; and are indeed to be preferred to the recommendations of the Commission,[35] which, indeed, strongly influenced the Thirteen Step NPT agenda that Australia still purports to support.

CONCLUSION: STRENGTHENING DISARMAMENT AND NON-PROLIFERATION POLICIES

While Japanese and Australian declaratory policies and voting patterns on disarmament and non-proliferation approaches at the UN have not changed dramatically in the five years of the US Bush administration, and both countries continue to be active in making important contributions to the UN disarmament/ non-proliferation agenda, particularly in such areas as disarmament education, early entry into force of the CTBT, verification initiatives and resources, support for strengthened IAEA safeguards (particularly in the Asia-Pacific region), and support for immediate negotiation of a FMCT, the two countries also have major weaknesses or inconsistencies in their disarmament and non-proliferation policies and approaches. These are often in areas that bear directly or indirectly on their alliance relationship with the United States.

Both countries appear to be moving away, at least in terms of practical action, from multilateral and cooperative security approaches and agendas towards a US-led emphasis on coercive, selective and military methods of achieving compliance with non-proliferation norms and conventions, and missile defence system approaches to dealing with nuclear threats. This is evident in both countries' active involvement in the PSI interdiction, and in their active involvement in research on, and even deployment of (in the case of Japan), missile defence systems. Both countries, of course, continued to be involved in the 'Coalition of the Willing' intervention in Iraq in a non-UN sanctioned operation that was ostensibly aimed at eliminating a WMD threat (subsequently discovered to be illusory).

This new emphasis risks undermining cooperative security strategies to achieve disarmament and non-proliferation objectives, and may indeed prove to be counter-productive in the sense of generating such hostility in potentially targeted countries that the whole NPT treaty regime collapses.

Both Japan and Australia have been selective in the parts of the UN agenda that they have chosen to actively support, avoiding some of the key issues that underpin the long-term viability of the NPT regime, such as the need for non-use and non-threat of use guarantees from all of the nuclear powers, the importance of establishing a wider Northeast Asian NWFZ in Japan's own vicinity, the need for coalition-building amongst like-minded countries to achieve eventual nuclear elimination, insistence on irreversibility principles in nuclear power negotiations on nuclear weapon reductions, reductions and bans on tactical nuclear weapons, and bans on developing new nuclear weapons.

Alternative Approaches

If both countries are to work more consistently and effectively on disarmament and non-proliferation objectives, there are some key ways in which they might do this, assuming sufficient political will, NGO pressure and civil society support:

- working with countries like Malaysia and Costa Rica on their proposal, advanced at the 2005 NPT Review Conference, for a more integrated 'incremental-comprehensive' approach to nuclear elimination, involving a framework convention guiding all aspects of the nuclear elimination process, and phased steps within each of the key dimensions;
- working with other NWFZ member-states on cooperative mechanisms to strengthen each zone; these could well include cooperative and domestic measures to prevent non-state actors acquiring nuclear weapons or precursor materials, a step that would certainly be supported by the United States despite its current lack of enthusiasm for multilateral arms control;
- working to establish new NWFZs, particularly in Central Asia, Northeast Asia, Middle East, and Central Europe, particularly given the fact that the NWS are now saying that this may be the only mechanism under which they are prepared to offer binding non-use guarantees;
- working to convene a Fourth UN Special Session on Disarmament to reinvigorate the international arms control and non-proliferation process;
- supporting greater civil society involvement and education on disarmament and non-proliferation issues, particularly involving people-to-people contacts across borders and conflict lines;

- aligning themselves with and eventually joining the New Agenda Coalition of countries that was so effective at the time of the 2000 NPT;
- convening conferences of like-minded countries on key disarmament or non-proliferation issues, such as small arms transfers, chemical and biological weapons, CTBT implementation, threats of accidental nuclear war, and proliferation to non-state actors.

Japan and Australia are caught between traditional security paradigms of relying on a traditional military alliance with a nuclear-armed state, and the potential for eliminating nuclear and other threats through cooperative diplomatic initiatives, such as the Six-Party talks with North Korea, and broader cooperative security measures through the NPT and United Nations. There is a very real danger of provoking even greater proliferation and nuclear instability through coercive military response to nuclear threats, such as the intervention in Iraq and the PSI, while missile defence is only like to result in increases in nuclear arsenals rather than reductions. The governments of both countries need to put more energy and commitment into measures that risk peace rather than war.

NOTES

1. UN Department of Disarmament Affairs, *2005 NPT Review Conference*, Section 5 'Final Document of the 2000 NPT Review Conference', New York: UN, April 2005, at www.un.org/events/npt2005 (sighted on 3 September 2005).
2. Ibid.
3. Douglas Roche, *Deadly Deadlock: A Political Analysis of the Seventh Review Conference of the Non-Proliferation Treaty, New York, May 2–27, 2005*, San Francisco: Middle Powers Initiative, June 2005, pp. 18–25.
4. UN Department of Disarmament Affairs, *2005 NPT Review Conference*, Section 5.
5. US Government, *Amendments Submitted by the United States of America to the Chairman's Working Paper of Main Committee I (NPT/CONF.2005/MC.I/CRP.3) and the Working Paper of the Chairman of Subsidiary Body I (NPT/CONF.2005/MC.I/SB/CRP.4)*, Working paper submitted to 2005 NPT Review Conference, 2–27 May 2005, New York: UN, NPT/CONF.2005/WP.62, May 2005.
6. 2005 Review Conference of the Parties to the Treaty on the Non-Proliferation of Nuclear Weapons, *Chairman's Working Paper of Main Committee*, NPT/CONF.2005/MC.I/CRP.3, and *Working Paper of the Chairman of Subsidiary Body 1*, NPT/CONF.2005/MC.I/SB/CRP.4, New York: UN, May 2005.
7. Roche, *Deadly Deadlock*, pp. 4–6.
8. UN Department of Disarmament Affairs, at http://disarmament.un.org:8080/vote.nsf (sighted on 13 August 2005).
9. Japanese and Australian Governments, *Further Measures to be Taken to Strengthen the Treaty on the Non-Proliferation of Nuclear Weapons Regime (Main Committee I issues)*, Working paper submitted to 2005 Review Conference of the Parties to the Treaty on the Non-Proliferation of Nuclear Weapons, NPT/CONF.2005/WP.34, UN, New York, 19 May 2005.
10. Australian Government, Working papers and reports submitted to the 2005 Review Conference of the Parties to the Treaty on the Non-Proliferation of Nuclear Weapons, NPT/

CONF.2005/13, NPT/CONF.2005/2, NPT/CONF.2005/WP.10, NPT/CONF.2005/WP.15, NPT/CONF.2005/WP.16, NPT/CONF.2005/12, New York: UN, May 2005.
11. Japanese Government, Working papers and reports submitted to the 2005 Review Conference of the Parties to the Treaty on the Non-Proliferation of Nuclear Weapons, NPT/CONF.2005/WP.34, NPT/CONF.2005/WP.30, NPT/CONF.2005/WP.31, NPT/CONF.2005/19, NPT/CONF.2005/WP.34, UN, New York, May 2005; Japanese Permanent Mission of Japan to the UN, *Working Paper of Japan for Submission to the 2005 Review Conference of the Parties to the NPT,* New York: UN, May 2005.
12. 2005 Review Conference of the Parties to the Treaty on the Non-Proliferation of Nuclear Weapons, *Final Document,* NPT/CONF.2005/57, New York: UN, 2005.
13. UN General Assembly, *Resolution 59/69, 10/12/04,* UN Department of Disarmament Affairs, at http://disarmament.un.org:8080/vote.nsf (sighted on 13 August 2005).
14. Ian Anthony, 'Major Trends in Arms Control and Non-Proliferation', *SIPRI Yearbook 2004,* New York: Humanities Press, 2004, pp. 581–584; John Bolton, US Undersecretary of State for Arms Control and International Security Affairs, 'Proliferation Security Initiative: Statement of Interdiction Principles', remarks at Proliferation Security Initiative Meeting, Paris, 4/9/03, cited in Anthony, ibid., p. 582.
15. Gillian Bird, Deputy Secretary, Department of Foreign Affairs and Trade, Australian Government, 'Global Threats and Regional Challenges: An Asia-Pacific Perspective', address to the 2005 Australian Group Plenary, Sydney, 20th April 2005, at www.dfat.gov.au/department/050420_ag.html (sighted on 17 August 2005).
16. Peace Depot, *Japan's Report Card on Nuclear Disarmament,* Yokohoma: Peace Depot, April 16 2004, p. 10 (also at www.peacedepot.org).
17. Japanese and Australian Governments, *Further Measures,* p. 2.
18. Shannon Kile, 'Nuclear Arms Control, Non-Proliferation and Ballistic Missile Defence', *SIPRI Yearbook 2003,* New York: Humanities Press, 2003, pp. 655–656.
19. UN General Assembly, *Resolution 59/75,* 10th December 2004, UN Department of Disarmament Affairs, at http://disarmament.un.org:8080/vote.nsf (sighted on 15 August 2005).
20. UN Department of Disarmament Affairs, *2005 NPT Review Conference,* Section 5.
21. Jozef Goldblat, *Arms Control: The New Guide to Negotiations and Agreements,* London: Sage, 1994, pp. 109–112.
22. Claire Applegarth and Rhianna Tyson, *Major Proposals to Strengthen the Nuclear Nonproliferation* Treaty, Arms Control Association/WILPF at www.reachingcriticalwill.org, April 2005, p. 25.
23. UN General Assembly, *Resolution 59/76,* 16th December 2004, UN Department of Disarmament Affairs, at http://disarmament.un.org:8080/vote.nsf (sighted on 12 August 2005).
24. UN General Assembly, *Resolution 59/77,* 16th December 2004, UN Department of Disarmament Affairs, at http://disarmament.un.org:8080/vote.nsf (sighted on 15 August 2005).
25. Applegarth and Tyson, *Major Proposals,* p. 25.
26. Michael Hamel-Green, 'The South Pacific: The Treaty of Rarotonga', in Ramesh Thakur (ed.), *Nuclear Weapons-Free Zones,* London: Macmillan/St Martin's Press, 1998, pp. 59–80.
27. Australian Department of Foreign Affairs and Trade, at www.dfat.gov.au/security/nwfz.html (sighted 13 August 2005).
28. Australian Government, *Implementation of Article VI of the Treaty on the Non-Proliferation of Nuclear Weapons,* report to 2005 NPT Review Conference, NPT/CONF.2005/13, New York: UN, 28th April 2005, p. 1.
29. Peace Depot, *Japan's Report Card,* p. 65.
30. Medical Association for the Prevention of War, 'Australia Refuses to Attend International Meeting on Nuclear Weapons Free Zones', *Media Release,* 13th April 2005, at www.mapw.org.au www.mapw.org.au (sighted 18 April 2005).
31. Conference of States Parties and Signatories to Treaties That Establish Nuclear-Weapon-Free Zones, *Declaration for the Conference of Nuclear-Weapon-Free Zones, CZLAN/CONF/5,*Tlatelolco, Mexico, 26–28 April 2005, at www.opanal.org (sighted on 3 September 2005).

32. Peace Depot NGO Presentation at 2005 NPT Review Conference by Keiko Nakamura, Takao Takahara and Hiromichi Umebayashi from Peace Depot Japan and Wooksik Cheong from Civil Network for Peaceful Korea, *'Move Towards a Northeast Nuclear Weapon-Free Zone,* New York: UN, May 2005.
33. UN General Assembly, *Resolution 59/514,* 17th December 2004, UN Department of Disarmament Affairs, at http://disarmament.un.org:8080/vote.nsf (sighted on 18 August 2005).
34. Alexander Downer, Minister for Foreign Affairs Australia, *The Threat of Proliferation: Global Resolve and Australian Action,* Speech to the Lowy Institute, Sydney, 23 February 2004, p. 3, at www.foreignminister.gov.au (sighted on 23 September 2005).
35. Canberra Commission on the Elimination of Nuclear Weapons, *Report of the Canberra Commission,* Canberra: Australian Government Printer, August 1996.

9. Japan, Australia and Niche Diplomacy in the South Pacific

Allan Patience

INTRODUCTION

Writing over forty years ago, Richard Rosecrance proposed what was, then, a revolutionary idea: that Australia should commit itself to 'an eventual end to the absolutist character of White Australia and an even more cordial response to Asian nations'.[1] Just over a decade ago, Joseph Nye made an equally radical recommendation: that 'the Japanese have to develop broader foreign policy attitudes despite their past hesitation to think about a broader global role'.[2] Some progress has been achieved on these issues. For example, the White Australia Policy legislation was repealed in 1973. Recently Japan has begun adopting a more active role in international peacekeeping operations. But it has mostly been progress at a snail's pace. The result is that Japan and Australia remain estranged states in the Western Pacific, tolerated and ambiguously regarded by their neighbours; rarely are they warmly embraced by them.[3] To borrow British philosopher Michael Oakeshott's terminology, the friendships they elicit in the region are 'utilitarian', not 'dramatic'.[4]

This estrangement largely arises from the fact that Japan and Australia share a flawed belief that their separate but similar alliances with the United States mark them out as unique, even superior, in the region. The security alliance each has with its 'great and powerful friend' has led to widespread beliefs in both countries that because each has a special relationship with the United States, each therefore has a special standing in regional and global affairs. This arrogation of superior standing in world affairs, based on assumed American regard, puts the rest of the region offside. Japan and Australia's estrangement is further aggravated by other entrenched diplomatic and cultural contradictions.

Japan's complacent sheltering under the protection of the American security umbrella stems from the signing of the 1951 Security Treaty. Kishimoto notes that that Treaty 'determined Japan's postwar course and became the basis of the so-called mainstream conservatism that dominated Japanese government for decades thereafter'.[5] Gerald L. Curtis has warned that any disruption to the relationship with the United States 'might generate a bipolar division in Japan'.[6] Even today, Japan's security reliance on the United States remains at the forefront of Japanese politics.

The 'mainstream conservatism' highlighted by Kishimoto reinforces Japan's quixotic diplomacy (or lack of it) in failing to offer an adequate apology for its wartime atrocities. This remains a major diplomatic sticking point in the region – particularly for China, the two Koreas, and parts of Southeast Asia.

From 1901 up to 1973 Australia maintained the White Australia Policy, prohibiting the settlement of non-Europeans.[7] David Walker has explained that: '(f)or well over a century, Australians have had 'Asia' on their mind, nervously aware that their 'title deed' to the last continent available for mass migration was not impregnable'.[8] The fears, insecurities, and paranoia this has variously engendered in its foreign policy history have kept Australia at a diplomatic and cultural arm's length from Asia. Despite some attempts to address this hiatus in Australian security and diplomatic posturing, the gap remains.[9]

Indeed, right from the origins of self-government in Australia (the 1850s), *separateness* from Asia was energetically fostered, overwhelmingly on racist grounds. The original intention was to maintain Australia as an 'organic' part of the British Empire. This was fostered by an ideology of 'British race patriotism' that underpinned Australia's national identity, from the time of British settlement of the Australian continent. This ideology socialised Australians into believing that they were essentially white and British and therefore superior to the peoples and politics in the newly emerging states in their regional neighbourhood.[10] There are similarities in this race patriotism to Japan's wartime ultra-nationalism.

Residues of race patriotism continue shaping Australian consciousness towards Asia and in keeping Australians thinking of themselves as constituting a distinctive and therefore separate and special form of middle power in the Western Pacific. This is evident in the anti-Asian politics that flared into the public arena during the late 1990s when the Pauline Hanson–One Nation phenomenon entered Australian electoral politics.[11] And vestiges of it have surfaced most recently in demands by right-wing politicians to ban Muslim girls from wearing headscarves in Australian public schools.

In the late 1990s, assertions by the Australian prime minister of the so-called 'Howard doctrine' pointed to the persistent Australian separateness from Asia that alienates many Southeast Asian leaders. This doctrine claimed for Australia the role of a 'deputy' (on some readings, 'deputy sheriff') of the United States in the region. As the Chairman of the National Savings Bank of Malaysia noted, it appears to assume for Australia the status of 'an outpost of the Western world here in South-East Asia'.[12] During the 2004 federal election, Howard insisted that Australia had the right to strike preemptively at potential terrorist targets in the territories of neighbouring states, ruffling many diplomatic feathers in Southeast Asia. And in 2005 the Howard government had to be cajoled into signing the Asian Treaty of Friendship and Cooperation (a motherhood statement, if ever there were one) before an invitation to the East Asian foundation summit was finally – and grudgingly – forthcoming.

Australia's persistent cultural distancing from Asia – a distancing with serious diplomatic consequences – was set in concrete at the signing of the ANZUS Treaty in September 1951. Ever since, this has cultivated a 'dependency' on the United States that has 'helped to establish the psychological and intellectual environment so essential to the public acceptance of the political, economic and security nexus tying Australia to the United States'.[13] This belief system has remained ingrained in the face of events like New Zealand's expulsion from ANZUS in 1985 and the ending of the Cold War. It has resulted in 'uncritical support for American military-strategic policies'.[14] Such support is underlined by Australia's strong commitment to the United States in the war in Iraq and, earlier, in the Korean War, the Vietnam War, the first Gulf War, and the war in Afghanistan. The late Donald Horne's words are terribly apposite: 'Australians could get into the habit of seeing themselves as a virtuous, nervous but belligerent island in a threatening world'.[15]

In Australia, this means that former foreign ministers have operated on the assumption that 'Australia is a middle power'.[16] This mind-set has led to what has been appropriately described as 'the intellectual over-extension of Australian foreign policy',[17] resulting in an exaggerated understanding of Australia's significance in the region and globally.

That Japan has become an economic superpower, but without an offensive military capacity to reinforce its economic and diplomatic credentials, suggests that Japan also may be categorised as a form of middle power, in the way Evans and Grant employ the term. They assert:

> It is a matter of balancing out GDP and population size, and perhaps military capacity and physical size as well, then having regard to the perception of others.[18]

Yet by these very criteria, it is arguable that neither Japan nor Australia can be helpfully categorised as middle powers. Australia's population size (approximately 20 million people in a land mass almost as big as the United States) is not persuasively that of a middle power. Japan's military capacity remains hedged about by historical, constitutional and political limitations.

Australia and Japan would benefit from comprehensively rethinking their dependence on US security arrangements, in order to construct different middle power profiles in their region. The highly questionable (even bogus) middle power profiles they both have assumed – mostly explicitly (in Australia's case) and mostly implicitly (in Japan's case) – are a stumbling block to a more active and positive role in the region, particularly as it comes to grips with the rise of

China. Avoiding being drawn into a Sino–American conflict – say over Taiwan – should be as high a priority for both Japan and Australia, as it certainly is for all the other states in the region, including the United States and China themselves.

This means that Japan and Australia could each profit from aspiring to a different kind of middle power status in the Western Pacific. They can do this jointly, developing multilateral approaches to the small states in South-Western Pacific where they already play major aid donor roles. By starting in this region, they can lay the foundations for a stronger multilateralism in the Western Pacific generally that could be of real benefit to themselves, to all the states in the region, and globally.

WHAT IS A MIDDLE POWER?

The middle power concept in international relations is opaque and to some extent passé. It is redolent of nineteenth century diplomatic theorising that extolled 'great powers' which looked down imperiously on smaller, less significant states. Smaller states without the trappings of empire and without plausible imperial pretensions – Portugal, for example, Italy, and Belgium – nonetheless wanted to be taken seriously on the world stage. Size mattered, terribly, in this ruthless discourse.

States deliberately assuming a middle power profile today – like Australia – have inherited the status (or size) anxieties of less powerful nineteenth-century states scrambling to be taken seriously by their imperial counter-parts. Like smaller, ambitious nineteenth-century states, they are anxious to be seen as having consequence – gravitas – in world affairs. While not of 'big' or 'great' (much less of 'super') power status, they assume that, under certain circumstances, they can take a lead – or at least exercise influence. Along the way, they stress indicators like GDP, population size, military capacity, and the perceptions of others in laying claim to a form of middle power mystique in regional and world affairs.[19]

In an earlier study, Carsten Holbraad identified eighteen middle powers based on similar indicators: Britain, Canada, Australia, France, West Germany, Poland, Italy, Spain, South Africa, Nigeria, Brazil, Mexico, Argentina, Iran, Japan, India, China, and Indonesia.[20] The problem with this list is that these states have very little in common except their differences. It also ignores some smaller or less salient states (like Denmark and Norway) that play distinctive roles from time to time, giving them a legitimate placing in what might be seen as a middle power league.

In contemporary attempts to find new meaning for the middle power concept, some scholars have emphasised the 'like-mindedness' of certain (special) states, on issues like the freeing up of international agricultural trade.

Within this vague like-mindedness, these scholars think they have found a new meaning for the concept. For example, Australia, supported by Canada, has been successful in establishing the Cairns Group of agriculture-exporting nations and this group has been able to bring considerable influence to bear on some of the richer agriculture-exporters like the EC and the United States.[21]

Related to like-mindedness is the view that special (or intimate) relations with a great or super power confer middle power status. As noted earlier, it is taken for granted by Japan and Australia that their special alliance with the US superpower attracts to them middle power kudos – they are like fawning courtiers at the superpower court, convinced that they have all the attendant prestige from belonging to that court.

All of these factors come into play when the prevailing but historically redundant idea of a middle power is under consideration. For all this moving of theoretical deck chairs on the *Titanic* of international realism, the concept is without substance.

NICHE DIPLOMACY

There is a different way of looking at the middle power concept that is giving it new currency. In an intellectual climate that is fast shuffling off the limitations of a simplistic realism in international relations theory, this way of looking at middle powers gives the concept greater substance than all of the other features put together. This is *niche diplomacy*.

Niche diplomacy is an alternative form of diplomatic agency in a world where big power politics dominate the main game-plays, even as less mighty players come and go, sometimes to notable (even noble) effect. It comes into play when states successfully punch above their weight in persuading (or cajoling, or shaming) a cynical, materially-obsessed, self-interested rich and powerful world to act less selfishly or belligerently than it might otherwise act. There are flickerings of this behaviour in the interstices of Britain's championing of debt relief for poor African states in the 2005 G8 summit.

Andrew Cooper notes that niche diplomacy issues include 'poverty and human welfare, ecology and human rights'.[22] We must add to this the closely related issue of *governance* – that is, measuring the capacity and willingness (or incapacity and unwillingness) of states to adequately care for their own citizens. As the report of the International Commission on Intervention and State Sovereignty (ICISS) has noted:

> Millions of human beings remain at the mercy of civil wars, insurgencies, state repression and state collapse . . . What is at stake here is not making the world safe for big powers, or trampling over the sovereign rights of small ones, but delivering practical protection for ordinary people, at risk of their lives because their states are unwilling or unable to protect them.[23]

Cooper cites 'the article of faith that middle powers act as good multilateralists or international citizens, and that they have the national will and capability to act in this responsible fashion'.[24] He argues that:

> Under conditions of complexity and uncertainty, middle powers have a greater necessity and greater opportunities to act skilfully and quickly, and to do so in concert with a wide range of actors and institutions. While the expressions and targets of this diplomatic activity vary considerably, according to national capabilities and preferences, the features of niche-building statecraft provide a common core. In carving out these segmented areas of attention, middle power diplomacy provides a rich source of empirical innovation and conceptual insight.[25]

Cranford Pratt advocates 'a revived and refurbished middle power effort to engender greater responsiveness to the development needs of the Third World from the industrialised states of the West'.[26] He also notes that niche diplomacy 'employs the language of human rights in its discussion of contemporary obligations towards the poor and oppressed'.[27] It is a form of diplomacy that emerges from a growing sense that the world has to resolve some of the profound problems confronting the contemporary human condition right around the globe.[28] In its more realist forms, it acknowledges that 'free and sustainable [human] agency emerges as a major engine of development'.[29] There is growing support, right across the globe, for the view that such norms are beginning to achieve increasing acceptance in the emergent international civil society.[30]

Before ambitions for niche diplomacy by middle powers acting as what may be described as moral-states are written off as irrelevant idealism, it is as well to observe that Pratt's 'humane internationalism' has a realist edge to it. As we cope with the aftermath of the events of September 11, it needs to be realised that there are desperate people, in large numbers in the world, confronting the self-regarding rich states in ways that are destabilising the entire globe. The main source of this desperation is not a simplistically elaborated 'clash of civilisations' but a denial of access to reasonable living standards and ways of authentically living out complex identities in rapidly evolving circumstances. Middle powers acting as moral states can draw attention to the fact that there are real remedies for overcoming some of the worst causes of contemporary global conflict. If the rich world is not shown how to act responsibly and effectively, the consequences will be catastrophic.

Thus we can look to middle powers as potentially 'good international citizens' that engage in effective niche diplomacy to bring about a world that is significantly safer from threats from areas that produce desperately marginalised peoples, some of whom have been, are, and will continue to be, easily cajoled into becoming terrorists if the world doesn't change.

HELL IN PARADISE

Viewing Japan and Australia through this prism, we may usefully take stock of the contemporary South Pacific region. Both Japan and Australia have been variously intervening in the region for well over a century. Some of the most concentrated and destructive violence of the Pacific War was focused on the region. Thousands of South Pacific peoples were its innocent victims. As Crocombe notes:

> the Japanese invasion of 1941-45 and the Allied defence brought massive environmental destruction to some islands. Tarawa in Kiribati and Guadalcanal in the Solomon Islands were the turning points of the war on land. They and other battlefields saw unprecedented ruin, the evidence for which is still apparent.[31]

From the 1960s, newly independent states have been emerging within the region. They are all struggling with issues of 'governance' – many failing to develop and deliver even the most basic kinds of services and security to their citizens.[32] Japan and Australia are the two largest aid donors and trading partners for these states.[33] A great deal of Japanese and Australian tourism occurs in the region (for example, Fiji), and the South Pacific is host to a not insignificant volume of Japanese and Australian trade and investment. In the making of South Pacific identity in the world, Australia and Japan are major influences.[34]

The region is popularly caricatured as a tropical paradise. And yet there is a growing hell amidst the apparent idyllic tranquillity of the region. A range of governance problems have brought many states in the region to the brink of failing or ruined state status. This means that their infrastructure (roads, communications networks, schools, hospitals, police forces, government offices, and related facilities) are inadequate and collapsing and that human capacity is not able to deal with the developmental problems confronting them all. Many of them are struggling with problems created by global warming – for example some small island states face total inundation by the sea in the near future. Many are also in danger of being overwhelmed by a rapidly rising HIV/AIDS pandemic and other major health crises in the region.[35]

The South Pacific states are regionally grouped into the Pacific Island Forum (PIF). The PIF includes Australia, the Cook Islands, Micronesia, Fiji, Kiribati, the Marshall Islands, Nauru, New Zealand, Niue, Palau, Papua New Guinea, Samoa, Solomon Islands, Tonga, Tuvalu, and Vanuatu.

If Australia and New Zealand are removed from this list (as developed states), what are left are states shouldering some of the most intractable and worrying governance crises in the world today. One of the very worst of these is Papua New Guinea (PNG).[36]

PNG celebrated the thirtieth anniversary of its independence from Australia on 16 September 2005. The past thirty years have been pretty much a story of sustained decline, as law and order problems have erupted, the education system has been tragically run down, health services are collapsing in the face of looming pandemics, and state services have shrunk even as demand and need has been increasing exponentially. Corruption is endemic at all levels of government. The result is widespread collapse in the delivery of basic services, right across the country, and law and order breakdowns that are entrenched and worsening. There is an effective absence of the state in some parts of the nation. A recent report sums up the governance issues confronting contemporary PNG:

> Despite reform efforts, the country continues to record negative growth in GDP per person and has Human Development Indicators (HDIs) that are among the lowest in the world. With a population of 5.2 million (up by 36 percent since the last census in 1990) and a growth rate of 3.1 percent compared to 2.7 percent in the last decade, the Asian Development Bank (ADB) declared that over a third of the population now live in absolute poverty (ADB 2001). The country's average income fell . . . from a high of US$1,300 in 1994 to US$774 in the new millennium as the economy entered a non-transitory period of recession . . . The country's rural infrastructure has collapsed and macroeconomic management has produced unsustainable results with inflation oscillating between 9–21 percent within short-time ranges coupled with a public debt ratio of over 80 percent of GDP.[37]

Some argue that it means that PNG is on the brink of becoming, or has become, a failing state.[38] A failing state can be depicted as one that has neither the financial/material resources nor the human capacity to adequately care for its people. PNG probably fits this description. But it may equally be argued that PNG is becoming a ruined state. This is a state whose political elite has begun to cannibalise the state's resources for its own purposes. Contemporary Zimbabwe is a stark example of a ruined state. North Korea, Haïti, and Myanmar could also be placed in this category. With little to show for ending rampant corruption spreading throughout its political and administrative structures, PNG displays worrying evidence of heading in the ruined state direction.

AUSTRALIA AND THE POST-SEPTEMBER 11 ORDER IN THE SOUTH PACIFIC

Following Papua New Guinea's independence in September 1975, Australia adopted a determinedly hands-off policy towards its former colony.[39] Although it continued to provide a sizable aid package each year (approximately 30 per cent of the PNG government's annual budget, plus considerable project aid targeting perceived needs or responding to natural disasters), the over-all strategy of successive Australian governments was to leave PNG to get on with governing itself. This strategy did not falter in the face of the growing governance crisis in PNG. The central justification for this was that Australia, as the former colonial power, did not want to leave itself open to charges of neo-colonial interference in PNG affairs.

This aloofness from PNG was generalised to the entire South Pacific region. Australian prime ministers were only desultory attendants at Pacific Island Forum meetings throughout the last three decades of the twentieth century. During the Hawke – Keating governments, the focus was on multilateralising ties with East and Southeast Asia, within the framework of the ANZUS alliance. During the Howard government, the focus has been intensively on the US alliance and, more recently, an acceptance of the need for a more cooperative approach to East and Southeast Asia. It was as if the South Pacific was insignificant, even irrelevant to Australia's higher foreign policy concerns.

But then September 11 happened. As Gerard Henderson has expressed it, in ways that both shape and are shaped by the thinking in the Howard government:

> Without question, following 9/11, Australia finds itself as part of a new order. Rightly or wrongly, the US regards itself at war with Islamism but not, of course, with the Muslim faith. This view is shared, to a degree, by the governments headed by Tony Blair and John Howard.[40]

The Howard government responded swiftly to this 'new order' by becoming preoccupied with what it perceived to be mounting terrorist threats as it committed itself more deeply to the United States' international war against terrorism – first in Afghanistan, then in Iraq. With the Bali bombings in 2003, and the bomb attack at the entrance of the Australian Embassy in Jakarta in 2004, Australian concerns about terrorism becoming a potent reality in the region began to intensify. It is also noteworthy that Australia suddenly began to feel conveniently responsible for security in the South Pacific just as pressure increased from the Bush administration for Australia to become more deeply involved in the Iraq war. It was perhaps easier to rebuff American advances if you could show you had a demanding suitor in the South Pacific.

It is at this moment that the Australian government began to notice the serious governance problems emerging in the 'arc of instability' to its north-east. From PNG through to Fiji, states were clearly struggling, and often failing, to deal with problems that were in part a consequence of what Richard Falk has described as 'predatory globalisation', and in part home grown.[41] As Gyngell and Wesley note: '(c)learly the Western-derived model of the secular sovereign state with supreme authority over and responsibility for all in society, acting impartially towards its citizens, and expected to deliver a range of policy outcomes for security to education and health, is severely tested in some of these states'.[42] The Howard government became anxious that Australia may be vulnerable to terrorist attacks through weak (or fragile or failing) states in the

South Pacific where law and order problems were burgeoning, corruption was flourishing, and administrative capacity was in decline.[43]

The first case in point was the Solomon Islands. From independence in 1978, governance in the Solomon Islands had been deteriorating. By 2003, it was clear that the Solomon Islands state was in a parlous condition. Crime, violence, corruption, collapses in state services, ethnic conflicts, and social breakdown were all reaching crisis points – in some cases surpassing them. Elsina Wainwright notes that the Solomon Islands crisis challenged Australia's defence planners because of its 'proximity to our shores'. Second it meant that the Solomon Islands could become a base for international criminal activity. Third, a bankrupt Solomon Islands could be bribed into providing bases for foreign interests potentially antipathetic to Australia. And finally, regional security became a priority, 'as awareness arose of how weak and failing states can destabilise the broader region'.[44] It was in this context that Australia began to play a leading role in what was to become a regional commitment to the Solomon Islands to restore governance capacity. This was to become known as the Regional Assistance Mission to the Solomon Islands (RAMSI). Australia's involvement in RAMSI attracted warm praise from the United States. As former Deputy Secretary of State, Richard Armitage noted: '(w)e realize failed states can reach out and touch us badly, and Australia is . . . reaching out to produce a better future for the region'.[45] But this also echoed a position stated in the 2000 Australian Defence White Paper which stated very bluntly: '(w)e have a key interest in helping to prevent the positioning in neighbouring states of foreign forces that might be used to attack Australia'.[46]

THE ECP

The apparent early and easy successes of RAMSI emboldened Australian security planners to try their hand at another intervention in the South Pacific, this time in PNG. The result was the Enhanced Cooperation Program – the ECP. This Program entailed sending 170 Australian police officers and 30 senior public servants to PNG.[47] The police were to be placed in law and order 'hot spots' (Port Moresby, Mt Hagen and Bougainville), to reinforce the PNG police who constitute a notoriously under-resourced and demoralised force. The public servants were to be placed in in-line positions in strategic government departments (for example, treasury and finance) to help improve government financial programs.

The deployment of ECP personnel commenced early in 2005. The Australian police were cautiously welcomed by a majority of Papua New Guineans who are too often the victims of gratuitous violence, muggings, break-ins, and worse. However, an influential minority began to campaign against the ECP, publicly arguing that the presence of foreign police officers in PNG compromised PNG sovereignty and contravened the Constitution. Undoubtedly, some wanted to see it closed down because it posed a threat to their corrupt dealings with and in government.

On Friday 13 May 2005, the PNG High Court found that the legislation under which the ECP deployment was operating was contrary to the PNG Constitution. The Australian police were immediately withdrawn and the ECP put on hold. Recently the Australian and Papua New Guinean Foreign Ministers have announced that a scaled-down version of the ECP (ECP 2) will be put in place. The minority opposing any form of ECP is likely to maintain its criticisms of the deployment and will probably continue to explore legal grounds on which to bring it to an end.

What is particularly noteworthy about the ECP is that it demonstrates that Australia has revised its attitude towards PNG, radically.[48] The old hands-off policy up to the events of September 11 has been abandoned. Australia judges that its interests are at stake in a PNG in which there is a 'fragile' state that is clearly incapable of addressing the mounting security threats. In the wake of September 11 the proposal in the White Paper suddenly became an imperative. Australian security was seen to be threatened by the increasing fragility of the PNG state. Moreover, Australia was taking its 'deputy' role in the region seriously – as the words of another report make evident:

> Other countries in the Asia Pacific region and beyond, including the United States, expect that Australia, as the largest and richest country in the immediate region, will take the leading role in ensuring that the region remains reasonably stable and its countries remain viable. We fed these expectations with the high profile and successful roles we have played in supporting East Timor and Solomon Islands in recent years. Other countries and governments will judge us on how well we manage similar issues in our immediate neighbourhood in the future and their judgments will affect our international standing to a significant degree.[49]

The language in this (ASPI) report is illustrative of the kind of 'manifest destiny' thinking that Australia is accruing to itself in regard to its standing in the South Pacific. Its assumption of middle power gravitas has led it into assuming that it can intervene, easily and successfully in the region, to shore up its own security interests and those of its major allies like the United States.

But the ECP – at least in its first manifestation – has been a bitter failure. It can even be described as a major bungle from the Australian side, and a constitutional shambles from the PNG side. It suggests that Canberra has little understanding of what is needed and what is likely to succeed in such a complex situation as contemporary PNG. It also demonstrates that Canberra has little understanding of the levels of suspicion and concern generated in PNG by its sudden and unilateral decision to instigate the ECP – simply as an Australian defence/security strategy.

The easy scenario would be for Australia to wash its hands of PNG, withdraw all ECP and related personnel, minimise its aid relationship, and shore up its own defences along the borders that it shares with PNG. As the ASPI Report notes: '(s)ome observers in recent years have argued that aid to countries such as PNG has done more harm than good'.[50] But for Australia to abandon PNG completely is an unlikely scenario. Equally unlikely is a more aggressive form of intervention, where Australia imposes its will on PNG, via some kind of force. In fact, ASPI is correct when it proposes that a new policy approach to PNG is necessary 'that would allow Australia to play a more active role in helping to strengthen PNG's government, without assuming a pro-consul-like role'.[51]

Arguably, the main reason for the failure of ECP 1 was its unilateralism. The ECP was unlike the seemingly more successful RAMSI program (though how successful that is and will continue to be is still not at all clear) in that RAMSI has always been a regionally mobilised multilateral intervention. The unilateralism of ECP 1 will also undermine any possible successes of an ECP 2.

If it wants to play an effective role in the South Pacific, one which seeks to alleviate human suffering and promote regional stability and prosperity, Australia now needs to look beyond its own resources and interests. This will require developing a massive sustainable development program for the entire South Pacific, in close consultation with the states in the region, and in close collaboration with a state or states who have both the resources and interests to create such a program and get it up and running.

CONCLUSION

At the outset of this chapter, attention was drawn to Australia and Japan's estrangement from the Western Pacific. Both have maintained a highly self-regarding set of policies in the region, each based on close security ties with the United States. It was proposed that it might be possible to imagine a different approach to the region, one that demonstrated that they are capable of sensitive niche diplomacy and attracting to them the status of *middle powers as moral states*. Australia's clumsiness in the handling of the ECP demonstrates that it lacks the skills and the capacity to mount a realistic rescue package for an increasingly vulnerable PNG state. It will face related limitations in relation to other parts of the South Pacific – even as the region becomes increasingly important strategically and economically, for Australia and the wider region. Australia needs partners to work with in the region, to come up with a multilateral approach to solving PNG's problems and similar problems across the South Pacific.

This is where Japan and Australia have an opportunity to work together, to mobilise the kind of multilateral international effort that will be required to halt the extremely serious governance declines that are currently hobbling sustainable development in PNG and the wider South Pacific. Let us be clear about the magnitude of the problems being faced. On almost any comparable per capita measure, they equate with the kinds of problems haunting the poor African states. It is vital that Australia and Japan start to work together, to coordinate aid programs and mobilise the international community to come to the aid of the region. This should be a central element in any 'broad framework agreement on defence and security that provides a road map for future cooperation' between the two countries, as advocated by Alan Dupont.[52] Japan and Australia can, and should work together on this issue. As Neville Meaney has explained:

> The Australian–Japanese relationship has in recent years matured into a political partnership of 'unprecedented quality'. During the last twenty years, both countries have begun to see that they share not only complementary economic interests but also a common vision for the Asia Pacific region.[53]

If they are able to build this 'common vision', they have much to gain. It will of course mean that they will have to carve out a leadership role for themselves that will give them moral state status in the Western Pacific, based on especially adroit niche diplomacy. This will help them overcome their estrangement from the Western Pacific as they collaborate with countries as diverse as China, Indonesia, the Philippines, and Malaysia in developing economic, political and regional strategies that will halt state failure and state ruination in the South Pacific and, in the process, enhance cooperative regionalism.

NOTES

1. Richard Rosecrance, *Australian Diplomacy and Japan,* Melbourne: Melbourne UP, 1962, p. 249.
2. Joseph S. Nye, 'Coping with Japan', *Foreign Policy,* 89, Winter 1992–3, pp. 96–115.
3. Michael Jacques and Allan Patience, 'From Estrangement to Engagement: Japan and Australia on the Edge of Asia', *Bulletin of the Faculty of Foreign Studies* (Sophia University), No. 37, 2002.
4. Michael Oakeshott, *Rationalism in Politics and Other Essays,* Indianapolis: Liberty Press, 1991, p. 537.
5. Kishimoto Koichi, *Politics in Modern Japan: Development and Organization,* Tokyo: Japan Echo Inc., 1997, p. 37.
6. Gerald L. Curtis, *The Logic of Japanese Politics: Leaders, Institutions, and the Limits of Change,* New York: Columbia UP, 1999, p. 167.
7. In the last two decades of its existence the Immigration Restriction Act (the legislative expression of the White Australia Policy) was honoured more in its breach than its observance – though there were still cases when it was deployed until its formal repeal in 1973. See Kenneth Rivett (ed.), *Australia and the Non-White Migrant,* Melbourne:

Melbourne UP, 1975; Jamie Mackie, 'The Politics of Asian Immigration', in James E. Coghlan and Deborah J. McNamara (eds), *Asians in Australia: Patterns of Migration and Settlement*, Melbourne: Macmillan, 1997. More recently, the treatment of asylum-seekers in Australian detention centres, as well as on-going discrimination against Aborigines and Torres Strait Islanders, might point to the fact that even though the law has been repealed, the culture that gave rise to it in the first place may still be significantly intact.

8. David Walker, *Anxious Nation: Australia and the Rise of Asia, 1850–1939*, Brisbane: University of Queensland Press, 1999, p. 11.

9. For example, Ross Garnaut, *Australia and the Northeast Asian Ascendancy*, Canberra: Australian Government Publishing Service, 1989; East Asia Analytical Unit, *Australia and North-East Asia in the 1990s: Accelerating Change*, Canberra: Department of Foreign Affairs and Trade and Australian Government Publishing Service, 1992. See also Alison Broinowski, *The Yellow Lady: Australian Impressions of Asia*, Melbourne: Oxford UP, 1992; Anthony Milner (ed.), *Australia in Asia: Comparing Cultures*, Melbourne: Oxford UP, 1996; Anthony Milner and Mary Quilty (eds), *Australia in Asia: Communities of Thought*, Melbourne: Oxford UP, 1996; and Anthony Milner and Mary Quilty (eds), *Australia in Asia: Episodes*, Melbourne: Oxford UP, 1998; Rawdon Dalrymple, *Continental Drift: Australia's Search for Regional Identity*, Aldershot: Ashgate, 2003; Paul Keating, *Engagement: Australia faces the Asia-Pacific*, Sydney: Macmillan, 2000; Alison Broinowski, *About Face: Asian Accounts of Australia*, Melbourne: Scribe Publications, 2003.

10. The consciousness shaped by British race patriotism is evident in former Prime Minister Robert Menzies' diary musings on a sea voyage to Britain, via Colombo (the capital of what was then Ceylon) in 1935. He describes Colombo: 'Here is a golf course, there a soccer football ground (in this climate) there a cricket ground. The town is clean. A few hundreds of Englishmen rule it and clean it and water it. The more I see of such people the more satisfied I am that while doctrinaires and theorists speculate about self-government for natives (who are chiefly experts in idleness and the demanding of baksheesh) the British calmly go on their way giving to these peoples what they never give themselves' (quoted in David Goldsworthy, *Losing the Blanket: Australia and the end of Britain's empire*, Melbourne: Melbourne UP, 2002, p. 22).

11. Michael Leacher, Geoffrey Stokes and Ian Ward (eds), *The Rise and Fall of One Nation*, Brisbane: Queensland UP, 2000.

12. Azim Zabidi, quoted in 'There Goes the Neighbourhood', *The Bulletin*, 14 March 2000.

13. Joseph A. Camilleri, *Australian-American Relations: The Web of Dependence*, Melbourne: Macmillan, 1980, p. 19.

14. Philip Bell and Roger Bell, *Implicated: The United States in Australia*, Melbourne: Oxford UP, 1993, p. 152.

15. Quoted by David Marr in 'All in the Cause of a Better Australia', *The Sydney Morning Herald*, 9 September 2005.

16. Gareth Evans and Bruce Grant, *Australia's Foreign Relations in the World of the 1990s*, 2nd edition, Melbourne: Melbourne UP, 1995, p. 344. It appears that the Hon Tony Street, Foreign Affairs Minister in the Fraser government, was the first to apply the term 'middle power' publicly to Australia. However its origins stretch back at least to the enacting (by the British Parliament) of the Statute of Westminster in 1931 that encouraged Britain's self-governing colonial dominions to take on the responsibilities of full sovereignty. Australia did not adopt the Statute until 1943, and then reluctantly. (Alan Watt, *The Evolution of Australian Foreign Policy: 1938-1965*, Cambridge: Cambridge UP, 1967, p. 268). As the (British) 'Commonwealth of Nations' evolved, especially after the Second World War, a distinction arose between the 'old dominions' (Australia, Canada, New Zealand, South Africa – that is, settler-colonial states/societies) and newly independent republics like India and Singapore. As Goldsworthy explains: 'the idea of a special imperial affinity among the old dominions, or perhaps more exactly the sense of a common British descent and shared allegiance to the Crown, still retained its potency among many who lived in these countries. Indicatively, in later years, Menzies would sometimes refer to the old-dominion group of states as the 'Crown Commonwealth', in order to distinguish them from the ranks of the Commonwealth republics' (Goldsworthy, *Losing the Blanket*, p. 22).

17. Richard Leaver and Dave Cox (eds), 'Introduction', *Middling, Meddling, Muddling: Issues in Australian Foreign Policy*, Sydney: Allen and Unwin, 1997, p. 6.
18. Evans and Grant, *Australia's Foreign Relations*, p. 344. See also Carsten Holbraad, *Middle Powers in International Politics*, London: Macmillan, 1984.
19. Evans and Grant, *Australia's Foreign Relations*, p. 344.
20. Holbraad, *Middle Powers*.
21. See, for example, Andrew Cooper, Richard Higgott, and Kim Nossal, *Relocating Middle Powers: Australia and Canada in a Changing World*, Melbourne: Melbourne UP, 1993. See also Andrew F. Cooper, 'Niche Diplomacy: A Conceptual Overview', in Andrew F. Cooper (ed.), *Niche Diplomacy: Middle Powers After the Cold War*, London: Macmillan, 1997.
22. Cooper, 'Niche Diplomacy', p. 2.
23. International Commission on Intervention and State Sovereignty (ICISS), *The Responsibility to Protect*, Ottawa: International Development Research Centre, 2001, p. 11.
24. Cooper, 'Niche Diplomacy', p. 6.
25. Ibid.
26. Cranford Pratt, 'Has Middle Power Internationalism a Future?', in Cranford Pratt (ed.), *Middle Power Internationalism: The North-South Dimension*, Kingston and Montreal: McGill-Queen's UP, 1990, p. 144.
27. Pratt, 'Middle Power Internationalism and Global Poverty', in *Ibid.*, p. 6.
28. For some useful accounts of growing global poverty, see Jeffrey Sachs, *The End of Poverty: How We Can Make it Happen in Our Lifetime*, London: Penguin, 2005; Fred R. Dallmayr, 'Globalization and Inequality', *International Studies Review*, 4(2), 2002; United Nations Development Program, *Human Development Report 2005*, New York: UNDP, 2005; Andrew Hurrell and Ngaire Woods, 'Globalization and Inequality', *Millennium*, 24, 1995.
29. Amartya Sen, *Development as Freedom*, New York: Anchor Books, 2000, p. 4.
30. See, for example, Alejandro Colas, *International Civil Society*, Cambridge: Polity Press, 2002; Mary Kaldor, *Global Civil Society: An Answer to War*, Cambridge: Polity Press, 2003.
31. Ron Crocombe, *The South Pacific*, Suva: University of the South Pacific, 2001, p. 27.
32. Barrie Macdonald, '"Good Governance" and the Pacific Island States', in Peter Larmour (ed.), *Governance and Reform in the South Pacific*, Canberra: National Centre for Development Studies, ANU, 1998; Peter Larmour, 'Corruption and Governance in the South Pacific', *Pacific Studies*, 20(3), 1997; Sinclair Dinnen, 'Threatening the State: Crime and Public Order in Papua New Guinea', in Beno Boeha and John McFarlane (eds), *Australia and Papua New Guinea: Crime and the Bilateral Relationship*, Canberra: Australian Defence Studies Centre, 2000.
33. See, for example, Sinclair Dinnen, 'Lending a Fist? Australia's New Interventionism in the Southwest Pacific', *State, Society and Governance in Melanesia Project*, Discussion Paper No. 5, Canberra: Research School of Pacific and Asian Studies, Australian National University, 2004; Ian Frazer, 'The Struggle for Control of Solomon Island Forests', *The Contemporary Pacific*, 9(1), 1997; Australian Government: Department of Foreign Affairs and Trade, Economic Analytical Unit, *Papua New Guinea: The Road Ahead*, Canberra: DFAT, 2004; Donald Denoon, *A Trial Separation: Australia and the Decolonisation of Papua New Guinea*, Canberra: Pandanus Press, 2005.
34. Crocombe, *The South Pacific*, especially Chapter 17.
35. See, for example, Peter Bauer et al., *Aid and Development in the South Pacific*, Sydney: CIS, 2003; Peter Dauvergne, 'Weak States, Strong States: A State-in-Society Perspective', in Peter Dauvergne (ed.), *Weak and Strong States in Asia-Pacific Societies*, Sydney: Allen and Unwin, 2003; Elsina Wainwright, 'Responding to State Failure – the Case of the Solomon Islands', *Australian Journal of International Affairs*, 57 (3), 2003.
36. See, for example, Maxine Pitts, *Crime, Corruption and Capacity in Papua New Guinea*, Canberra: Asia Pacific Press, 2002; Susan Windybank and Mike Manning, 'Papua New Guinea on the Brink', *Issue Analysis*, 30, 12 March 2003; Henry Okole and David Kavanamur, 'Political Corruption in Papua New Guinea: Some Causes and Policy Lessons', *South Pacific Journal of Philosophy and Culture*, 7, 2003; R. J. May, 'Disorderly Democracy: Political Turbulence and Institutional Reform in Papua New Guinea', *State,*

Society and Governance in Melanesia Project, Discussion Paper no. 3, Canberra: Research School of Pacific and Asian Studies, Australian National University, 2003; Sinclair Dinnen, 'In Weakness and Strength – States, Societies and Order in Papua New Guinea', in Dauvergne, *Weak and Strong States,* 2003; Helen Hughes, 'Can Papua New Guinea Come Back from the Brink?' *Issue Analysis,* No. 49, 2004.

37. David Kavanamur et al., *Understanding Reform in Papua New Guinea: An Analytical Framework,* Port Moresby: Institute of National Affairs, 2004, p. 2. See also Human Rights Watch, 'Making Their Own Rules: Police Beatings, Rape and Torture of Children in Papua New Guinea', 2005, at http://hrw.org/reports/2005 (sighted 2 September 2005).
38. See Windybank and Manning, 'Papua New Guinea on the Brink'; Hughes, 'Can Papua New Guinea Come Back'.
39. If we count Japan's wartime occupation of parts of PNG we may also argue that Japan is a former colonial presence in the country, with all the obligations that entails. But Japan has also mostly adopted a hands-off policy towards PNG, offering mainly aid, in return for (sometimes especially predatory) access to the rich PNG logging industry. As two former colonial powers, Japan and Australia have much to answer for in accounting for the governance failures now besetting PNG – for example, in the inadequate infrastructure they left behind when they each withdrew and the inadequate support they have offered the country since.
40. Gerard Henderson, 'World Order – From the Old to the New', *Australian Journal of International Affairs,* 57(3), 2003, p. 480.
41. Richard Falk, *Predatory Globalization: A Critique,* Cambridge: Polity Press, 1999.
42. Allan Gyngell and Michael Wesley, *Making Australian Foreign Policy,* Cambridge: Cambridge UP, 2003, p. 220.
43. Sinclair Dinnen, 'Lending a Fist?'.
44. Wainwright, 'Responding to State Failure', p. 489.
45. Quoted in ibid., p. 494.
46. Australian Government, Department of Defence, *Our Future Defence Force,* Canberra: Australian Government Publishing Service, 2000, para. 4.8.
47. Michael Potts, *The Enhanced Cooperation Package: An Australian Perspective,* Address by the Australian High Commissioner to PNG to the University of Papua New Guinea, 10 September 2004.
48. Allan Patience, 'The ECP and Australia's Middle Power Ambitions', *State, Society and Governance in Melanesia Project,* Discussion Paper no. 4, Canberra: Research School of Pacific and Asian Studies, Australian National University, 2005.
49. Australian Strategic Policy Institute, *Strengthening Our Neighbour: Australia and the Future of Papua New Guinea,* Canberra: Australian Government Publishing Service, 2004, p. 18.
50. Ibid., p. 39.
51. Ibid.
52. Alan Dupont, *Unsheathing the Samurai Sword: Japan's Changing Security Policy,* Sydney: Lowy Institute Paper 3, 2004, p. 59.
53. Neville Meaney, *Towards a New Vision: Australia and Japan Through 100 Years,* Sydney: Kangaroo Press, 1999, p. 137.

PART IV

Global Governance and Sustainability

10. The Role of the United Nations in the Twenty-first Century

Tetsuya Yamada

This chapter focuses on the new roles that have emerged for the United Nations in the post-Cold War era and on the difficulties it faces in carrying out those roles – particularly with regard to the types of conflict that have recently emerged. It questions the school of thought which sees the United Nations as a panacea for the world's ills but equally the school that simply dismisses the United Nations as ineffectual, hence irrelevant. It examines the varying roles of the superpower, middle powers and the small and developing countries in the United Nations with a view to showing that differing interests, particularly of the superpower and the developing countries, constitute obstacles to UN reform. It then assesses the movement towards UN reform and shows how these conflicting interests have impeded progress towards reform and even agreement on the goals of reform. It concludes with a discussion of possible roles for middle powers, particularly Japan, in the context of the current impasse.

INTRODUCTION

Since the end of the Cold War, the possibility of a 'new world order' has been repeatedly canvassed, either enthusiastically or sceptically. One important feature of this discussion has focused on how the United Nations might contribute to such a new order. As O'Neill and Rees have observed, the United Nations became active in its role as peacekeeper with the disappearance of the East–West rivalry.[1] Expectations that the United Nations would play an important role in maintaining or restoring international peace and security were heightened when a response was required to the Iraqi invasion of Kuwait in August 1990. The newly found assertiveness of the UN Security Council was considered a relative 'success' in the sense that the United Nations was able to carry out its role in accordance with Chapter VII of the UN Charter.[2] What seemed to emerge in this process was a 'new world order' with the following three distinguishing features. First, the new international order would be characterised by the further expansion of liberal-democratic values in the political sphere and free market mechanisms in the economic sphere. Second, multilateral fora such as the United Nations would play an important role in formulating and implementing rules and norms which would realise this dual expansion. Third, if any violation of these rules and norms occurred, it would be corrected by multilateral processes and multilateral action. In sum, multilateral institutions would play a key role in formulating and implementing values and norms shared by all members of international society.

Since the emergence of these expectations of a 'new world order', however, we have also witnessed a number of dramatic failures on the part of this multilateral framework and inaction by international society – particularly in Somalia, the former Yugoslavia and Rwanda – with tragic consequences. These events have highlighted the short-term 'success' of the United Nations in Iraq and Kuwait. The collective action taken by the United Nations has come to be seen as, at best, a partial success, and perhaps nothing more than an unattainable ideal. One question to be solved in this regard is the tension between non-intervention as the traditional and fundamental norm of inter-state relations on the one hand and the maintenance of international peace and security by multilateral intervention in intra-state conflicts on the other. We have had to face an even more difficult question – legally and politically as well as ethically: how could or should we cope with internal conflicts where the vulnerable members of local communities, notably women and children, are involved as casualties, soldiers, refugees or internally displaced persons (IDP), and when no international action can be taken given political disagreements among the big powers?

Kosovo offers the clearest example. NATO's bombardments in 1999 – with vague mandates and authorisations from the UN Security Council – seem to have succeeded in improving the humanitarian situation in Kosovo. The legality of this event was later evaluated by the Independent International Commission on Kosovo, whose final report concluded that 'the NATO military intervention was illegal but legitimate.'[3] This conclusion indicates how difficult it is to speak of the legality and legitimacy of 'humanitarian intervention' in the face of defective procedures which persist despite the fact that the values and norms involved are so undeniably noble.

The events of September 11 have thrust even more complex questions before us. In the pre-September 11 world, the task was one of maintaining the collaborative approach of the permanent members of the UN Security Council, and so enabling the council to act or to respond to conflicts occurring outside their territories. However, September 11 was an attack against a permanent member of the Security Council – indeed against the most powerful of them. After September 11, the United States came to perceive itself as the target of terrorist attacks. In the face of this threat, the United States decided to react unilaterally.

It is easy to criticise the unilateral behaviour that has been characteristic of the Bush administration since September 11. But what is at question here is whether the UN Security Council can be a workable mechanism when one of the permanent members is the object of a direct external attack. To make matters worse the country under attack was the world's sole superpower.

The terrorist attack has exposed another problem. It has shown that innocent civilians living in relatively safe developed countries can be just as much at risk as those living in the unstable political and socio-economic conditions of weak or failed states. Unlike inter-state conflicts in poor countries, the 'war on terror' can escalate without limit because the architects have the resources and capacity to wage this war anywhere and anytime they perceive there is a terrorist threat. At the same time, terrorists are also likely to escalate their attacks against the centres of power and wealth for as long as they feel alienated in the globalised international community. Thus, a not unlikely scenario for the immediate future is the simultaneous escalation of both terrorism and counter-terrorism – in other words, increased terrorist actions against the United States and its allies and increased reaction by these states against terrorists and their supporters, actual or suspected. If this sketch of the emerging world is at all accurate, what is on the horizon is nothing short of unbridled barbarism.

The focus of the analysis here is the direction in which the United Nations seems to be headed, and the factors that appear to be moving it in that direction. Elsewhere the author has examined the role of the United Nations in maintaining and restoring international peace and security, using East Timor and Kosovo as case studies. However, it is not the author's intention to explore the hermeneutics of the UN Charter, or to address the questions of positive law *(lex lata)* surrounding the legality of particular UN decisions. Here we consider preferable law *(lex feranda)* – how the United Nations should act. This approach is taken because the United Nations itself now faces the question of 'our shared responsibility' for 'a more secure world' and 'larger freedom'.[4]

The first question to pose is whether the United Nations is the appropriate body to deal with the 'new' threats that have emerged since the end of the Cold War. As Article 1, paragraph 1 of the UN Charter stipulates, the foremost purpose of the United Nations is:

> to maintain international peace and security, and to that end: to take effective collective measures for the prevention and removal of threats to peace, and for the suppression of acts of aggression or other breaches of the peace, and to bring about by peaceful means, and in conformity with the principles of justice and international law, adjustment or settlement of international disputes or situations which might lead to a breach of the peace.[5]

Even though this paragraph says nothing about internal conflicts, refugees and IDP – or even about terrorism – it does not follow that the United Nations should be silent on these issues or pass them onto other (international) institutions, or to a group of willing states. Rather, as Sriram points out, conflict prevention, placed in its wider context, is a central goal of the United Nations.[6] During its first 45 years, the United Nations was not at all active in dealing with internal conflicts. This was in part the result of the Security Council's paralysis and its preoccupation with the East–West confrontation. It did not reflect a belief that the United Nations was not the appropriate body to deal with those issues. On the other hand, the trend since the end of the Cold War of giving the United Nations responsibility to address new threats has come to constitute a challenge which the drafters of the Charter did not foresee in 1945.[7] The UN Charter, the various organs of the United Nations including the structure of the Secretariat, and the various procedures under the Charter, have come under close review in order to fit better with the new situation. This review process has in turn led to a debate over the future role of the United Nations.

One school of thought asserts that the United Nations can do little or nothing because of the inefficiency, bureaucracy and corruption in the UN Secretariat. These claims come principally come from the US neo-conservatives. Another school of thought, which can be best described as UN-centric utopianism, erroneously views the United Nations as constituting something akin to a world government. The present author questions the validity of both views. This chapter instead takes a more modest approach concentrating on what the United Nations is, what challenges it currently faces, and what individual memberstates, particularly Japan, could do for the betterment of the organisation.

RELATIVE STRENGTHS OF POWERS IN THE UNITED NATIONS

The United Nations and its predecessor, the League of Nations, represent a compromise between lofty ideals and immediate realities. They also represent a compromise between the idealism of the United States, and the realism of Europe.[8] While noting that there were also differences within the United States itself, it is important to remember that it was the United States that promoted the establishment of these two international organisations. Even today, the United States acknowledges the significance of the United Nations, at least to the extent that it does not regard the United Nations as unnecessary.

One of the mistakes that multilateralists often make is to assume that multilateralism is capable of deterring superpower autocracy. The facts suggest the contrary. Regimes and institutions are established to enable the superpower/s and its/their allies to maintain their vested interests and preserve the status quo in international relations. This applies as much to multilateral systems for maintaining international peace and security as to any other international regime. Since the Concert of Europe in the nineteenth century, the victors have taken the lead in establishing the postwar international order. The organisation created to maintain peace and international order provides the forum and the procedures that preserve the fruits of military victory.[9]

Rules and procedures established within multilateral institutions can confer legitimacy relatively easily, unlike actions based unilateral enforcement.[10] Superpowers and dominant states are therefore willing to shoulder the responsibility of making financial contributions, both assessed and voluntary, despite the financial burden, simply because they find these institutions useful for advancing their own policy goals – and not because they are motivated by sympathy, charity, or some notion of the international common good.[11] Obviously, the United States has been the main contributor to the UN regular budget since its establishment. In 2004 and 2005, the US contribution amounted to 22 per cent of the total regular budget. The United Nations has faced severe financial crises whenever the United States refused to disburse its assessed contribution. References to a theoretical dichotomy between UN-led multilateralism and US unilateralism has become fashionable in discussions of current and future world order. However, looking at financial realities, the simple fact is that the United Nations cannot ignore the wishes of the superpower and the dominant states. Though it is politically easy to condemn Washington's domineering attitude to the United Nations, no one has seriously proposed reducing the amount of the US assessed contribution for the purpose of freeing the United Nations so that it can pay less attention to its political and financial master.

Unlike the superpower, no single middle power is able to dominate international organisations such as the United Nations, or the international order in general. This means, conversely, that middle powers can take the lead in standard-setting by forming flexible *ad hoc* groups of like-minded countries on an issue-by-issue basis. A good many examples point to a pattern of middle power behaviour. One such example is the role of the Nordic countries in the promotion of human rights issues and another is the role of Japan in initiating the adoption of the resolution for the overall abolition of nuclear weapons despite opposition from the five nuclear weapons states. Middle powers behave in these ways because they believe that they can function as a bridge between the superpower and the small and underdeveloped countries. This also means that, for the middle powers, they can utilise multilateral institutions in order to pursue their own foreign policy goals, which can gain legitimacy through multilateral debate and decision making.

The position of small and underdeveloped countries, formerly known as the Group of 77 (G-77), within the United Nations is delicate. Many Third World countries gained independence as a consequence of the vigorous efforts of the UN decolonisation process during the 1950s and 1960s. For these newly independent states, admission to the United Nations was a symbol of independence. They enjoyed sovereign equality with their former colonial masters. As the number of these countries increased, they formed a majority in various UN fora, notably the General Assembly. Financially their contribution is marginal. On the other hand, these states have utilised the General Assembly as a forum to make their voices heard in international society. As a result of their initiatives many resolutions aimed at changing the basic underlying structure of international order, including the resolutions of 'permanent sovereignty over natural resources' in 1962[12] and of the 'new international economic order' in 1974,[13] were adopted at the General Assembly as counter-arguments to existing arrangements. The establishment of the UN Conference on Trade and Development (UNCTAD) was another example of this trend. However, the end of the Cold War has severely weakened their ability to make their voices heard.

This division of the UN membership (superpower, middle powers, small and underdeveloped countries) casts a shadow over all discussions on UN reform. The United States and other advanced industrial states seek to reorganise the United Nations so that their financial contribution promotes their own political agendas. For this purpose, principles and mechanisms are proposed to fit with their policy goals. On the other hand, small and underdeveloped countries are opposed to any UN reforms which would jeopardise their equal status within the UN body. The principles of sovereign equality and non-interference in the internal affairs of other countries are the two biggest prizes gained by independence and guaranteed by the UN Charter. At the same time, no reform plan requiring a General Assembly resolution will ever be implemented without the support of this group since they constitute the vast majority of the Assembly. Therefore, a key to the success of the UN reforms under current consideration is whether they have the support of the small countries. This division, which can be seen as a new North–South faultline, must be overcome if UN reform is to succeed. Such a task is further complicated by the fact that the North–South gap has become much wider since the end of the Cold War – precisely at a time when the United Nations has become preoccupied with a number of internal conflicts and other new threats.

IS A 'STRENGTHENED' AND 'REFORMED' UNITED NATIONS VIABLE?

Plans for Reform

In 2003, Kofi Annan, the UN Secretary-General, convened a high-level panel to assess the threats which the international community faced and to put forward a concrete set of proposals to enable the United Nations to assume the role of providing collective security for all. This panel, composed of well-known former diplomats, statesmen, retired generals and scholars,[14] met six times from December 2003 to November 2004. Its final report was submitted to the Secretary-General on 1 December 2004.[15] In a note attached to his *A More Secure World* report, the Secretary-General explained that he had set up the panel because he felt a 'deep division among the Member States on the nature of the threats that we face and the appropriateness of the use of force to address those threats'.[16] Annan was clearly referring to the unilateral use of force against Iraq by the United States in 2003. In all likelihood, he also had in mind NATO's Kosovo air campaign. Annan's hope was that the deliberations of the panel would find a way to keep the United States within the multilateral process of collective security at the Security Council. How the United Nations can engage the United States is a critically important question not only for the international community as a whole but also for the United Nations' own authority and even survival.

It is safe to conclude that the panel's report was designed to secure the support of the United States and other developed countries. In other words, its conclusions and recommendations seemed sufficiently sensitive to US positions to secure Washington's support. The debates which followed, including the Secretary-General's own report presented in March 2005, were also US-friendly. The United States itself has been quite enthusiastic about proposing a reform plan for the United Nations.[17] Not surprisingly, the draft outcome document prepared for the high-level plenary meeting of the General Assembly of September 2005[18] coincides with and employs various proposals made by the United States. While the United States is reluctant about Security Council reform, in accordance with the proposal made by Japan, Germany, India and Brazil (the G4 countries), upgrading the Commission on Human Rights to the Council on Human Rights and establishing a Peace-Building Commission and an office supporting it, appeared both in the United States' proposal and in the draft outcome document.

What is implied in these commonalities is quite indicative. First, any reform plan not gaining US support cannot be implemented even if it gains a majority of the vote. In other words, in addition to the majority vote, US support is key to the realisation of any reform. Secondly, current mainstream arguments and proposals for UN reform are never acceptable to small countries, simply because some of the ideas will bring about the transformation of the nature of the United Nations from an organisation of cooperation among the member-states based on (classical) sovereign equality to that of interference, coercion and enforcement. Also, we must not forget that small and underdeveloped countries have refused to legitimise so-called 'humanitarian interventions,' which are contrary to the 'non-use of force' principle of Article 2, paragraph 4 of the UN Charter, as well as to the principle of non-interference in internal matters under paragraph 7 of the same Article. Thirdly, even countries opposed to the idea of a US-dominated United Nations find it difficult to challenge the basic idea of reform. The Secretary-General's report, and the United States' own report contain so many words and phrases reaffirming the importance of fundamental values, such as democracy, peace and human rights, that countries opposed to US policies must take care not to be perceived as if they are denying the importance of those values themselves.

What Was Achieved in the World Summit

At the close of the World Summit, in September 2005, the Outcome Document was adopted by consensus. However, its content was considered unsatisfactory to most member-states. Some 178 paragraphs were spent 'reaffirming' how the member-states regard the United Nations as the 'indispensable foundation of a more peaceful, prosperous and just world'. However, it is difficult to arrive at a positive evaluation of this Outcome Document in so far as the future road map for UN reform is concerned.

Most striking is the fact that the paragraphs on disarmament were in the end completely deleted because of the strong opposition from one powerful state. For Japan, there was no concrete achievement on Security Council reform. Even though paragraph 153 of the Outcome Document requested 'the General Assembly to review progress on the reform set out (in the previous part) by the end of 2005', there was no concrete proposal to be 'reviewed'.

Why did UN reform come up against a brick wall? Is there any future for UN reform? Or even any future for the United Nations itself? Many answers could be given to these questions. During the negotiations over the Outcome Document, member-states, from the largest to the smallest, tried to pursue their own particular goals rather than 'common' goals for a 'common' future. As the diversity of the UN's membership becomes greater, it becomes more difficult to establish universally acceptable principles, norms, rules and procedures accepted by all countries.

NEW DIVISIONS OR THE RECURRENCE OF THE PAST?

Before presenting a set of conclusions or policy proposals, some salient points, both practical and theoretical, are placed here for further consideration and discussion. These inter-linked problems seem to suggest that we are now facing a new division between the rich North and the poor South. This division resembles the hierarchical international order which used to be called imperialism. However, an important difference between these new and old divisions is that imperialism has now lost its political legitimacy with the rise of new international norms, notably the self-determination of peoples.[19]

Here, the key question appears to be how we observe and interpret the changing character of today's world. Looking and judging from one vantage point of international society, we often use terms like 'the end of history' or 'the clash of civilisations' as shortcuts for describing post-Cold War international society. 'Globalisation' is another term that falls into the same category, although it expresses not only the consequences but also the processes which characterise international society.

Numerous criticisms have been made, politically and intellectually, against the particular policies and legal frameworks that are accelerating and reinforcing the trend towards globalisation. Chimni, for example, argues that the function of international institutions is to constitute a nascent global state whose current task is to realise the interests of an emerging transnational capitalist class to the disadvantage of subaltern classes in the third and first worlds.[20] International economic institutions, in particular the International Monetary Fund (IMF), the World Bank and the World Trade Organisation (WTO) are regarded as the main instruments of this trend.

In addition to these socio-economic aspects, questions of 'peace and security' and the role of international institutions such as the United Nations pose the same challenge. As previously discussed, international society at the end of the Cold War had expectations of a multilateral approach for maintaining or restoring international peace and security. During the past fifteen years, in which the United Nations has experienced many new pressures, a new political jargon has emerged with the use of such words and phrases as 'failed state', 'humanitarian intervention', 'peace-building', 'human security', and 'transnational territorial administration'. These words and phrases and the activities called for and legitimised by this jargon are seemingly difficult to criticise. No one can deny the importance of extending humanitarian assistance to refugees and internally displaced persons. It is clearly humane for people who inhabit the world of the 'haves' to assist with the reconstruction of war-torn societies through the United Nations and its agencies and programmes, through NGOs, or even through national armed forces dispatched as a part of peacekeeping operations.

However, here again, we should not ignore criticisms targeting some of the activities aiming at the reconstruction of postwar countries, whatever the jargon in which they are 'dressed up'. These criticisms target, among other things, international commitments and interventions carried out in the name of peace-building. While Western writers tend to emphasise the role of peace-building rooted in such values as democracy, respect for human rights and gender equality,[21] the recipient countries/societies review these ideas as interference in internal affairs, even if the particular peace-building mission is properly authorised by a resolution of the Security Council. Moreover, transitional territorial administrations, as in Kosovo, Bosnia-Herzegovina and East Timor, often face the criticism that such operations are a continuation of the 'imperial past'.[22]

The key question to have emerged in the current discourse on international relations is the contemporary relevance of the twin notions of sovereignty and the equality of states. Of course, much has been written (by Western scholars) on this subject.[23] However, we should take care to note that their arguments are often used to legitimise policies espoused by particular states. What is needed now is a normative approach to policies and operations that sees through the camouflaging jargon and takes serious account of opposing views.[24]

CONCLUSION

In December 2005, the United Nations faced a difficult moment regarding its draft biennial budget. The United States had threatened to oppose the proposed draft budget unless concrete results were achieved in reforming of the UN Secretariat. Other member-states were critical of the US attitude on the grounds that the United States had taken the budget hostage in order to gain UN reform. Only Japan expressed sympathy for US tactics. As the second largest contributor to the United Nations, Japan seems to have good reason to act in concert with the United States.

It is too early to conclude, or predict, whether the approach favoured by the United States and Japan is likely to succeed in getting the UN Secretariat to undertake serious reform. However, it would be fair to characterise their approach as a double-edged sword. If the General Assembly votes for the draft budget without making major modifications in line with the US request, the United Nations will face a serious financial crisis with the possibility of the United States and, somewhat less likely, Japan withholding payment. At the same time, the United States and Japan will be severely criticised by other member-states for their arrogance. Japan may see a decline of its political influence within the United Nations.

On the other hand, if the General Assembly accepts even part of the request from these two countries, there is no surety that reform of the UN Secretariat will actually succeed. Taking these possible negative consequences into consideration, Japan, instead of doggedly following the US lead, could undertake a mediating role between the United States and other UN member-states. Middle powers such as Australia, Canada and even EU countries could add their weight to Japan's efforts and so enhance the quality of the debate on Security Council reform.

This is a practical illustration of the role that middle powers such as Japan and Australia can play. As indicated earlier middle powers have most to gain from multilateralism. To this end, these countries have two tasks ahead of them. One task would be to keep the superpower, or hegemon, engaged in the multilateral process, and the other would be to conduct themselves in ways that do not disappoint smaller countries, which exert effective political influence only through participation in the multilateral process. Putting aside the question of the possible inclusion of Japan in an expanded Security Council, Japan and Australia should cooperate more closely by placing UN reform in a broader context, and so give satisfaction to both the hegemon and the smaller countries. All this said, the administrative and financial reform of the United Nations remains an urgent matter. Establishing new international norms relating to the maintenance of peace and security under the framework of the UN Charter is also an inescapable task, given the circumstances which have divided the world since the end of the Cold War and especially since September 11.

NOTES

1. John Terence O'Neill and Nicholas Rees, *United Nations Peacekeeping in the Post-Cold War Era*, New York: Routledge, 2005, p. 41.
2. This did not necessarily mean that the whole crisis in the region was resolved. Sustained problems such as the Kurdish population issue, the abolition of weapons of mass destruction (WMD) and UN inspection thereto, and the Hussein regime itself led to the 'Second' Gulf War in 2003.
3. Independent International Commission on Kosovo, *Kosovo Report: Conflict, International Response, Lessons Learned*, New York: Oxford UP, 2000, p. 4.
4. These words and phrases are taken from two reports relating to the current discussion on UN reform, *A More Secure World: Our Shared Responsibility: The Report Of The High-Level Panel On Threats*, U.N. Doc. A/59/565, 2 December 2004, and *In Larger Freedom: Towards Development, Security and Human Rights For All*, U.N.Doc. A/59/2005, 21 March 2005, with a review of what the UN has done or has failed to do during the past fifteen years of the so-called 'post-Cold War period'.
5. Charter of the United Nations, at un.org/aboutun/charter (sighted on 30 January 2006).
6. Chandra Lekha Sriram and Karin Wermester (eds), *From Promise to Practice: Strengthening UN Capabilities for the Prevention of Violent Conflict*, Boulder, CO: Lynne Rienner Publishers, 2003, p. 1.
7. Ibid., p. 1.
8. For more detailed analysis on the establishments of respective organisations, see Hidemi Suganami, *The Domestic Analogy and World Order Proposals*, Cambridge, UK: Cambridge UP, 1989.
9. This corresponds to the historical facts that many international organisations belonging to the so-called 'UN system' or 'UN family' are the successors of the wartime cooperation among the United Nations.
10. See, more generally, Nico Krisch, 'International Law in Times of Hegemony: Unequal Power and the Shaping of the International Legal Order', *European Journal of International Law*, 16 (3), 2005, pp. 369–408.
11. The US and British withdrawal from the United Nations Educational, Scientific, and Cultural Organization (UNESCO) explains this formula from the reverse angle. In addition to the inefficiency and lax management of the Secretariat, 'anti-Westernised' UNESCO was abandoned by two of the most powerful and dominant member-states.
12. UN General Assembly Resolution 1803 (XVII), 14 December 1962.
13. UN General Assembly Resolution 3281(XXIX), 12 December 1974.
14. Sadako Ogata, former UN High Commissioner for Refugees, and Gareth Evans, former Australian minister for foreign affairs, were the members of the Panel from Japan and Australia. They participated in the Panel in their personal capacities.
15. UN Doc. A/59/565, 2 December 2004.

16. Paragraph 1 of 'Note by the Secretary-General', contained in *A More Secure World: Our Shared Responsibility: The Report Of The High-Level Panel On Threats, Challenges And Change*, UN Doc. A/59/565, 2 December 2004.
17. See, for example, *American Interests and UN Reform: Report of the Task Force on the United Nations*, The Endowment of the United States Institute of Peace, 2005.
18. This document without UN document number is available from http://www.un.org/ga/president/59/draft_outcome.htm (sighted on 28 July 2005).
19. This new division may remind us of the international order in the 19th century, which divided states and countries into 'civilised', 'barbarian' and 'savage', asserted by, for example, James Lorimer, *The Institutes of the Law of Nations: A Treatise of the Jural Relations of Separate Political Communities*, Vol. 1, Edinburgh: William Blackwood and Sons, 1883, pp. 101–133.
20. B. S. Chimni, 'International Institutions Today: An Imperial Global State in the Making', *European Journal of International Law*, 15 (1), 2004, pp. 1–37.
21. See, for example, Samuel H. Barnes, 'The Contribution of Democracy to Rebuilding Postconflict Societies', *American Journal of International Law*, 95, 2001, pp. 86–101.
22. William Bain, *Between Anarchy and Society: Trusteeship and the Obligations of Power*, Oxford: Oxford UP, 2003, p. 192.
23. Steven D. Krasner, *Sovereignty: Organised Hypocrisy*, Princeton: Princeton UP, 1999, would be the most important contribution to this topic. The same author contributed 'Sharing Sovereignty: New Institutions for Collapsed and Failing States', *International Security*, 29(2), Fall 2004, pp. 85–120. He is now at the US State Department.
24. In addition to Chimni, 'International Institutions Today', Antony Anghie, *Imperialism, Sovereignty and the Making of International Law*, Cambridge: Cambridge UP, 2005, and Balakrishnan Rajagopal, *International Law from Below: Development, Social Movements and Third World Resistance*, Cambridge: Cambridge UP, 2003, are important works on this subject. Also, Nico Krisch criticises current US unilateralism from the point of sovereign equality in Nico Krisch, 'More Equal than the Rest? Hierarchy, Equality and US Predominance in International Law', in Michael Byers and Georg Nolte (eds), *United States Hegemony and the Foundations of International Law*, Cambridge: Cambridge UP, 2003, pp. 135–175.

11. Foreign Policy in Search of a Sustainable World

Shigeko Fukai

INTRODUCTION

Realpolitik nationalists like Condoleezza Rice advise that American foreign policy 'proceed from the firm ground of the national interest and not from the interest of an illusory international community'.[1] Implicit in this kind of statement is the assumption that there is an inevitable conflict between the pursuit of national interest and commitment to the interests of an international community. This chapter argues against this assumption. It argues that, in the face of rapidly worsening global environmental degradation and social inequity, we are now compelled to think in terms of longer-term and more enlightened self-interest and construct foreign policy on the basis of a broader conception of national interest that incorporates global public interest at its core.

NATIONAL INTEREST AND GLOBAL INTEREST

Definition of National Interest: Whose Interest Is It?

Conventionally, national interest with national survival and security as its main pillars is the primary concern of foreign policy. Hans Morgenthau, for example, has argued that since struggles between states to secure their conflicting national interests are inevitable and power determines which country prevails, it is imperative for any state to aim at increasing, keeping and demonstrating power in foreign relations. He emphasises military, economic and territorial power. Others emphasise national prestige, soft power, power based on technology, information, and the ability to influence public opinion.

However, the reality of the pursuit of national interest must be explored. Who actually determines the concrete content of national interest that the state pursues with the tax money of its citizens? Joseph Nye observes for the case of the United States:

When the majority of the American public is indifferent and complacent about international affairs, the battlefields of foreign policy are left to those with special interests. The result is a narrow definition of the US national interest that often alienates other countries. Take the apparent paradox of American refusal to pay UN dues in the 1990s, despite a consistent majority being in favor of the United Nations.[2]

Thus, Nye notes, often it is the voice raised by special interest groups that Congress pays attention to in determining the national interest. He also notes an important additional role of such ideologues as Senator Jesse Helms in the important committees in amplifying their voice. Henry Kissinger concurs with Nye by saying that 'What is presented by foreign critics as America's quest for domination is very frequently a response to domestic pressure groups.'[3]

It is true that national survival is the most vital national interest, but national interest is broader than national survival. It includes what the citizens feel as vital to their identity and wellbeing – both material and spiritual. It should be determined by the citizens through democratic debate and deliberation, muddled and time-consuming though the procedure may be. It is essential that the citizens be well informed – a difficult condition to achieve but the situation has been improved by progress in the information disclosure system and Internet access to information.

International Public Good and Global Public Good

In the past, the terms international public goods (IPG) and global public goods (GPG) have been used interchangeably. For example, peace, law and order, financial stability, ecological soundness, prevention of epidemics have been cited as typical examples of both IPG and GPG.[4] Other more concrete examples cited as both IPG and GPG are the international health surveillance systems, the international traffic rules for ships and airplanes, surveillance (and control) systems of narcotics trafficking and other trans-national crimes, as well as a variety of treaties on environmental protection. All of these qualify as public goods, as their benefits are shared by all and do not promote international rivalry. There are many examples like these that qualify as both IPG and GPG in conventional usage of the terms.

However, in order to clarify the nature of current global challenges that compel us to think and make policies – not only domestic but also foreign – as members of the human race rather than as members of a nation or a state, it is of vital importance to distinguish between a state-centred concept of IPG (defined as the interests presumably shared by all the member-states of the international community) and a global community-centred concept of GPG (defined as benefiting all peoples, present and future, on the earth). This is necessary because international public goods are defined as such by states, and hence reflect the values and interests of the ruling elites of those states and may well disregard or suppress those of the powerless. It is therefore critical to formulate the concept of global public goods in a way that reflects the values and the needs of the powerless on the planet. What, then, are the criteria for a good to qualify as a global public good? While two criteria – who benefits and who provides – come to mind immediately, the most important is who benefits. If it benefits all the people, present and future, on the earth, regardless of socioeconomic, national, regional, and other status, it qualifies as a global public good.

If it benefits only certain socio-economic classes, states, or regions, it does not qualify as a global public good, although it may qualify as an IPG, as indeed formulated by the theory of hegemonic stability – one of the most influential theories on IPG. This theory identifies such global services as maintaining the free trade system, making loans to countries in need, providing markets for exports from other countries, and defending sea lanes for international trade as the core international public goods.[5] Underlying this is the assumption that the free trade system benefits all the member-states, in the long run if not in the short run. This assumption has been falsified by the past performance of the free trade system. The free trade system as practiced today does not benefit all the states of the global community; it benefits mostly those industrialised countries already better off, and the tiny elite segments of the poorer countries well connected to those states. The globalisation of unfettered competition for profit maximisation promoted in the name of free trade has not only accelerated deterioration of critical environmental systems but also expanded inequality between and within nations.[6]

Growing inequality generates a 'force impelling the deprived to demand a better life from the powers that be,' as Nelson Mandela has warned.[7] If the ruling elites of the current system disregard this demand and the deprived become convinced that change through peaceful means is impossible, it would be natural also that they may choose to resort to violent means. If we accept peace as a vital global public good, we must recognise that global distributive justice, indispensable for achieving sustainable peace, constitutes a crucial global public good as the UNDP contends.[8] If all the states pursue their national interests defined in a shortsighted, narrowly self-interested way and avoid paying the cost for those public goods, it is certain that social and environmental disintegration will accelerate the collapse of our civilisation and of critical life-support systems.

Threats to Global Well-being

The global public goods are coming under threat today. There are three dimensions to the global crisis giving rise to this threat: the social and ecological dimensions and the dimension of legitimacy.

The Social Dimension

The social dimension is most apparent in the North–South disparity. The North here refers to the wealthy and industrialised, economically developed countries (EDCs), while the South symbolises the economically less developed countries (LDCs). There is a vast expanding economic gap between North and South. Richard Barnet and John Cavanagh have documented how powerful US corporations along with those from England, France, Germany and Japan are integrating about one-third of humanity into complex chains of production, shopping, culture and finance.[9] In consequence, Broad and Cavanagh note, the North–South divide has evolved into a new divide between,

> (t)he roughly one-third of humanity who make up a 'Global North' of beneficiaries in every country, and the two-thirds of humanity from the slums of New York to the favelas of Rio who are not hooked into the new global menu of producing consuming, and borrowing opportunities in the 'Global South'.[10]

Conventional wisdom classifies the citizens of the EDCs in the category of winners, the beneficiaries of this global system. However, both the social and ecological foundations of wellbeing of their citizens are rapidly eroding under the intensifying tide of neo-liberal globalisation. This process has shrunk the middle-income strata and expanded the poverty enclave in the EDCs, what Barnet and Cavanagh call the 'Global South' in the geographical North, where in fact many immigrants from the geographical South reside.

The North–South economic divide of this nature has complex ramifications in the realms of environmental and security issues. The vicious cycle of poverty and environmental deterioration is well known. The perceived injustice in the current global economic system also provides a rich source of motivation and support for terrorist actions. Economic grievances moreover can be mixed with cultural ones, as economic integration arouses the fear of cultural homogenisation. The fear of losing religious and cultural identity could translate into a strong motive for joining or supporting terrorist groups. Given that highly industrialised and centralised societies are most vulnerable to terrorist attacks, it is imperative that major states cooperate in tackling these social inequity problems at both the global and national levels.

The Ecological Dimension

The Limits to Growth – a 1972 report for the Club of Rome by Donella Meadows and her colleagues at MIT – warned of an impending disaster unless we immediately reduce resource-intensive industrial activity. The only way to avoid disaster, according to the report's prescription, is for conservation and pollution control to be combined with a halt in economic growth.

In 1992 and 2004, the group published 20 - and 30-year updates of the report entitled *Beyond the Limits*, in which the authors concluded that the two decades of history mainly supported the original conclusions and that humanity had already overshot the limits of Earth's support capacity. Even optimists must concede that the challenge would be tremendous if we were to raise the standard of living levels of the nearly 5 billion people living in poverty in the South up to the levels of the North. If the North keeps using most of the resources and creating most of the pollution, how can the South develop without exacerbating resource depletion and ecological deterioration? The North–South issue and environmental problems are inextricably intertwined.[11]

The Dimension of Legitimacy

The gravest among the global political issues is the lack of legitimacy of the current global capitalist system. The sustainability of a political system depends on the legitimate monopoly of coercive power or the apparatus of violence (military, police and tax power) and legitimacy. In the Westphalian international system the apparatus of violence is divided among sovereign states which claim a monopoly over the legitimate use of force in their territories. That is, the first condition is absent. The second condition, legitimacy, is therefore evermore important in achieving the stability and sustainability of the world order. Legitimacy for the nation-state is 'the feeling on the part of the people that the government which is acting in the name of the state and exercising the power of the state is rightly entitled to do so.'[12] With this feeling, the citizens are inclined to accept peaceably and as binding the decisions made by the authorities and institutions of the government.[13]

In the contemporary world, legitimacy depends on a sense of fairness and the degree of democratic accountability as well as on the quality of governance. At a global level, legitimacy requires a sense of fairness in the members of the global society and is therefore inseparable from the issues of achieving sustainability, eradicating poverty, and reducing North–South disparities through 'a new kind of democratisation of the global economy.'[14] It will require raising the living standards of the South, while reducing the rate at which the global stock of resources is depleted and the capacity of the physical world to accommodate human wastes is exhausted. Ultimately, values need to change, as commented by a Pulitzer Prize winning journalist:

> Much more of our gratification – especially in the wealthier nations – must come from sources other than the acquisition and consumption of an endless stream of products, most of which depend on artificially created demand and many of which are superfluous to our personal happiness. It seems to require, instead, that we look to our intellectual pursuits, our creative activities, our recreational competitions, and our expanding web of relationships for personal fulfillment.[15]

Only with such changes can a cohesive civilisation and a sense of community in global society be expected to emerge.

To restore the legitimacy of global governance, the first step would be to 'create and maintain some explicit conception of the common interest' as the shared goal among the policy makers and peoples of different nations.[16] The 'common interest' must be so basic and primordial in nature that it can appeal to anybody as such regardless of his/her culture or social status.

The most obvious common interest of such primordial nature in global society is our own survival. Our shared goal is to find the systemic causes that are making our globe unsustainable and build a vision and strategy for necessary structural changes. This would reveal the answers to the questions, 'who should get what out of the stock of scarce resources, how, when, and why?' Most likely, the issue of redistribution of resources and ecological space from the North to the South will emerge as prominent policy targets to be tackled.

Responsibility and Obligation of the Developed Countries

With the biological and social foundations of our existence destroyed, what value or significance could national interest have? Global interests can and should be incorporated into a broad and long-sighted concept of the national interest.[17] Global warming, infectious diseases, pollution, terrorism, to cite a few obvious examples, hurt the entire world community. Who should take the initiative and pay the cost for saving our biosphere and rectifying the imbalance in the distribution of global wealth?

The answer is clear: industrialised nations should, as they are mostly responsible for the destruction of nature by using a far greater amount of resources and generating far more pollution than the developing nations. The North has clear moral obligations to the South for other reasons as well. Most developing states are ill-equipped to deal with the problems of preservation, conservation, regulation of manufacturing processes, construction, waste disposal and other sustainability issues. Many of their governments are inefficient, wasteful, and corrupt, and many rules and institutions governing the international economy – designed to protect the interests of the industrialised countries of the North – are disadvantageous to developing countries.[18]

Singer points out that the very existence of structural inequalities in the international economy means that industrialised states have a duty to take action.[19] Pogge finds the North's moral failure in its imposition on the South of 'a skewed global order that obstructs and hampers their development'[20] and its refusal to address its role in creating the conditions for political repression and poverty in the South.[21] In addition to moral responsibility, industrialised nations are both equipped with the financial and technical capability to affect necessary reforms and positioned to benefit most from the stability of the global system.

Inhabitants in the affluent North have been able to avoid many adverse impacts of environmental deterioration by exporting their wastes and dangerous jobs and importing industrial goods.[22] They can afford stricter regulations and greener technologies. Little wonder their citizens and policy makers lack an incentive for taking initiatives in changing the situation by paying the short-term costs for restructuring the system. Little wonder also that they opt for the neo-liberal belief in market mechanisms and technological progress. Nonetheless, the fact remains that both responsibility and capability reside with industrialised states. Japan is in a perfect position to assume leadership in a joint endeavour among nations in pursuit of global environmental sustainability and social justice.

IN PURSUIT OF A SUSTAINABLE WORLD

The pursuit of a sustainable world will require what Blondel calls a revolutionary/ transformative-type of political leadership, the successful exercise of which will require social vision-making as a vital complement to effective political strategy.[23] The vision must show how to change the foundation and the framework of the system itself in practical and morally appealing ways.

In this section, I will sketch a vision. It must be both revolutionary and achievable through within-system strategies – that is, through changes carried out within the current framework of capitalist market economies and the Westphalian sovereign state system.

Vision

Steady-state Economy

The type of economy envisioned is a steady-state economy. Herman Daly has defined the steady-state economy as an economy in which total population and the total stock of physical wealth are maintained constant at some desired level by a 'minimal' rate of maintenance throughput.[24] Throughput is the flow of energy and material, which begins with depletion (resulting from production and consumption) and ends with an equal amount of waste effluent or pollution.[25]

Currently gross domestic product (GDP) is quantitatively associated with throughput, paying little attention to the depletion of low-entropy stocks. Institutions and theories are oriented toward maximising throughput, driving us to expansionary behaviour that causes feedbacks from the rest of the system in the form of pollution, breakdown of local life-support systems, and deepening social ills caused by massive dislocation from ever-accelerating technological, social and economic changes.[26] It is unsustainable to have unlimited economic growth that means unlimited inputs of energy and matter into economic production and unlimited outputs of wastes into the environment. The concept of limits was familiar to such classical economists as Adam Smith, Thomas R. Malthus and David Ricardo but totally abstracted away in neo-classical economics.[27]

Over millions of years of evolution, the biosphere has adapted itself to living off the fixed income of solar energy but in the last two centuries, human beings have ceased to live within the annual solar budget. What has enabled us (and conventional neo-classical economists) to forget these limits and helped generate what Daly calls the growth paradigm has been the availability of seemingly abundant (though non-renewable) fossil fuels.[28]

To convert this unsustainable economy into a sustainable one, it is necessary to lower the level of throughput flow and move toward a steady-state economy with a simpler frugal sustainable society. William Ophuls lists five features shared by a variety of 'frugal sustainable societies': (1) decentralisation and local autonomy; (2) a simpler, smaller-scale, face-to-face life closer to nature; (3) labour-intensive modes of production; (4) a de-emphasis on material things; (5) individual self-sufficiency (versus dependence on complex systems for the fulfilment of basic needs); and (6) cultural diversity.[29] A transition of the affluent North into such a frugal society is the only way to enable the poverty-stricken Third World nations to raise their living standard without increasing either the total depletion of resources or the burden on the environment.

Strong Government/Grass-roots Democracy
Each regional economic community will aim at realising utmost self-sufficiency. A highly decentralised system in which autonomous, self-reliant regional and local economic units coexist in several layers is envisaged. The world would consist of decentralised, self-reliant nations. The principle of subsidiarity would apply to the relationship between local, regional, national, and global levels of the economy. A combination of strong government and direct grass-roots democracy is envisaged not only at the local, regional and national levels but also at the global level. Strong government, endowed with unbending regulatory and coercive power, is a must in the initial stages of undertaking such a radical change as reversing the current trend away from economic growth and expansion towards lowering the material consumption level in pursuit of local or regional self-sufficiency.

To prevent a strong state from becoming too powerful and oppressive, it is necessary to found the political system 'on common consent on a set of principles designed to foster the common interest of the steady state instead of the particular interests that would destroy it.'[30] This is where grass-roots democracy comes in to ensure that the system operates on the basis of the consent of the ruled. It would be necessary to have citizens participate in the stage of agenda setting, policy making and implementation through evaluation. Information disclosure and the right to know must be incorporated as key elements of the political system. To prevent direct democracy from degenerating into fascism, a variety of institutional designs are conceivable, but one premise is to have citizens with a certain level of knowledge, information, a critical mind, and analytical skills. One way to foster and support such citizenship is what Morrison calls associative democracy, based on the empowerment of community-based democratic (one-member-one-vote) associations, involved in all kinds of social and economic activities.[31]

Global Parliament
David Held, Jürgen Habermas, and Noberto Bobbio, among others, argue that globalisation has undermined the democratic gains won over the last century and advocate the extension of democratic forms beyond nation-states.[32] To restore the democratic project they argue for international institutions ruled by the people and empowered to regulate the global markets in labour, money, goods, and ideas that have dramatically expanded in the past decades.[33]

At this stage, however, legislation of concrete policies at a global parliament is politically infeasible. The main role of the global parliament proposed here, therefore, would be to prepare for such institutional development by serving as an arena for debate and deliberation at the agenda setting stages. Its members would be elected directly by the citizens acting independently of any national government. By providing the parliament with broad power to inspect, report, and coordinate transnational projects and cooperative efforts at all levels, it could help generate and promote new trends and movements among diverse groups towards a sustainable world.

Preservation of the Environment

Is it possible to solve global environmental problems within the fragmented sovereign state system? The past history of international cooperation is not promising. How to narrow the mismatch between globalisation of the environmental issues and the fragmentation of governance is the task that we need to address, but that has been ignored or resisted almost unanimously by states. Greater and deeper restriction (or curtailment) of sovereignty is necessary to ensure effective international cooperation. Japan should take a lead in supporting such restriction of sovereignty in behalf of global public interests.

It is necessary to restore balance between nature's service and economic activity through a radical restructuring of the current system of global capitalism, which needs to transform its linear system of mass production, mass consumption, mass waste production into a circular system that reduces the amount of use of virgin resources and comes close to eliminating waste production.

To reverse the current global trends of ecological unsustainability, we need also to critically examine the current political system of green diplomacy. The conventional political wisdom is to focus on one specific, limited, and manageable problem at a time. Broadhead critiques this incrementalism as having served to perpetuate the growth model and continual profit-seeking underlying the environmentally destructive political, economic and social structures.[34]

A practical first step for Japanese initiative may be to work with the EU to make, for instance, its four principles of environmental policy into international rules. They are the precautionary principle, the prevention principle, the ratification at source principle, and the polluter pays principle. The OECD's proposals on the combined use of economic instruments and regulations would provide another practical basis for starting the environmental reform movement at the state level.

Naturally, this kind of initiative will face strong resistance. One of the strengths of foreign policy in pursuit of global public interests, however, is the moral weight they carry. The pursuit of global sustainability has potentially a universal moral as well as practical appeal, as everyone understands that the destruction of the ecological support base would affect everyone on the planet, even if initially the poor would be the worst hit and the rich may manage to keep their delusions of sustainable affluence a short while.

Global Security, Global Inequality, Limitless Growth

Henry C. Wallich writes:

> Growth is a substitute for equality of income. So long as there is growth, there is hope, and that makes large income differentials tolerable.

Herman E. Daly writes:

> We are addicted to growth because we are addicted to large inequalities in income and wealth. To paraphrase Marie Antoinette: let them eat growth. Better yet, let the poor hope to eat growth in the future.

In addition to the limits to growth imperative,[35] if growth were used as a substitute for distributive justice, the first step in transforming the economy into a steady-state economy would be to treat the addiction to inequality by identifying it as a deadly social malaise. The only way to cure this disease is to implement a redistribution of income and wealth to make the world more equal from the national to the global levels. This kind of treatment would have not only environmental effects but also important security implications. Today's irony is that global security may have little to do with military might. It is time to address the global security issues emanating from global poverty and inequality, by raising the redistribution of income and wealth as the global political issue to be tackled in earnest.

SOME STEPS TOWARD A SUSTAINABLE WORLD

Structural Changes in the Economy

The first task to tackle is dematerialisation of the economy. Many analysts observe that dematerialisation is well under progress with the shift of the industrialised economies into a post-industrial stage and the rise of the knowledge industry – although this change should not be overrated.

The second task is a radical reform of economic indicators, creating a new set of economic indicators that properly internalise social and environmental costs and are capable of measuring not only material affluence but also social, intellectual, and spiritual dimensions of change.

GDP is nothing but an undifferentiated indicator of material throughput, which regards growth of any type of consumption to be positive.[36] Jan Tinbergen and Roefie Hueting observe the consequences of the economic policy that places the highest priority on the growth of national income:

> The production of man made goods and services has increased unprecedentedly, but has been accompanied by an unprecedented destruction of the most fundamental, scarce, and consequently economic good at human disposal – namely, the environment. This process has already caused much human suffering. Much of what is called natural disasters – such as erosion, flooding, and desertification – is caused by mismanagement of the environment. This process threatens the living conditions of generations to come. Furthermore, part of the growth of national income consists of production increases in arms, alcohol, tobacco, and drugs. Few people consider this progress. Part of the growth in gross national product (GNP) is double counting. Thus, environmental losses are not written off as costs, but expenditures for their partial recuperation or compensation are written up as final consumption. The same holds true for expenditures on victims of traffic accidents and diseases caused by consumption, such as smoking.[37]

It is time to replace this unsophisticated indicator to measure progress with a more information-rich quality-measuring indicator.[38]

A third possible task would be to use taxation to correct some skewed aspects of the economy. Lester Brown recommends using taxes to incorporate in the prices the environmental costs of producing goods or providing services, to enable the market to send the right signals. For instance, when we buy furniture made of wood, normally we do not pay the costs of the flooding downstream caused by the logging of the trees. He suggests, 'If we restructure the tax system and raise taxes on clearcutting timber so that its price reflects the cost to society of the resultant flooding, this method of harvesting timber likely would be eliminated.'[39]

Another task would be to shift the allocation of subsidies in fiscal policy. The authors of the 1997 Earth Council report on environmentally destructive governmental subsidies observed, 'There is something unbelievable about the world spending hundreds of billions of dollars annually to subsidise its own destruction.'[40] Governments spend some $800 billion of taxpayers' money each year to encourage the use of water in the countries where water tables are falling, the burning of fossil fuels (despite rising concern about atmospheric carbon dioxide levels and climate change), and the use of pesticides, fishing, and driving. It is time for governments to shift subsidies away from the current list of recipients to a new list of environmentally constructive activities, such as investing in renewable energy, tree planting, family planning and the education of young women in developing countries.

Changes in the Rules on Trade and Investment

Along with structural reforms to promote changes toward steady-state economies, an alternative vision incorporates trade and investment mechanisms to reduce gross disparities in individual life opportunities, access to power, and socioeconomic fairness currently so striking between the North and the South. An alternative trade system is based on self-sufficiency for communities, nations, and economically integrated regions, on the one hand, and the free trade of ideas, information, knowledge, and services among nations, on the other. Developed countries that have accumulated substantial material resources that can be recycled could take a lead in implementing this. Already many parts of the industrialised world are moving toward 'an economy that emphasises reduction in the absolute amount of materials processed,' as Stephan Schmidheiny of the Business Council for Sustainable Development (BCSD) notes.[41]

Another pillar of reform is the rule of localisation on foreign direct investment (FDI). FDI should be conducted in such a way as to promote self-reliant development of the local host community (and country), reducing its vulnerability to world economic fluctuations. Rather than simply cut production costs or to evade the home country's pollution controls or labour regulations, FDI should be conducted to produce goods needed and consumed by the local people, using technology appropriate to local conditions that creates jobs and is environmentally sustainable. In fact, there is a broad recognition in the developing countries that the Western resource-intensive, high-consumption, high-waste model is unsustainable and untenable for their development. Usually, this recognition is keener among the grass roots than among the ruling groups.

Profits, except for an equitable return for the capital and technology supplies, should be retained and used in the host country. The concept of an equitable return on investments needs to be articulated as a criterion for legitimate business conduct, and as a conceptual tool for transforming the international business culture. It may be made a corporate norm to allocate a certain portion of reinvestment for education, health and research and development. It would lead to an improved investment environment through the improvement of the labour quality, the market, and social capital.

The localisation principle ought to be applied to management and technology transfer as well, by actively promoting the appointment of local personnel to management and technical positions. To preserve local culture and tradition, ways should be found to incorporate indigenous knowledge and production/recycling methods used during the self-sufficiency era into a new production/recycling system. Indigenous beliefs or understandings of the meaning of life and death, of time and eternity, and of how human beings should relate to the forces of the cosmos are unique from one another. From different understandings of these matters, emerge different conceptions of the good life and the good society. A code of conduct should be made to ensure foreign investors or aid agencies pay attention to these cultural differences.

The significance of the localisation rules is that they promote a transformation of the current shortsighted investment pattern that seeks to exploit developing countries' resources, cheap labour, cheap costs, and weak regulations, into an enlightened investment strategy aiming at long-term profit returns by fostering the domestic markets of the developing countries. This is the only natural outlet for the surplus capital of the North where domestic markets are saturated and investment opportunities are narrowed (indeed moving toward a steady-state).

Some Short-term Benefits of this Vision

The paradigm shift from narrow national interest to the construction of a sustainable world would bring about not only long-term benefits but also short-term benefits to affluent countries.

FDI conducted on the principle of localisation would help reverse the current tendency of economic globalisation to destroy indigenous culture. Also, home countries could avoid de-industrialisation and indirect trade friction with a third country.

The self-sufficiency and localisation principle would help alleviate the pressing problem of massive labour migration from the South to the North by creating more job opportunities and raising living standards in the former, while lowering the level of material consumption of the latter.

Industrialised affluent welfare states ironically have generated a society of lonely crowds. People have lost a sense of being needed and often become uncertain about their own *raison d'être*, as the state provision of social welfare has usurped them of the intimate sense of need to care for each other. In the past, mutual help was a must for 'survival'. Today, people exhaust themselves in endless competition in pursuit of narrow self-interest or instant pleasure. What is called the atomisation of society, the loss of community or social capital, is afflicting many affluent societies. The simpler frugal society would help regenerate the social ties and sense of solidarity. It would restore face-to-face communication and mutual help as part of daily living. In the small-scale communities, self-sufficient in basic necessities, links between producers and consumers would be revived. Less traffic and noise as well as less energy consumption would be another benefit.

For Japan, building a sustainable society as a test case for the world to study and learn from would be a challenging goal worth trying on its own. It would help fill the void left by the successful achievement of the postwar goal of catching up with the West in material affluence. It would promote a sense of solidarity with the developing world, and strengthen a sense of solidarity with a broad range of actors – in government, civil society, and business worldwide – who are committed to a shared project of sustainable world-building.

Japan, as most industrialised countries, has been able to create a seemingly sound environment and safe living conditions within its borders, while importing resources and exporting polluting industries and wastes, relegating the environmental costs to other, mostly developing, countries. It is therefore hard for most Japanese to comprehend the seriousness of the sustainability crisis confronting humankind. People lack the critical attitude necessary to re-examine the viability and sustainability of the current system and its values. Placing the construction of a sustainable world as its national goal, so to speak, would break this parochialism. A new social vision of what can be done to make our world sustainable can serve as the 'ultimate concept of the common interest' as it is tied to the most primal of needs – survival.

What is generally called global civil society has been on the opposing side of Japan's foreign policy, as demonstrated in Seattle in 1999 and a series of G7 or G8 summits. However, an alternative approach oriented towards sustainability at all levels from local to global would change this situation. By giving direction to the energy and aspirations of the people for a better life and a better world the orientation outlined here has a potential to succeed in generating broad public support and creating a genuinely democratic society.

NOTES

1. Peter Ludlow, 'Wanted: A Global Partner', *Washington Quarterly*, 24 (3) 2001, p. 167.
2. Joseph S. Nye, 'The American National Interest and Global Public Goods', *International Affairs*, 78 (2), 2002, p. 234.
3. Henry Kissinger, 'America at the Apex', *The National Interest*, 64, 2001, p. 15.
4. Inge Kaul, Isabelle Grunberg, and Marc A. Stern (eds), *Global Public Goods: International Cooperation in the 21st century*, Oxford: Oxford UP, 1999, p. xxv.
5. Charles P. Kindleberger, 'International Public Goods Without International Government', *The American Economic Review*, 76(1), 1986, pp. 1–13.
6. John Cavanagh and Jerry Mander (eds), *Alternatives to Economic Globalization: A Better World is Possible*, San Francisco: Berrett-Koehller, 2002, p. 4.
7. 'Mandela Says U.S. Must Aid World's Poor', *New York Times*, October 7 1994; John T. Rourke, *International Politics on the World Stage*, Guilford CT: Dushkin/McGraw-Hill, 1997, p. 209.

8. Debi Barker and Jerry Mander, *Invisible Government*, San Francisco: International Forum on Globalization, 1999.
9. Richard J. Barnet and John Cavanagh, *Global Dreams: Imperial Corporations and the New World Order*, London: A Touchstone Book, 1994.
10. Robin Broad and John Cavanagh, 'Development: The Market is not Enough', in Cavanagh and Mander (eds), *Alternatives*, p. 34.
11. Jack M. Hollander, *The Real Environmental Crisis: Why Poverty, not Affluence, is the Environment's Number One Enemy*, Berkeley: University of California Press, 2003, p. 14. He argues that economic growth is the only way to solve the environmental problems.
12. W. Andrew Axline and James A. Stegenga, *The Global Community*, New York: Dodd, Mead, and Co., 1972, p. 13.
13. Legitimacy is seen as related to social solidarity and cultural homogeneity, which in turn are related to the existence of community, a commitment on the part of the individuals in the society to each other and to the institutions of the society, Ibid.
14. Ross Gelbspan, *Boiling Point: How Politicians, Big Oil and Coal, Journalists, and Activists are Fuelling the Climate Crisis – and What we can do to Avert Disaster*, New York: Basic Books, 2004, pp. 197–198.
15. Ibid., p. 199.
16. Miles Kahler and David A. Lake, 'Globalization and Governance', in Kahler and Lake (eds), *Governance in a Global Economy: Political Authority in Transition*, Princeton: Princeton UP, 2003, p. 8.
17. Nye, 'The American National Interest', p. 236.
18. Vivien Collingwood, 'Achieving Global Economic Justice: Assistance with Fewer Strings Attached', *Ethics and International Affairs*, 17(1), 2003, p. 65.
19. Hans Singer, quoted in Collingwood, 'Achieving Global Economic Justice', pp. 64–65.
20. Thomas W. Pogge, 'Rawls on International Justice', *Philosophical Quarterly*, 51, Part 203, 2001, p. 253.
21. Thomas W. Pogge, *World Poverty and Human Rights: Cosmopolitan responsibilities and reforms*, Cambridge: Polity Press, 2002.
22. Paul R. Josephson, *Resources Under Regimes: Technology, Environment, and the State*, London: Harvard UP, 2004, p. 25.
23. Blondel has classified leaders into three categories: (1) saviours, who seem to be able to solve a major problem facing the nation or the state, such as the threat of total annihilation; (2) ideologues/revolutionary transformers, who are interested in bringing about major changes in the basis on which society is organised; and (3) paternalists/populists, who wish to introduce some changes but do not want to upset the whole society. J. Blondel, *Political Leadership*, London: Sage, 1987, p. 97. See also Shigeko N. Fukai, 'Building the war economy and rebuilding postwar Japan: A profile of pragmatic nationalist Nobusuke Kishi', in Ofer Feldman and Linda O. Valenty (eds), *Profiling Political Leaders: Cross-cultural studies of personality and behaviour*, London: Praeger, 2001, p. 168.
24. In other words, it is characterised by birth and death rates that equal at the lowest feasible level, and by physical production and consumption rates that are equal at the lowest feasible level.
25. Daly traces the part of constant stocks to the idea of John Stuart Mill and classical economics, and the part of 'minimal' flow of throughput to Kenneth Boulding. See John Stuart Mill, *The Principles of Political Economy*, Harmondsworth: Penguin, 1848; J. E. de Steiguer, 'Three Theories from Economics about the Environment', *Bioscience*, 45 (8), September 1995, p. 552; Kenneth E. Boulding, 'Income or Welfare?', *Review of Economic Studies*, 17, 1949–50, pp. 77–86.
26. Herman Daly, *Steady-State Economics: The Economics of Biophysical Equilibrium and Moral Growth*, San Francisco: W. H. Freeman, 1977, pp. 110–111.
27. Charles Sokol Bednar, *Transforming the Dream: Ecologism and the Shaping of an Alternative American Vision*, Albany NY: SUNY Press, 2003, p. 18.
28. Herman Daly, 'The Steady-State Economy: Toward a Political Economy of Biophysical Equilibrium and Moral Growth', in H. Daly (ed.), *Toward A Steady-State Economy*, San Francisco: W.H. Freeman, 1973, p. 153; Bednar, *Transforming the Dream*, p. 18.

29. William Ophuls, 'The Politics of the Sustainable Society', in Dennis Clark Pirages (ed.), *The Sustainable Society: Implications for Limited Growth,* New York: Praeger, 1977, p. 165.
30. William Ophuls and A. Stephen Boyan, *Ecology and the Politics of Scarcity Revisited: The Unravelling of the American Dream,* New York: Freeman, 1992, p. 286.
31. Roy Morrison, *Ecological Democracy,* Boston: South End Press, 1995, p. 142; Bednar, *Transforming the Dream,* p. 57.
32. Craig N. Murphy, 'Global Governance: Poorly Done and Poorly Understood', *International Affairs* 76(4), 2000, p. 790.
33. David Held, *Democracy and the Global Order: From the Modern State to Cosmopolitan Governance,* Cambridge: Polity Press, 1995, part 3; Murphy, Ibid.
34. Lee-Anne Broadhead lists four assumptions at the basis of the current approach to global environmental problems: (1) the role of instrumental logic will provide answers to scientific and technological questions, ensuring that ecological balance is sustained; (2) market structures, if properly managed, can respond to such problems that present themselves as ecological externalities; (3) the concept of sustainable development provides us with the framework within which the market can develop along ecologically sound lines; and (4) green diplomacy – that is, the multilateral efforts at finding collaborative agreements (regimes) to place effective limits on human action – will succeed in establishing the necessary bureaucratic mechanisms to ensure environmental protection. She criticises all four as products of a fundamentally unenlightened worldview that leads the modern world to disaster. Lee-Anne Broadhead, *International Environmental Politics: The Limits of Green Diplomacy,* London: Lynne-Rienner, 2002, p. 23.
35. The only way to increase one's income or wealth without taking from another is through economic growth or enlargement of the social pie. But if the pie cannot grow, the only option is redistribution. Joel Jay Kassiola, *The Death of Industrial Civilization: The Limits to Economic Growth and the Repoliticization of Advanced Industrial Society,* Albany NY: SUNY Press, 1990, p. 77.
36. Dennis Pirages, 'Building Sustainable Societies: The Third Revolution in Human Affairs', in Joel Jay Kassiola (ed.), *Explorations in Environmental Political Theory: Thinking About What we Value,* London: M. E. Sharp, 2003, p. 62.
37. Jan Tinbergen and Roefie Hueting, 'Wrong Signals for Sustainable Economic Success that Mask Environmental Destruction', in Robert Goodland, Herman E. Daly, and Salah El Serafy (eds), *Population, Technology, and Lifestyle: The Transition to Sustainability,* Washington DC: Island Press, 1992, p. 53.
38. In the US, the genuine progress indicator was developed in an attempt to foster debate over the quality of growth. Clifford Cobb et al., quoted in Pirages, 'Building Sustainable Societies', p. 62.
39. Lester Brown, *Eco-Economy: Building an Economy for the Earth,* London: W. W. Norton, 2001, p. 235.
40. Ibid., p. 240.
41. Stephan Schmidheiny with the Business Council for Sustainable Development, *Changing Course: A Global Business Perspective on Development and the Environment,* Cambridge, MA: The MIT Press, 1992. The group supports free trade but recognises the inherent conflict between ecological goals and free trade practice. They argue that internalising environmental costs and making polluters pay must remain the responsibility of individual governments and that environmental protection and resource management need international agreements; if the governments fail in such agreements, the pressure for trade barriers will mount *(Changing Course,* p. 26). Cynics may contend that those global corporations may weed out smaller competitors by using their technological edge to push stricter environmental regulations, although the group emphasises fostering small and medium-sized enterprises in developing countries.

Conclusion

12. Between Alliance and Regional Engagement: Current Realities and Future Possibilities

Joseph A. Camilleri

As the previous chapters have indicated, the post-Cold War period has seen important changes in the international organisation of human affairs, in the global balance of economic and political influence, and in regional governance, not least in the Asia-Pacific region. To a greater or lesser extent, all states, regardless of size, location or stage of economic development, have experienced the impact of these changes. Some have adjusted to the new environment with greater ease and speed than others. Some have actively sought to embrace the changing pattern of economic and security relationships, while others have sought refuge in the arrangements and relationships of an earlier era. In Asia, a critical factor in the responses of states has been the attitude to the alliances painstakingly constructed by the United States in the late 1940s and early 1950s as part of its containment of Chinese and Soviet power. One of the most intriguing themes running through many of the preceding chapters has been the extent to which the alliances of the Cold War period have continued to influence the region's security landscape, and as a consequence the extent to which the United States and its allies have used the alliance infrastructure to consolidate their respective power positions and set foreign policy priorities. In this respect, Japan and Australia offer particularly instructive case studies, and this for three reasons. First, they reflect the lingering hold of alliance discourse and practice on the political imagination of junior allies, that is, on the way they perceive and respond to change. Secondly, they show how the domestic politics of these societies – their political culture and institutions – is intimately connected with alliance management. Thirdly, they help to explain how alliances often constrain the willingness or capacity of junior allies to pursue active, let alone independent policies of regional engagement.

Alliances, however, cannot be viewed in isolation. The role that alliances continue to play in Japan's and Australia's relations with the outside world must be set in a wider historical and political context. If, as we shall argue in these pages, both Japan and Australia have encountered immense difficulty in responding to the exigencies of the post-Cold War period, it is in large measure because the two societies have yet to reconcile the often contradictory influences of history and geography. This chapter assesses the challenges facing the state and civil society in both countries, and explores the more imaginative policy options open to them in relation to three key signposts: relations with the United States, reform of the UN system, and cooperative regionalism. These options, however, are in no sense limited to Japan's and Australia's special circumstances. They are also relevant to other states and civil societies in the region, since they too will need to give increasing attention to the problem-solving capacities of regional and global processes and institutions.

AUSTRALIA AND JAPAN: THE WEIGHT OF HISTORY

In many respects Australia and Japan are as different as any two countries can be. Japan is a relatively small, densely populated archipelago located in the temperate latitudes, whereas Australia is, except for its coastal regions, a sparsely populated, arid island continent. Japan has a long, uninterrupted history, with agriculture introduced more than 2000 years ago, whereas European settlement in Australia occurred just over 200 years ago, in circumstances that created a sharp and lingering divide between the indigenous and non-indigenous communities. Though Japanese society bears the imprint of several waves of migration from the Asian continent and nearby Pacific islands, followed by heavy importation of culture from China and Korea, Japanese society experienced a long period of relative isolation from the outside world, during which a distinctive culture emerged. Modern Australia, on the other hand, has until recently developed largely as a European outpost in the South Pacific, patterned on British legal, political and cultural institutions. The Australian colonies and later the Australian Federation which came into being in 1901 continued to see themselves as an integral part of Western civilisation generally and of the British empire in particular. The arrival of a substantial number of Chinese in the nineteenth century merely served to reinforce Australia's sense of whiteness. Japan had by the early twentieth century achieved a high level of industrialisation, whereas Australia even today remains, despite its affluent lifestyle, heavily dependent on the export of primary commodities.

The differences in the historical trajectories and geographical and demographic circumstances of the two countries are as striking as they are numerous. Yet, they also share a number of equally striking similarities, which significantly colour their political outlook on the world: a certain insularity characteristic of island nations, a profound sense of dependence on American power, and a deeply entrenched incapacity to acknowledge the darker side of their recent histories, all of which has severely impeded a coherent sense of national identity, and prompted a marked ambivalence towards Asia.

Australia

In Australia's case, a deeply ingrained racism continued to hamper reconciliation with 'Indigenous Australia'. The ensuing culture of *dependency*, combining a high degree of insularity with reliance on great and powerful friends, was symptomatic of a deeper and lingering ailment, namely the psychologically and culturally unresolved tension between the country's history and geography. It is only by placing it in this context that we can make sense of Australia's troubled relationship with Asia, and begin to identify the anxieties and insecurities that continue to shape Australia's image of itself and its place in the world.[1]

At the risk of oversimplifying a tumultuous and highly complex period of Australian history, it may be said that from the late 1960s to the mid-1990s Australian governments attempted, however cautiously, to reshape the rhetoric and symbolic imagery that had traditionally underpinned the domestic and foreign policy agenda. With John Gorton's prime ministership (1968–71), we see the first tentative steps to construct a more independent Australian foreign policy, one less tied to America's apron strings and less committed to treating Asia as an arena of subversion and instability posing a direct threat to Australian security. After the brief aberration of McMahon's prime ministership, Gough Whitlam sought again, but in more forceful and eloquent language, to chart a new course 'with less emphasis on military pacts', based on 'an independent outlook in foreign affairs', and directed towards 'a new regional community'. Fraser too, though hostile to the Soviet Union and a strong advocate of the American alliance, was nevertheless prepared to voice a distinctively Australian perspective, not least on issues of race and Third World poverty, and to canvas possibilities for a much closer relationship with China.

Under Hawke and Keating the themes first elaborated by Whitlam were given added flesh. A stream of government initiatives suggested an unprecedented commitment to a policy of engagement with Asia. The decade of Labor government was labelled a 'remarkable decade of transition' that had witnessed 'an explosion of Asia consciousness'. Several indicators pointed in this direction: Australian firms were increasingly attracted by Asia's booming markets; the social and political life of Asian countries was given more extensive media coverage; the study of Asian languages became more popular; the immigrant community of Asian origin expanded significantly, as did the number of Asian tourists and students visiting Australia.[2]

None of this is to suggest that engagement with Asia was a fully coherent policy, that relations with great and powerful friends had been adequately reconceptualised, or that Australia's vision of an Asia-Pacific community accorded fully with East Asian notions of regional cooperation.[3]

Well before Keating's election defeat, numerous voices could be heard questioning each and every aspect of the new discourse. Constitutional change, even of the symbolic variety, recognition of indigenous rights,

Australia's changing demographic composition, and the complexities of the new regional diplomacy were seen by certain sections of society as at best irrelevant diversions from the more pressing concerns of everyday life or at worst as disturbing trends which ought to be reversed. For the best part of a decade Australia's profound ambivalence towards Asia would resurface with a vengeance. It is as if many Australians, frightened by the discourse of the 1980s and early 1990s, were only too keen to return to more familiar terrain.

Japan

Japan's imperial policies in the first half of the twentieth century, its aggressive thrust into Asia, and the atrocities it committed during the Second World War are by no means unique to it. However, there is reason to suggest that Japan has found it more difficult than Germany to exorcise the demons of the past and has tended to persist with what many regard as an inadequate or at least highly selective memory of its conduct. A key contributing factor has been the Cold War or, to be more precise, the role of the United States which, as the occupying power, was more concerned to consolidate its position in the country by forming alliances with established elites than in encouraging Japan to undertake the painful task of revisiting its past.[4] In sharp contrast to the position advocated by its wartime allies, the United States was intent on absolving Emperor Hirohito, in whose name Japan had conducted its military activities. Both Japanese and Western historians for example, John W. Dower, Herbert Bix, Yutaka Yoshida, Osamu Watanabe have in recent years emphasised that the Japanese Emperor was a knowing participant in a violent expansionist regime, the full record of which was deliberately obscured by Japanese and US authorities on the grounds of national security.[5]

Throughout the Cold War years, Japan was content to take advantage of the shield provided by the US umbrella. The truncated war crimes trials in Tokyo (1945–48) and subsequent compensation payments to some 27 governments were widely seen in Japan as adequate exoneration of its militarist past. Concentrating instead on the imperatives of economic reconstruction, Japanese governments and Japanese society more generally preferred to evade the issue, just as they had circumvented the full implications of the US-imposed peace Constitution.

The net effect of the strategy of evasion was to prevent Japan from healing the wounds that still festered in its relations with East Asia generally. Japanese actions dating back to the late nineteenth century and the 1895 Treaty of Shimonoseki had left a deep scar in Sino–Japanese relations.[6] Both China and Korea have since remained highly critical of Japan for its failure to face up to its conduct before and during the Second World War.

It was only in August 1993, four years after the demise of Emperor Hirohito, that a significant transformation took place in Japan's official interpretation of the nation's role during the Second World War. That month, Hosokawa

Morihiro, the first prime minister to break the post-occupation period of Liberal Democratic Party (LDP) rule, formally described the Sino–Japanese War and the Pacific War as 'a war of aggression'. He went on to apologise on a number of separate occasions for Japan's past aggression and subjugation of Asian countries. In 1995, the Diet passed a resolution on Japan's responsibility for the Second World War that acknowledged the nation's guilt for 'acts of aggression' and 'colonial rule'. This was widely seen as a compromise statement, widely criticised internationally for failing to use the word 'apology' and to refer to specific brutal acts committed by Japanese troops during the war. The same year on 15 August, in a speech marking the 50th anniversary of the end of the Second World War, Prime Minister Murayama Tomiichi went much further than the resolution by stating:

> During a certain period in the not-too-distant past, Japan, through its colonial rule and aggression, caused tremendous damage and suffering to the people of many countries, particularly those of Asia. In the hope that no such mistake will be made in the future, I regard, in a spirit of humanity, these irrefutable facts of history, and express here once again my feelings of deep remorse and state my heartfelt apology.[7]

While this statement was endorsed by South Korea in a Joint Declaration with Japan three years later, historical tensions have endured.[8] In any case, Japan's more conciliatory approach would soon provoke an intense reaction from Japanese conservatives and nationalists. The failure to resolve the textbooks controversy and statements in the media glossing over or even justifying past Japanese imperialism merely served to accentuate tensions with Asian neighbours.[9]

FROM BERLIN TO BAGHDAD TO BEIJING

The fall of the Berlin Wall dramatically altered the political landscape in Europe, and gave rise to a period of remarkable optimism about the prospects of a more peaceful world order. The impact of these events was less immediate but no less evident in the Asia-Pacific region. Though Japan remained highly suspicious of Soviet (later Russian) intentions, it could not indefinitely insulate itself from the post-Cold War euphoria. In both Japan and Australia the domestic winds of change combined with international influences to produce a more relaxed strategic outlook, and a greater willingness to consider new institutional arrangements that would take advantage of the available window of opportunity. However, these welcome initiatives would soon falter as more conservative political elites came to office, and as economic or social constraints weakened the national impulse for innovation as much in foreign as in domestic policy.

Australia

Under Howard, Australia once again opted for a conception of the world, as much psychological as intellectual, in which Western and in particular American notions of cultural and political superiority constituted the central frame of reference.[10] This conception in part reflects a deeper sense of white Australia's cultural and racial identity, and helps to explain the awkwardness – not to say reticence – with which the political phenomenon of Hansonism[11] was handled. The triumphalism that accompanied Australia's intervention in East Timor, the insensitive way in which the entire relationship with Indonesia was recalibrated following Suharto's fall from power, the 'deputy sheriff' pronouncements which came to be known as the 'Howard doctrine', the treatment of asylum seekers of Muslim provenance, the 'children overboard' affair, and the threat to take anti-terrorist pre-emptive action in the region all attest to the same mindset.[12] The net effect of these and other policies was twofold: it created the impression that the Howard government was intent on retreating from constructive engagement with Asia, except for the promotion of Australia's trade interests;[13] it significantly limited Australia's support for multilateralism, except for when such support was in line with alliance priorities.[14]

When Howard spoke of Australia's 'national character', of its 'distinct and enduring values', and of 'an Australian way', he was using code language to refer to key aspects of the white Anglo-Australian heritage. In this context, the United States assumed a pervasive presence in the Howard cosmology precisely because it provides much-needed psychological comfort and sustenance. By identifying so closely with the great and powerful friend, Australia once again placed the US alliance at the centre of its diplomatic, strategic, economic and cultural connections with the outside world.[15] The United States as a European, English-speaking superpower offered Australians racial, cultural and ideological affinities, that is, the comfort zone they so desperately sought to occupy. The result was familiar enough: renewed dependence in almost every area of policy – from Iraq and the 'war on terror' to civil liberties, the role of the United Nations, global warming, international trade, missile defence,[16] attitudes to Islam and Southeast Asia, and much else.[17]

There was more, however, to the umbilical connection with the United States than cultural or ideological empathy. Power is the other pivotal dimension. For the Howard government, and one suspects for a large segment of Australian society, the United States dazzles and comforts by virtue of its economic, technological and military prowess.[18] As I have argued elsewhere, for many Australians

> ... the unchallengeable power of the United States is doubly reassuring: it provides protection against the ultimate threat to 'national security', and enables Australia to speak and act in its neighbourhood with a louder voice than would otherwise be the case. Australia's little stick is reinforced and legitimised by America's big stick.[19]

The reassurance, however, was not purely or even primarily economic and political. It was fundamentally psychological, for it provided Australians a way out of the dilemma which they would otherwise need to confront, namely, the unresolved tension between history and geography. To put it crudely, but not inaccurately, the attachment to America as 'hyperpower' helped to postpone the evil day when Australia would need to come to terms with its indigenous heritage, its recent demographic and cultural evolution, and its Asian neighbourhood.

Japan

It is arguable that at least three contradictory currents have shaped Japan's hesitant attempts to adjust to the post-Cold War world. The first reflects the intricate nexus of political, bureaucratic and military interests that has over the years made a strong and enduring investment in the alliance with the United States.[20] The second current is nurtured by an increasingly forceful expression of Japanese nationalism,[21] which has seen a growing number of influential voices within and outside the LDP calling for an expansion of the Self-Defense Forces, greater capacity for military power projection, including participation in international peace operations, and, more recently, changes to the Japanese Constitution. All of this has become part of a wide-ranging vision to transform Japan into a 'normal' state.[22] The new nationalist wave has gathered strength partly in response to the faltering performance of recent governments, the prolonged stagnation of the Japanese economy, and an inchoate sense that the time has come for Japan to regain a sense of national identity which need no longer bear the burden of an aggressive military past. The third current, whose political influence and psychological resonance have steadily diminished over the last two decades, is represented by those who would wish Japan to adopt an internationalist stance, but one that remains firmly anchored in the renunciation of war as an instrument of policy.[23] It is reasonable to suggest that the present government's orientation represents for the most part an ambiguous oscillation between the contradictory but also complementary pressures exerted by the first two currents.

During the Cold War years Japan had allowed itself to become in Chalmers Johnson's words 'an ally, satellite and agent in the confrontation with the Soviet Union and China.'[24] Japan's regional role was in some respects more important to the United States than Britain's or even Germany's role in Europe. With the Cold War at an end, the US military presence in Japan – the 45,000 US troops and their related air and naval bases – has come to matter more to US strategic planners than any comparable presence in Europe. At stake is the capacity of the United States to project military power across a region riddled with actual or potential conflicts. This legacy has left the United States with enormous influence on a society 'that is unable to set national objectives and define a political role commensurate with its economic weight'. It is worth noting in parenthesis that Japan's economic leverage vis-à-vis the United States is not negligible, were it inclined to exercise it. Since the mid-1980s the export of Japanese capital has played a crucially important role in easing the impact of the 1987 Wall Street crash on the US economy and in maintaining the buoyancy of its financial markets.[25] More significantly still, Japanese financial flows have in part offset the inadequacies of domestic savings in the United States, thereby allowing it to persist with its otherwise unsustainable external deficits.

Some believed that the election of the eccentric Junichiro Koizumi would change the culture of dependence in Japanese foreign policy. The appointment of Makiko Tanaka as foreign minister seemed to point in this direction. However, her sacking in January 2002, precisely because of her more independent attitude to the United States, made it clear that any change in Japanese policy would be largely cosmetic.[26] Indeed, the Japanese Prime Minister soon made it plain that he intended a further strengthening of the relationship with the United States.[27] Notable the steady flow of actions and pronouncements that first punctuated his years in office, were:

- the decision to respond to the North Korean[28] threat by launching Japan's first spy satellites in order to develop an independent capacity for surveillance over North Korea;[29]
- the decision to join the Proliferation Security Initiative, a multilateral effort to interdict North Korean ships suspected of carrying weapons or contraband;
- the law passed in February 2004 allowing the government to impose – unilaterally and without any UN resolution – economic sanctions on North Korea;
- a string of counter-terrorism measures, including the special law passed soon after September 11 authorising ships from the Maritime SDF to assist US naval deployments in the Indian Ocean – though the law restricted cooperation to refuelling and logistics, the Japanese navy may be said to have in effect provided rear support for the invasion of Afghanistan;[30]
- the decision to deploy about 600 SDF troops near the town Samawah in southern Iraq, the country's first troop deployment under its own flag rather than the UN's since the Second World War – unlike previous Japanese peacekeeping missions, which have always been deployed in post-conflict non-combatant situations, this particular involvement raises the possibility of Japanese troops using weapons for self-defence in a hostile environment;[31]
- the announcement that cooperation with the United States on developing anti-missile defence technology was aimed at the threat from China (hitherto, joining Washington's Theatre Missile Defense program has used the North Korean threat as its justification);[32]

- the string of measures and announcements (including rising military budgets and the 10-year defence program released in December 2004 which openly labels China as a potential threat to Japanese interests), making it clear that Japan is intent on strengthening its military capabilities so as to enable it to respond to a much wider range of situations;
- the string of measures aimed at enhancing Japanese–US defence and security cooperation;[33]
- the joint statement with the United States that Taiwan was a 'common security issue' and therefore highly relevant to the US–Japan military alliance;[34]
- the announcement in February 2005 that the Japanese Coast Guard would officially take control of the disputed Senkaku Islands;
- the strong diplomatic support extended to the United States in opposing the European Union's plan to end the arms embargo imposed against China in the wake of the Tiananmen events of June 1989.

The net effect of these initiatives was to signal an enhanced regional policing role for Japan and a greater willingness to participate in future conflicts under US leadership.[35] Though Tokyo might justify these attempts at policy innovation by reference to any number of emerging threats (for example, international terrorism,[36] nuclear proliferation, North Korean roguishness),[37] the net effect was to compound the rising and widespread displeasure of a number of neighbouring countries, notably China and South Korea.[38] For them at least, Japan's actions reflected an attempt to assume a more assertive role on the international stage in ways that were oblivious to their historically grounded sensitivities or current preoccupations.[39] The double-edged sword in all of this was China's prodigious economic growth, and its political and strategic implications.[40] Were current trends to continue into the next decade, China would become the dominant influence in East Asia, thereby confronting Japan with a decidedly unfavourable shift in the Asian balance of power. The repositioning of Japanese security policy under the Koizumi prime ministership may be interpreted in part as an attempt to anticipate and neutralise this possible, no to say likely, reconfiguration of the power balance.[41]

It is doubtful, however, whether a strategy so patently tied to the fortunes, not to say whims, of imperial power or to the undisguised reassertion of narrowly conceived national interests and preferences will achieve the desired result.[42] Even from a purely self-interested perspective, the sheer weight of China's economic presence suggests that a cooperative approach is likely to yield a better return than the politics of confrontation. A recent CIA forecast suggested that China's GDP would equal that of Britain in 2005, Germany in 2009, Japan in 2017 and the United States in 2042.[43] Already the Chinese market has attracted many of Japan's giant corporations as well as countless of its small and medium-size firms. Apart from some 110 joint ventures, Japanese companies have established sub-contracting arrangements with some 3,000 China-based suppliers, are increasingly looking to China for their software outsourcing, and are rapidly setting up research and development laboratories in China. By 2004, some $66.6 billion of Japanese investment had entered China, but this may not necessarily translate into decisive leverage, given that total foreign investment had exceeded $560 billion.[44]

RECONCEPTUALISING THE FUTURE

What emerges from this all too brief survey of the overall direction of Japan's and Australia's external relations is a striking ambivalence in adapting to the rapidly evolving economic, political and strategic landscape. It is arguable that the political elites of both countries, though in different ways and to different degrees, have yet to internalise the far-reaching implications of an increasingly multipolar world. Despite much loose talk about the unipolar moment, US power is not quite as unchallengeable as some have come to believe.[45] The extraordinary difficulties the Bush administration has encountered in Afghanistan, Iraq and the 'war on terror' are indicative of imperial decline. The multiple sources of resistance to US policies in the Middle East and elsewhere show no sign of abating. In the longer-term, the wider geo-political landscape looks less than promising. Washington's unilateral responses to terrorism and the actions of 'rogue' states has already exacted a heavy financial and human price at home, which may prove beyond the tolerance of the American electorate. In Europe, governments and populations alike are gradually losing faith in America's capacity to lead. In East Asia, China's rise as the dominant regional power and developments in the Korean peninsula and Southeast Asia suggest that US power is being effectively bypassed. In a world in which power and influence are increasingly diffuse, a relationship with the United States that breeds a culture of dependence and emulation, is likely to deepen the gulf that separates Japan and Australia from their neighbours, and close doors to fruitful interaction.

This then may be an appropriate moment for these two strategically placed allies of the United States to reassess the present functioning of the alliance relationship, especially in the Asia-Pacific context.[46] In proceeding with such reassessment each country may have much to gain from observing how the other is weighing up its options, and even from considering the feasibility of joint initiatives.[47] Several courses of action suggest themselves. At one extreme is the possibility of abandoning the alliance and severing most, if not all, of the numerous and intricately interwoven legal, institutional and infrastructural arrangements that connect the Japanese and Australian defence forces with the US military establishment, its doctrines, basing requirements, weapons systems, communications facilities and intelligence operations. Though an abrogation of existing alliance arrangements may have much to commend it in the abstract, and may one day come to pass, it is difficult to envisage such an outcome emerging in the present political climate of either country. A more feasible scenario would be one in which Japan and Australia, as both states and civil societies, undertake a thoroughgoing re-examination of the alliance with the United States in order to develop a more independent security policy, one that more closely reflects the needs and aspirations of the two countries, while at the same time contributing to global and regional security.[48] If the relationship between these two US allies were to develop the necessary intimacy that goes beyond trade and defence cooperation, it might become possible for the two partners to engage in a private and public dialogue with the difficult questions that each has in the past been inclined to evade.[49]

In conditions of globalisation, or to be more precise in an environment of steadily rising technological, economic and ecological interconnectedness, states, buffeted by pressures which they cannot adequately control, have with varying degrees of skill and enthusiasm sought to pool their efforts and resources and create both global and regional collaborative frameworks and mechanisms. Japan and Australia have at different times contributed in significant ways to this process, but in recent years their contribution has been less than imaginative or enthusiastic.[50] Nowhere is this more apparent than in the restricted and at times grudging role that they have played within the UN system.[51] Here we content ourselves with a few general observations as to important signposts for a more effective contribution.

In the aftermath of the failure of the UN Summit in September 2005 to fulfil any of the widespread expectations for UN reform, both Japan[52] and Australia[53] could begin by unambiguously accepting the broad outlines of the UN Secretary-General's report *In Larger Freedom*, and in particular the need for a more focused approach to the implementation of the Millennium Development Goals (MDGs), which goes beyond existing aid programmes and, in Japan's case, substantial contributions to humanitarian relief.[54]

Beyond the specifics of the MDGs, the two governments could enunciate their unequivocal adoption of the principle of human security, and its far-reaching policy implications. The 1994 UNDP's Human Development Report identified two key dimensions of human security (freedom from fear and freedom from want) and seven areas where human security was under challenge: economic security, food security, environmental security, health security, personal security, community security, and political security. In his 2000 UN Millennium Report, UN Secretary-General Kofi Annan pointed to 'a new understanding of the concept of security' which now embraced 'the protection of communities and individuals from internal violence' and recognised 'the continuing dangers that weapons of mass destruction, most notably nuclear weapons, pose to humanity'.[55] Each of these security dimensions has special relevance to East Asia's societal needs and geopolitical circumstances.[56]

As Hamel-Green makes clear, Japan and Australia have at different times expressed a strong commitment to the nuclear disarmament and arms control agenda. Japan's three non-nuclear principles and Australia's advocacy for a comprehensive test ban treaty as well as Keating's decision to establish the Canberra Commission[57] are indicative of initiatives which could be strengthened to meet present circumstances. The deeply disappointing outcome of the 2005 NPT Review Conference and the UN Summit a few months later[58] calls for a fresh approach, especially on the part of US allies. The notion that would-be nuclear powers can be coerced into renouncing the acquisition of nuclear weapons, if necessary by the threatened use of nuclear weapons, while nuclear weapons states can retain a free hand to refine or even expand their nuclear arsenals is a contradictory and counter-productive position, which requires sustained reassessment.[59] The abolition of all nuclear weapons is an objective to which Japan and Australia should subscribe, and actively pursue in concert with like-minded governments in Asia and the South Pacific. Equally welcome would be a more active and systematic approach to the establishment of new nuclear weapon-free zones and the strengthening of existing ones.[60] In Japan's case, a first yet crucial step would be to dispel mounting regional anxieties about the possibility of a future Japanese nuclear weapons capability[61] by unambiguously renouncing this option and by terminating current policies predicated on the processing of spent nuclear fuel and accumulation of plutonium stockpiles.

The United Nations is clearly in need of urgent reform as Yamada incisively points out. Japan has endeavoured to bolster its case for permanent membership of the Security Council by pointing to the need for UN reform,[62] but its proposals have been singularly lacking in depth or detail[63] The Australian government has similarly made noises about the virtues of UN reform,[64] but often by way of tarnishing the image of the world body or deflecting criticism periodically levelled against it for its treatment of indigenous Australians, refugees and asylum seekers.[65] A more promising approach would be one which addresses the detail of Kofi Annan's package of proposals, especially those designed to enhance the international human rights regime and its monitoring capabilities, to lay down the strict principles that should govern the international community's use of force in humanitarian catastrophes, and to establish more clearly the principles of legitimacy and accountability that should govern the UN's peace operations. So far as the international human rights regime is concerned, the two countries could usefully begin by reviewing the major international human rights instruments, and ensure that ratification is followed by the necessary steps that would enshrine their relevant provisions into domestic law. Especially relevant here are the two international covenants and their accompanying protocols, and the recent Rome Treaty establishing the International Criminal Court.

In the light of the unfortunate experience of the last few years, whereby US administrations have sought to circumvent the authority of the United Nations in sanctioning the use of force, it behoves both Japan and Australia to distance themselves from Washington's unilateralist inclinations. The close support that Tokyo and Canberra have extended to US actions in Afghanistan and Iraq, and more generally to the 'war on terror', has thus far yielded few positive results either in the specific theatres of conflict or for Japanese and Australian security. One of the less controvertible effects of these adventures has been the increasing diplomatic isolation of the United States and its close allies. In responding to the terrorist threat, both Japan and Australia would be better advised to pursue a longer-term approach which places the emphasis on prevention rather than cure and on causes rather than symptoms.

Side by side with the development of global processes and institutions (that is, globalism) – most strikingly evident in, but by no means confined to, the activities of the UN system – has been the growth of regionalism. Though Europe, in particular the European Union, is often viewed as the precursor of this trend, no region, regardless of size, stage of development or civilisational outlook, can now be said to be immune to the trend. Asia Pacific is no exception to the rule.

Among the more significant region-wide organisations to have emerged in Asia since the end of the Cold War are the Asia-Pacific Economic Cooperation group (APEC), the ASEAN Regional Forum (ARF), ASEAN+3 (comprising the ten ASEAN countries plus China, Japan and South Korea) and the Asia-Europe Meeting (ASEM).[66] The steady advance of Asia-Pacific regionalism makes it clear that the US strategic presence in the region offers no substitute for multilateral cooperation.[67]

In this part of the world, however, regionalism has given rise to a number of unresolved tensions, notably the tension between two different geographical/ institutional models, each representing distinct configurations of power and interest. One model, which carries the label 'Asia Pacific', serves as a bridge between 'residual US hegemony' and East Asia as an emerging centre of economic and political influence. The other model, best known as 'Pacific Asia', is centred primarily, if not exclusively, on East Asia, and may be said to reflect the economic dynamism and interdependence of the East Asian region and an explicit or implicit 'Asian' outlook. Relevant to an understanding of this phenomenon is the Asian versus Western values debate which gained prominence during the mid-1990s. Two other kinds of tension are worth noting here. These may be best encapsulated in the form of two questions (to which we shall presently return): what is to be the specific contribution (and relative importance) of states, markets and civil society in the task of regional integration? How are priorities to be set between competing notions of security?

At this point, it may be helpful to note ASEAN's critical role in the emergence and consolidation of Asian regionalism. Established in 1967, ASEAN has progressed from its humble origins to become an inclusive, geographically compact and functionally polymorphous organisation. It remains, despite its ups and downs and unevenness of performance, the principal engine of East Asian multilateralism, and continues to provide the most convenient litmus test for evaluating the prospects of any new regional proposal.[68]

These and other trends have now combined to create a unique historical conjuncture, the main elements of which may be summarised as follows:

(a) the growth of a pan-Pacific trading and investment region, which presently includes East Asia, North America and Oceania, but whose geographical boundaries and centre of gravity are susceptible to change given shifting patterns of economic activity and competitive advantage;
(b) the development in Asia Pacific of a 'zone of economic interdependence' (rather than a trading bloc or free trade area) whose dynamism rests on continuing access to the large US market, Japanese penetration of Asian supplier networks, and steady growth of the economic zone that is 'Greater China';
(c) a unique ASEAN approach to regionalism characterised by an emphasis on longer time horizons and policy perspectives, a preference for informal structures and processes, consensual forms of decision making, multidimensional or comprehensive notions of security, and a strong residual commitment to the principle of non-interference in the internal affairs of member countries – the net effect of which has been to produce a brand of multilateralism that is more enticing and less threatening to East Asian political elites than would otherwise have been the case;
(d) the increasingly prominent role of influential elements in the business and academic communities, and after a slow start the expanding number of civil society networks with an acknowledged stake in regionalisation.

Institutional innovation, viewed from the vantage point of either Asia Pacific or Pacific Asia, has come a long way, which is not to say that such arrangements are equal to the immense challenges that lie ahead. One need only think of large and unpredictable financial flows, rising military expenditures and acquisition of potentially destabilising offensive weapons systems and platforms, the actual and potential proliferation of nuclear capabilities, and the multiple and extensive forms of environmental degradation. To this list can be added the disparities of wealth and income within and between states, and the consequent suspicions and fears harboured by the less prosperous and successful vis-à-vis those exercising economic dominance; latent bilateral tensions, many of them predating the Cold War (for example, Sino–Japanese rivalry, Japan–Korea tensions, the India–Pakistan conflict, competing territorial claims in relation to the Spratlys, the Kuriles or Northern Territories, and the Senkaku or Diaoyutai Islands; and a good many unresolved civil conflicts (for example, Tibet, Kashmir, Aceh, Papua) and issues of divided sovereignty (China–Taiwan, Korean peninsula). The inadequacy of regional security arrangements was strikingly evidenced in the violence that gripped East Timor in the period leading up to self-determination and eventual independence.

While East Asian regionalism has made considerable strides on many fronts since the end of the Cold War,[69] the existing regional architecture needs to be given a more solid normative foundation, a stronger institutional base, and a more coherent set of functions. Both Japan and Australia are well placed, despite the recent tentativeness of their respective approaches,[70] to make a considered response to these possibilities, though success will require extensive consultation with other parties in both Northeast and Southeast Asia, and with ASEAN in particular.

The framework envisaged here would be comprised of many elements. Foremost among these would be a clear acknowledgement of the principles of comprehensive security. As already indicated, particularly helpful would be a readiness to incorporate the principle of 'human security', which has now acquired widespread acceptance within the UN system. The proposed normative framework would encapsulate two other key requirements. First is the now widely shared understanding that the emerging regional architecture cannot countenance conditions of 'hegemonic control', whether of the kind associated until recently with US strategic dominance or of the kind that might emerge with the rise of a new centre of power. The rationale for such a normative principle should be readily apparent: the Asia-Pacific region has entered a delicate period of transition, in which, notwithstanding US unilateralist preferences, power will remain diffuse and decisions, to be legitimate, will have to rely on consensus rather than diktat.

Such a normative framework would operate most effectively if its key tenets were encapsulated in a formal charter or 'declaration of principles'. Such a document could be prepared specially for the purpose and become the focus of a carefully structured process of discussion and negotiation, or it could comprise or build upon a number of already established agreements, of which the now widely supported Treaty of Amity and Cooperation (TAC) is by far the most relevant.[71] Whichever route is followed, the declaration would seek to define norms of international conduct by giving moral, and in certain cases legal, force to three distinct but closely interrelated notions. First is the need for a strong commitment to the twin tasks of confidence-building and transparency, or, to put it a little differently, a willingness to implement both formal and informal measures – unilateral, bilateral and multilateral – to prevent and resolve tensions and uncertainties in inter-state relations. Secondly, existing mechanisms need to be extended and refined with a view to promote predictable and legitimate behaviour, particularly with respect to bilateral or regional conflicts as in the case of the Northern Territories and South China Sea, but also in highly sensitive conflicts considered by one or other party to be an internal matter (for example, China–Taiwan, Indonesia–Papua). In this context, it would be helpful to refer in such a declaration to the benefits and modalities of consultative and other mediatory processes. Thirdly, respect for fundamental social, economic, cultural, civil and political rights must be accepted as a keystone of state conduct, and appropriately reflected in mechanisms of accountability and participation at all levels of governance.

The precise formulation of the principles that would comprise such a declaration would no doubt prompt considerable debate and even disagreement, not least around the twin notions of sovereignty and non-interference in the internal affairs of other countries. The negotiating process, by seeking to reconcile diverging perceptions, interests and policies, is likely to prove as important as the outcome itself, especially if it were to engage the widest cross-section of civil society in each country and draw on the region's diverse religious and cultural traditions. In any case, any eventual agreement would not be the last word on the subject, but simply one more step or threshold in an on-going conversation. On the other hand, once reached, a normative consensus, however provisional, would offer governments useful guidance for the development of national human rights institutions, and the region as a whole a convenient benchmark with which to assess institutional performance.

The case for institutional reform is just as compelling, although here again it would be a matter of building on what already exists, rather than starting with a clean slate. To begin with, Asia-Pacific regionalism needs a highly visible roof or umbrella. One possibility would be to have the annual APEC summit renamed the Asia-Pacific Leaders Meeting. Such a forum would be expected to consider the entire gamut of economic, strategic and environmental concerns in line with the understanding that these are closely interconnected and form an integral part of a comprehensive security agenda. It is worth noting that recent APEC summits, with Japanese and Australian support, have been moving steadily in this direction, as evidenced by the willingness of all members to place such issues as East Timor, Korea and terrorism on the agenda and to incorporate them in public declarations.

As for APEC itself – a regional organisation whose establishment owes a great deal to Australian and Japanese initiative – the time has come for serious stocktaking.[72] Over a ten-year period it would not be unreasonable to expect the organisation to undertake a re-examination of its mandate, and in particular of its narrowly defined focus on trade and investment liberalisation. There is much to be said for APEC beginning to devote systematic attention to unconventional security issues that impinge directly or indirectly on economic policy (for example, environment, development, energy security, labour migration, labour laws, narcotics trade), and to do this in coherent fashion, where necessary in collaboration with other regional organisations. Though small steps have already been taken, the organisation's long-term relevance will also depend on it making a concerted opening to civil society, through the establishment of an APEC Civil Society Advisory Council, an APEC Trade Union Advisory Council, and the participation of non-governmental organisations.

In the case of the ARF, unconventional security issues (for example, environment, piracy, transnational crime and human rights) will increasingly intrude into all three stages of its development (confidence-building, conflict prevention and conflict resolution), but here a strong case can be made for a more integrated approach as well as for setting clear benchmarks for the more effective coordination of functions and for more effective and better resourced conflict prevention and conflict resolution initiatives. Here, close consultation and cooperation with ASEAN will be vital to the success of such an approach.[73] In second track diplomacy, CSCAP, which has thus far relied primarily on specialists in 'security studies', might consider the possibility of judiciously involving other epistemic communities – environmental and medical scientists, lawyers and judges, parliamentarians and civil servants, sociologists and psychologists, to name a few – with a view to widening the sources of available knowledge and expertise, and so increasing its own usefulness to first-track regional organisations, in particular the ARF, while at the same time enhancing its own legitimacy and connections with civil society. As the security agenda expands and the multilateral process gathers pace, there will be a greater need to develop other second-track functions, not least a systematic monitoring function.

As we have already noted, ASEAN+3 has emerged as the most significant political expression of 'pan-Asian' consciousness and of East Asian economic interdependence.[74] Over the next few years the membership of ASEAN+3 will have to determine whether the organisation can significantly contribute to the comprehensive security agenda. Perhaps the greatest test in this regard will revolve around its capacity to fashion a *modus vivendi* between its three major centres of power and influence (China, Japan and ASEAN) and to generate a sufficiently distinctive and coherent set of ideas that can guide its internal development as well as its external relationships, in particular its input into APEC, ASEM, the ARF and even the United Nations and other global institutions. It is to be hoped that ASEAN+3 will develop the political will, structures and policies which, though taking account of the close connections between several of its members and the United States, can nevertheless offer, in keeping with East Asia's cultural and political traditions, an independent approach to pressing international problems that distinguishes it from the priorities favoured by Washington or Brussels.

It remains to say a few words about the extra-regional dimensions of international cooperation. East Asia's relationship with other regions, including the rest of Asia, Africa and Latin America, will no doubt assume increasing importance. Complex issues will need to be addressed that go to the heart of the future relationship between the Global North and the Global South. Even more important will be ways of managing the relationship with the United States, for which several regional avenues are already available including APEC and ARF, and an even larger number of global fora. Let me confine these brief concluding observations to one inter-regional forum (ASEM) and one global (the United Nations).

In ASEM's case, three key functions are worth highlighting: (a) the intrinsic benefits to be derived from closer commercial, financial, technological and cultural links and exchanges between the two regional formations (EU and ASEAN+3); (b) a more mature inter-civilisational and human rights dialogue; (c) the potential to facilitate an East Asian–European collaborative relationship that might curb the excesses of US unilateralism, and over time persuade US policy makers of the virtues of an international concert of powers as a first step towards the progressive democratisation of global governance. One of ASEM's main challenges is to create the psychological and political conditions in which Asian and European policy makers find it comfortable and advantageous to place on their agenda the future structural and policy reorganisation of key global institutions, including the UN Security Council and other parts of the UN system, as well as the IMF, World Bank and WTO.

By virtue of its Charter and universal membership, the United Nations is the pre-eminent organisation concerned with fashioning a comprehensive approach to security – a view repeatedly reaffirmed in the declarations of the UN Secretary-General and the deliberations of UN Security Council, especially in the post-Cold War period. In *An Agenda for Peace,* Boutros Boutros-Ghali called for closer links between the United Nations and regional organisations, partly with a view to strengthening the legitimacy of the international organisation, and directly or indirectly enlarging the pool of resources at its disposal. This, however, need not be a one-way street. Regional organisations have themselves much to gain from closer interaction with the world body. Events of the last fifteen years have made this abundantly plain. The Cambodian peace process, the Comprehensive Action Plan on Indo-Chinese Refugees, the international community's efforts to address the continuing problems facing East Timor, the unfinished business of bringing to trial the perpetrators of monstrous crimes in Pol Pot's Cambodia, and the UN's coordinating function in response to the Tsunami tragedy all attest to the UN's important role in the region, a role which both Japan and Australia have normally welcomed, and at times even strongly advocated.

More systematic and effective coordination between regional and global processes may be especially helpful in relation to arms control (notably around the issue nuclear non-proliferation and small arms), conflict prevention (for example, Law of the Sea) and peace-building (for example, application of international criminal law with respect to Cambodia and East Timor). Other opportunities for fruitful cooperation exist in relation to such issues as uncontrolled or illegal migration, narcotics smuggling, border disputes, monitoring of human rights standards,[75] resource management, and protection of the environment. The attention intermittently given by the ARF to the peacekeeping agenda is suggestive of other possibilities. One is the establishment of a regional peacekeeping centre (to oversee preparation and development of systematic training programmes, and provide early warning about latent local and regional conflicts). Another is greater cooperation between the United Nations on the one hand and the ARF, ASEAN or Pacific Islands Forum on the other in handling a number of intra-state conflicts, whether in Indonesia (Aceh, Papua), the Philippines (Mindanao), or in what is sometimes referred to as the 'Melanesian arc of instability', including Papua New Guinea/Bougainville, the Solomons, and potentially Fiji.

Asia Pacific, not despite but because of the plurality of religious and ethical traditions which it encompasses, is uniquely placed to put to constructive use both differences and complementarities. Several possibilities readily suggest themselves. A human rights dialogue grounded in the cultural traditions of the Asia-Pacific region would enhance the comprehensiveness of the international human rights regime, and in the process help to establish a better fit between human rights and human needs, between rights and obligations, and between individual and community. Much would also be gained from a concerted effort to strengthen second and third track diplomacy. This would help to inject into the multilateral project the energies and resources of the legal, medical, educational, scientific and other professions, not to mention religious, cultural and social organisations concerned with issues of economic development, health, environment, media, urban planning, or industrial relations.

A more encompassing approach that incorporates Asian perspectives could over time help to moderate the legalistic and individualistic ethos which still dominates much of Western human rights discourse – a third generation of human rights might emerge, which affirms the related rights to security, survival and sustainability, that is, the right of groups and individuals – even those of unborn generations – to be reasonably confident of their prospects of physical well-being, now increasingly under threat by terrorism, weapons of mass destruction, disease, poverty and environmental degradation. To complement and underpin the aforementioned proposals, an independent Regional Centre for Cultural Dialogue and Co-operation might be established to perform specific research and training functions. With appropriate funding from one or more of the developed economies, not least Japan and Australia, such a centre would promote debate, research and analysis across the full range of rights and responsibilities (individual and collective), bringing to bear a strong inter-cultural, inter-civilisational focus. It would provide interested governments with a range of professional services, including facilitation of national educational strategies, regular briefs, policy papers and various forms of research and technical assistance, notably in the preparation of national and regional meetings and conferences.

Pacific Asia and Asia Pacific – the two conceptions of regionalism will remain in uneasy but hopefully productive tension for some time to come – have entered an era of unprecedented challenges and opportunities. Japan and Australia are under increasing pressure to forge a more coherent and constructive synthesis of their historical and geographic circumstances. Such a synthesis must encompass both domestic and foreign policy. In Japan's case becoming a 'normal' power in the international context cannot be allowed to overshadow the need for 'internal normalisation', that is, the need to come to terms with the cultural, social and political roots of its imperialist past.[76] In Australia's case, acceptance by regional neighbours will in good measure depend on its capacity to shed the anti-Asianism of the past, and fashion an educational and social agenda that is attuned to multicultural values and cross-cultural dialogue. In all of this, the adequacy of the response will be determined by the imagination of the governments involved, but at least as importantly by the imagination and perseverance of organised civil society both within and across national boundaries. For all the impediments that stand in the way, there is much that Japan and Australia can contribute to this dual undertaking. Such a contribution would be all the more effective to the extent that it encouraged a wider regional framework of inter-cultural interaction and policy coordination.

NOTES

1. This part of the argument is developed at greater length in J. A. Camilleri, 'The Howard Years: Cultural Ambivalence and Political Dogma', *Borderlands E-Journal Special Issue*, 3 (3), 2004, http://www.borderlandsejournal.adelaide.edu.au/vol3no3_2004/camilleri_howard.htm
2. See Gareth Evans and Bruce Grant, *Australia's Foreign Relations in the World of the 1990s*, Melbourne: Melbourne UP, 1995; Paul Keating, *Engagement: Australia Faces the Asia-Pacific*, Sydney: Macmillan, 2000.
3. See Joseph A. Camilleri, 'The Multilateral Dimensions of Australia's Security Policy', in Des Ball (ed.), *Maintaining the Strategic Edge: The Defence of Australia*, Canberra: The Australian National University Strategic and Defence Studies Centre, 1999, pp. 307–334.
4. See Philippe Pons, 'Japan's Creative Amnesia', *Le Monde Diplomatique*, October 2001.
5. See John Dower, *Embracing Defeat: Japan in the Wake of World War II*, New York, NY: W. Norton & Co., 1999; Herbert Bix, *Hirohito and the Making of Modern Japan*, New York, NY: HarperCollins Publishers, 2000; also Pons, 'Japan's Creative Amnesia'.
6. For further discussion of the history of Sino–Japanese tensions see Claude Leblanc, 'Unfriendly Neighbours', *Le Monde Diplomatique*, October 2004.
7. See Ministry of the Foreign Affairs of Japan, http://www.mofa.go.jp/announce/press/pm/murayama/9508.html (sighted on 1 September 2005).
8. A subsequent speech by South Korean President Roh Moo-Hyun in 2005 described both the speech and Joint Declaration as inadequate. See Gavan McCormack and Wada Haruki, 'The Strange Record of 15 Years of Japan-North Korea Negotiations', *JapanFocus.org*,

2 September 2005, http://www.japanfocus.org/article.asp?id=385 (sighted 3 September 2005).
9. For further discussion of the implications of the unresolved legacy of the Second World War, see Gilbert Rozman, *Northeast Asia's Stunted Regionalism: Bilateral Distrust in the Shadow of Globalization*, Cambridge: Cambridge UP, 2004, p. 303.
10. After the progress made by Labour governments during the 1980s and 1990s in Australia's relations with the Asia-Pacific region, the Howard government sought to differentiate itself from the Keating government by criticising what it saw as 'Asia first' or even 'Asia only' policies. See Richard Woolcott, 'Megaphone Diplomacy', *The Diplomat*, 3 (5), December 2004–January 2005, pp. 18–19.
11. Refers to the political phenomenon that was triggered off by the independent member of the Australian parliament, Pauline Hanson, whose strident anti-Asian sentiments struck a response chord in certain sections of Australian society.
12. I discuss these aspects of Australia's external outlook in Joseph A. Camilleri, *States, Markets and Civil Society in Asia Pacific: The Political Economy of the Asia-Pacific Region*, Volume 1, Cheltenham, UK: Edward Elgar, 2000, pp. 313–322.
13. See Richard Broinowski, *Fact or Fission: The Truth About Australia's Nuclear Ambitions*, Melbourne: Scribe Publications, 2003, pp. 217–218.
14. See, Bruce Grant, *Fatal Attraction: Reflections on the Alliance with the United States*, Melbourne: Black Inc., 2004, p. 87.
15. See, Department of Foreign Affairs and Trade (DFAT), *Advancing the National Interest: Australia's Foreign and Trade Policy White Paper*, Canberra, 2003, Chapter Six, 'Strengthening Our Alliance with the United States', http://www.dfat.gov.au/ani/chapter_6.html (sighted 7 September 2005) and DFAT, *Australia-United States Ministerial Consultations Joint Communique*, 2005, http://www.dfat.gov.au/geo/us/ausmin/ausmin05_joint_communique.html (sighted on 7 September 2005).
16. Alexander Downer, Media Release, 'Australia to Join US Missile Defence Program', 4 December 2003, at http://www.foreignminister.gov.au/releases/2003/fa151_03.html (sighted on 9 September 2005).
17. See Tony Kevin, 'Foreign Policy', in Robert Manne (ed.), *The Howard Years*, Melbourne: Black Inc. Agenda, 2004, pp. 295–7; also Mark Beeson, 'Australian Foreign Policy after Bali', *The National Interest*, 13 November 2002, at http://www.inthenationalinterest.com/Articles/Vol1Issue10/Vol1Issue10Beeson.html (sighted on 9 September 2005).
18. See Woolcott, 'Megaphone Diplomacy', p. 18 and Grant, *Fatal Attraction: Reflections on the Alliance with the United States*, p. 101.
19. See Joseph A. Camilleri, 'A Leap into the Past – in the Name of the National Interest', *Australian Journal of International Affairs*, 57 (3), 2003, pp. 431–453.
20. For further discussion of the US–Japan alliance, with a particular focus on the military dimension, see Christopher W. Hughes, *Japan's Re-emergence as a 'Normal' Military Power*, Adelphi Paper 368–369, Oxford & New York: Oxford UP, 2004, pp. 97–105.
21. For discussion of some of the domestic influences shaping current Japanese nationalism see Kiri Paramore, 'Stoking Tension', *The Diplomat*, 4 (2), 2005, 17–18; also Leblanc, 'Unfriendly Neighbours'.
22. See Hughes, Japan's Re-emergence as a 'Normal' Military Power, pp. 49–57.
23. See Hughes, Japan's Re-emergence as a 'Normal' Military Power, p. 59.
24. Chalmers Johnson, 'The American Shogunate', *Le Monde Diplomatique*, March 2002.
25. Japan's more recent financial contributions to reconstruction efforts in both the Balkans and Afghanistan have continued this trend. See Yutaka Kawashima, 'Japan's Security Environment', *CNAPS Working Paper*, The Brookings Institution, 1 March 2002, p. 4.
26. For full discussion of the Tanaka Makiko affair see Rozman, *Northeast Asia's Stunted Regionalism*, p. 304.
27. See Gavan McCormack, 'Remilitarizing Japan', *New Left Review*, No. 29, Second Series, September October 2004, pp. 33–4; Ministry of Foreign Affairs of Japan, *Statement by Prime Minister Junichiro Koizumi at the Ceremony Commemorating the 150th Anniversary of Japan–US Relationship*, 3 April 2004, http://www.mofa.go.jp/region/n-america/us/relation/150th/state0404.html (sighted 8 September 2005); Ministry of Foreign Affairs of Japan, *Speech by Foreign Minister of Japan Nobutaka Machimura on Japan's Global*

Strategy and the Japan-US Global Partnership on the 60th Anniversary of the End of World War II, April 29, 2005 http://www.mofa.go.jp/policy/un/fmv0504/speech.html (sighted 8 September 2005); also Ministry of Foreign Affairs of Japan, *Joint Statement: Strategic Development Alliance*, New York, 17 September 2005, http://www.mofa.go.jp/region/n-america/us/joint0509.html (sighted on 29 September 2005).

28. See Hughes, *Japan's Re-emergence as a 'Normal' Military Power*, p. 44, and McCormack and Haruki, 'The Strange Record of 15 Years of Japan-North Korea Negotiations', p. 9.

29. Koizumi's efforts to normalise diplomatic relations with North Korea (including visits to Pyongyang by the prime minister himself) failed to abate anti-North Korean sentiment in Japan particularly relating to the controversy over the return of Japanese citizens abducted by North Korea in the late 1970s.

30. For further discussion of Japan's response to September 11 and involvement in the invasion of Afghanistan, see Michishita Narushige, 'Japan's Response to 9-11', in Han Sung-Joo (ed.), *Coping with 9-11: Asian Perspectives on Global and Regional Order*, Tokyo & New York: Japan Center for International Exchange, 2003, pp. 40–42; also Rozman, *Northeast Asia's Stunted Regionalism*, p. 305. See also Treaty between Japan and the United States of America on Mutual Legal Assistance in Criminal Matters (Mutual Legal Assistance Treaty), 5 August 2003, http://www.mofa.go.jp/region/n-america/us/treaty0308.pdf (sighted on 10 September 2005).

31. For more on the political and historical significance of Japanese contribution to the war in Iraq see McCormack, 'Remilitarizing Japan', pp. 35–36; Tomohiko, Taniguchi, *Wither Japan? New Constitution and Defense Buildup*, Washington, The Brookings Institution, May 2005, http://www.brookings.edu/fp/cnaps/papers/taniguchi20050530.pdf (sighted on 12 September 2005) and Soeya Yoshihide, 'Japan as a Regional Actor' in Japan Center for International Exchange (JCIE), *ASEAN-Japan Cooperation: A Foundation for East Asian Community*, Tokyo & New York: Japan Center for International Exchange, 2003, p. 53. See also Ministry of Foreign Affairs of Japan, *Statement by Prime Minister Junichiro Koizumi (The Basic Plan Regarding the Measures Based on the Law Concerning the Special Measures on Humanitarian and Reconstruction Assistance in Iraq)*, 9 December 2003, http://www.mofa.go.jp/region/middle_e/iraq/issue2003/pmstate0312.html (sighted on 13 September 2005).

32. For discussion of Chinese perceptions of Japan's involvement in the US missile defence system, see McCormack, 'Remilitarizing Japan', p. 32 and Michael Krepon, 'Missile Defense and Asian Security' in Alan D. Romberg and Michael McDevitt (eds), *China and Missile Defense: Managing U.S.-PRC Strategic Relations*, Washington, Henry L. Stimson Center, 2003, www.stimson.org/china/pdf/CMDWP4.pdf (sighted on 13 September 2005).

33. See *Agreement Between The Government Of Japan And The Government Of The United States Of America Concerning Reciprocal Provision Of Logistic Support, Supplies And Services Between The Self-Defense Forces Of Japan And The Armed Forces Of The United States Of America*, 29 July 2004, http://www.mofa.go.jp/region/n-america/us/security/agreement.pdf (sighted on 14 September 2005); Ministry of Foreign Affairs of Japan, *Joint Statement U.S.-Japan Security Consultative Committee*, Washington DC, 19 February 2005, http://www.mofa.go.jp/region/n-america/us/security/scc/joint0502.html (sighted 14 September 2005); Japanese Minister of Foreign Affairs Machimura, Japanese Minister of State for Defense Ohno, US Secretary of State Rice & US Secretary of Defense Rumsfeld, *Security Consultative Committee Document U.S.-Japan Alliance: Transformation and Realignment for the Future*, 29 October 2005, http://www.mofa.go.jp/region/n-america/us/security/scc/doc0510.html (sighted on 14 September 2005).

34. For discussion of Chinese perceptions of Japan's involvement in the Taiwan issue see Michael Krepon, 'Missile Defense and Asian Security', p. 77.

35. See Kosuke Takahashi, 'Japan to Become "Britain of the Far East"', *Asia Times Online*, 24 February 2005, http://www.asiatimes.com/atimes/japan/GB24DL03.html (sighted on 13 September 2005).

36. See Hughes, *Japan's Re-emergence as a 'Normal' Military Power*, pp. 46–47.

37. Japanese–North Korean relations are perhaps more complex than such simple language suggests. For a more comprehensive discussion, see Gavin McCormack, 'Making Sense of the North Korean Crisis: An Interview', interview by Stephen R. Shalom and Mark

Selden, *JapanFocus.org*, 2004, http://www.japanfocus.org/article.asp?id=092 (sighted on 14 September 2005).
38. See Wang Jisi, 'China's Search for Stability with America', in *Foreign Affairs*, 84 (5), 2005, p. 44.
39. Sino–Japanese relations reached their lowest point in well over a decade in early 2005, with the enduring tensions over Japanese school textbooks (omitting details about the massacres in Nanjing and other atrocities and war crimes committed by the Japanese in the 1930s and 1940s) and Prime Minister Koizumi's visitations to the Yasakuni war memorial shrine boiling over into fierce anti-Japanese demonstrations in China. Japan's relations with South Korea also succumbed to historical feuds, particularly over a small group of islands called Tokdo by the Koreans and Takeshima by the Japanese. See Michael E. O'Hanlon and Mike Mochizuki, 'Calming the Japan-China Rift', The Brookings Institution, 21 April 2005, http://www.brookings.edu/views/op-ed/ohanlon/20050421.htm (sighted on 15 September 2005); Kosuke Takahashi, 'Japan-South Korea Ties on the Rocks', *JapanFocus.org*, 2005, http://japanfocus.org/246.html (sighted on 15 September 2005); Rozman, *Northeast Asia's Stunted Regionalism*, pp. 319–320; Taku Tamaki, 'Taking the "Taken-for-Grantedness" Seriously: Problematizing Japan's Perception of Japan-South Korea Relations', *International Relations of the Asia-Pacific*, 4, 2004, pp. 147–169; also Jason U. Manosevitz, 'Japan and South Korea: Security Relations Reach Adolescence', *Asian Survey*, 43 (5), 2003, pp. 801–825. This last piece, while focusing primarily on developments in the 1990s, gives a somewhat naïve assessment of the bilateral relationship, oblivious to the underlying tensions that had already become apparent.
40. See Zheng Bijian, 'China's "Peaceful Rise" to Great-Power Status', *Foreign Affairs*, 84 (5), 2005.
41. Hughes, *Japan's Re-Emergence as a 'Normal' Military Power*, p. 45.
42. In monetary terms alone, the costs of recent compliance with US military campaigns and defence commitments was in the order of tens of billions of dollars – a cost all the more burdensome given Japan's decade-long stagnation. See McCormack, 'Remilitarizing Japan', pp. 39–41.
43. Marquardt, Erich, 'East Asia's Power Plays', *Asia Times Online*, 7 April 2005, http://www.atimes.com/atimes/japan/GD07Dh01.html (sighted on 16 September 2005). The IMF's early GDP estimates for 2005 placed China as the sixth largest economy in the world (in terms of nominal GDP), but the third largest (after China and the European Union, and well ahead of the fourth largest, Japan) if GDP is based on purchasing power parity calculations. International Monetary Fund, *World Economic Outlook Database*, April 2005.
44. Zhibin Gu, George, 'Japan Inc in China', *Online Opinion*, 10 May 2005, http://www.onlineopinion.com.au/view.asp?article=3422 (sighted on 21 September 2005).
45. See Jisi, 'China's Search for Stability with America', p. 42.
46. For a detailed discussion of the negative implications of the Howard government's policies for Australia's engagement with Asia, see Kevin, 'Foreign Policy', pp. 299–303.
47. This would require going beyond the prevailing assessment of the scope of the bilateral relationship as articulated, for example, in Department of Foreign Affairs and Trade, *Advancing the National Interest: Australia's Foreign and Trade Policy White Paper*, Canberra, February 2003, chapter 5, 'Actively Engaging with Asia', p. 7, http://www.dfat.gov.au/ani/chapter_5.html (sighted on 19 September 2005).
48. Assessments of regional tensions often missed this point. Both Ted Osius and Joshua P. Rowan put forward proposals suggesting Japan–US initiatives to resolve particular problems (for example, cross-strait relations, South China Sea disputes), without, however, addressing the need to substantially rethink the role of Cold War alliances in finding lasting solutions to these problems. See Ted Osius, *The U.S.-Japan Security Alliance: Why it Matters and How to Strengthen it*, Westport CT & London: Praeger, 2002, p. 28 and Joshua P. Rowan, 'The U.S.-Japan Security Alliance, ASEAN, and the South China Sea Dispute', *Asian Survey*, 45 (3), 2005, pp. 414–436.
49. Particularly useful in this context are the analysis and recommendations offered by an informed Australian analyst Alan Dupont, *Unsheathing the Samurai Sword: Japan's Changing Security Policy*, Sydney: Lowy Institute for Strategic Policy, 2004 (see recommendations on pp. 53–64).

216   *Conclusion*

50. For recent examples see Australian Government, *Weapons of Mass Destruction, Australia's Role in Fighting Proliferation: Practical Responses to New Challenges*, Commonwealth of Australia, 2005, p. 42; Address by H.E. Mr Junichiro Koizumi Prime Minister of Japan at the High-Level Plenary Meeting of the Sixtieth Session of the General Assembly of the United Nations, 'Turning Words into Action', 15 September 2005, http://www.un.org/webcast/summit2005/statements15/jap050915eng.pdf (sighted on 23 September 2005) and Minister for Foreign Affairs, 'The Hon Alexander Downer MP, Speech, 'Reforming the United Nations and Building Cooperation Towards Peace and Security: A Speech to the Los Angeles World Affairs Council', Los Angeles, 19 January 2005 http://www.foreignminister.gov.au/speeches/2005/050119_reforming_un.html (sighted on 21 September 2005).
51. The UN's role in Asia in the post-Cold War era has been large and complex. It includes two of the UN's largest peace operations (Cambodia and East Timor) and responses to a range of non-traditional security threats, notably resource scarcity, drug trafficking and infectious diseases (including bird flu, SARS and AIDS). For a discussion of Japan's role within the UN including large financial contributions, see Michael Fullilove, *Angels and Dragons: Asia, the UN, Reform, and the Next Secretary-General*, Issues Brief, Sydney: Lowy Institute for International Policy, July 2005, http://www.lowyinstitute.org/Publication.asp?pid=282 (sighted on 3 September 2005).
52. For a discussion of Japan's possible approach to UN reform following the September 2005 summit, see Philip H. Gordon, 'After the UN Summit, Japan May Have to Lower its Sights', The Brookings Institution, October 2005, http://www.brookings.edu/views/articles/gordon/20051001.htm (sighted on 14 September 2005).
53. During the Howard years Australia tended to concentrate on those aspects of UN reform that dovetailed with alliance priorities. See Alexander Downer, 'Reforming the United Nations and Building Cooperation Towards Peace and Security'; also Alexander Downer, 'Statement to the Sixtieth Session of the United Nations General Assembly', New York, 21 September 2005, http://www.foreignminister.gov.au/speeches/2005/050921_16th_session.html (sighted on 26 September 2005).
54. See Kawashima, 'Japan's Security Environment', p. 4; also Statement by H.E. Mr Kenzo Oshima Permanent Representative of Japan at the Plenary Meeting of the General Assembly on the Report of the Secretary-General, 7 April 2005, http://www.mofa.go.jp/announce/speech/un2005/un0504.html (sighted on 1 September 2005).
55. Millennium Report of the Secretary General of the United Nations, *'We the Peoples': The Role of the United Nations in the 21st Century*, New York: United Nations, 2000, http://www.un.org/millennium/sg/report/full.htm (sighted on 4 September 2005).
56. Japan went some of the way to incorporating these concepts into policy in various areas. See Statement by H.E. Ambassador Koichi Haraguchi, Permanent Representative of Japan to the United Nations, delivered at the Plenary Meeting of the 58th General Assembly on the Follow-up to the Outcome of the Millennium Summit (Item 60) and the Report of the Secretary-General on the Work of the Organisation (Item 10), 6 October 2003, http://www.mofa.go.jp/announce/speech/un0310.html (sighted on 5 September 2005); also Statement by H.E. Mr. Kenzo Oshima Permanent Representative of Japan at the Plenary Meeting of the General Assembly on the Report of the Secretary-General, 7 April 2005, http://www.mofa.go.jp/announce/speech/un2005/un0504.html (sighted on 7 September 2005).
57. The recommendations of the Canberra Commission were not pursued by the Howard government which was elected just before the Commission presented its landmark report. For a discussion of the government's inadequate handling of the Canberra Commission, see Broinowski, *Fact or Fission*, p. 223.
58. See Gordon, 'After the UN Summit, Japan May Have to Lower its Sights'.
59. Australian Foreign Minister Downer's position in this regard was somewhat inconsistent, with the accent often more on rhetoric than on substance. Perhaps the clearest articulation of the Australian government's position was offered in *Weapons of Mass Destruction, Australia's Role in Fighting Proliferation: Practical Responses to New Challenges*, p. 34. For a critical assessment of Downer's approach to nuclear arms control and disarmament, see Broinowski, *Fact or Fission*, pp. 226–229.
60. Japan was somewhat more forthcoming than Australia in advancing practical proposals. See *Weapons of Mass Destruction, Australia's Role in Fighting Proliferation: Practical*

Responses to New Challenges, p. 42, and Statement by H.E. Ambassador Koichi Haraguchi, Permanent Representative of Japan to the United Nations (as delivered) at the Plenary Meeting of the 58th General Assembly on the Follow-up to the Outcome of the Millennium Summit (Item 60) and the Report of the Secretary-General on the Work of the Organisation (Item 10).

61. See Frank Barnaby and Shaun Burnie, *Thinking the Unthinkable: Japanese Nuclear Power and Proliferation in East Asia*, Oxford and Tokyo: Oxford Research Group & Citizen's Nuclear Information Center, August 2005, p. 7; also Kurt M. Campbell and Tsuyoshi Sunohara, 'Japan: Thinking the Unthinkable' in Kurt M. Campbell, Robert J. Einhorn and Mitchell B. Reiss (eds), *The Nuclear Tipping Point: Why States Reconsider Their Nuclear Choices*, Washington D.C., Brookings Institution Press, 2004, pp. 229–230, 237 & 243.

62. See Statement by H.E. Ambassador Koichi Haraguchi, Permanent Representative of Japan to the United Nations (as delivered) at the Plenary Meeting of the 58th General Assembly on the Follow-up to the Outcome of the Millennium Summit (Item 60) and the Report of the Secretary-General on the Work of the Organisation (Item 10); also Statement by H.E. Mr Kenzo Oshima Permanent Representative of Japan at the Plenary Meeting of the General Assembly on the Report of the Secretary-General.

63. The superficiality of the Japanese response to the reform agenda was strikingly evident in the lead up to the 2005 UN Summit. See Gordon, 'After the UN Summit, Japan May Have to Lower its Sights'.

64. See, for example, Australian Government, *Weapons of Mass Destruction, Australia's Role in Fighting Proliferation: Practical Responses to New Challenges*, p. 49. Here we see a noticeable reticence to articulate in any detail the kind of policies that the government would pursue or the way in which any conflict with US priorities and preferences would be dealt with.

65. See Spencer Zifcak, 'As Chair of the United Nations Commission on Human Rights, Australia's Performance Has Been Shameful', in *The Diplomat*, 3 (4), 2004, p. 18.

66. See Joseph A. Camilleri, *Regionalism in the New Asia-Pacific Order*, Cheltenham UK: Edward Elgar, 2003; also Rozman, *Northeast Asia's Stunted Regionalism*, pp. 345–347.

67. The relationship between US strategy and Asia-Pacific regionalism is examined in Rozman, *Northeast Asia's Stunted Regionalism*, p. 290.

68. Both Australia and Japan have a record of longstanding support for ASEAN. Partly prodded by China's increasing regional prominence, Japan became more proactive. See Sueo Sudo, *Evolution of ASEAN-Japan Relations*, Singapore, Institute of Southeast Asian Studies Publications, 2005, pp. 49–51; also Yoshihide, in JCIE, *ASEAN-Japan Cooperation*, p. 57; Mohamed Jawhar Bin Hassan, 'ASEAN's Political and Security Relations with Japan', in JCIE, *ASEAN-Japan Cooperation*, pp. 146–147.

69. Australia's contribution to this process has been conceptually and practically limited by its narrow emphasis on trade and more recently on counter-terrorism. See, for example, Department of Foreign Affairs and Trade, *Advancing the National Interest: Australia's Foreign and Trade Policy White Paper*, Chapter Five; also Minister for Foreign Affairs Alexander Downer and Minister for Trade Mark Vaile, Joint Media Release, 'Step Forward for Australia and ASEAN', 22 April 2004, http://www.foreignminister.gov.au/releases/2004/joint_asean.html (sighted on 28 September 2005); Australia-ASEAN Joint Declaration for Cooperation to Combat International Terrorism, 1 July 2004, http://www.dfat.gov.au/globalissues/terrorism/aus-asean_interr.html (sighted on 28 September 2005).

70. See Sueo Sudo, *Evolution of ASEAN-Japan Relations*, pp. 53–63.

71. After publicly deriding the treaty and refusing to sign for months, Australia eventually added its signature once it became apparent that its inclusion in the East Asia Summit in December 2005 would be conditional on taking this step. For an official explanation of the change of heart, see Media Release, 'East Asia Summit and Treaty of Amity and Cooperation', 26 July 2005, http://www.foreignminister.gov.au/releases/2005/fa096_05.html (sighted on 29 September 2005).

72. APEC reform is now an acceptable subject of discussion. The proposals advanced by Allan Gyngell and Malcolm Cook, 'How to Save APEC', *Policy Brief*, Lowy Institute for International Policy, October 2005, http://www.lowyinstitute.org/Publication.asp?pid=305

(sighted on 26 September 2005), though a step in the right direction, fall short of the more systematic re-examination of objectives advocated here.
73. Japan in particular is well placed to take a leading role. See Nishihara Masashi, 'Japan's Political and Security Relations with ASEAN', in JCIE, *ASEAN-Japan Cooperation*, pp. 152–157.
74. See Sueo Sudo, *Evolution of ASEAN-Japan Relations*, pp. 53–63.
75. This will require more than token infrastructure aid projects as has often been the norm. See Alexander Downer, Media Release, 'Protecting and Promoting Human Rights in Asia and the Pacific', 10 December 2004, http://www.ausaid.gov.au/media/release.cfm?BC=Media&Id=2817_3279_7560_3389_2085 (sighted on 23 September 2005).
76. See McCormack and Haruki, 'The Strange Record of 15 Years of Japan-North Korea Negotiations'.

Select Bibliography

Agamben, Giorgio, *Homo Sacer: Sovereign Power and Bare Life*, trans. Daniel Heller-Roazen, Stanford, CA: Stanford University Press, 1998.

Agnew, John and Stuart Corbridge, *Mastering Space: Hegemony, Territory, and International Political Economy*, London: Routledge, 1995.

Alan Dupont, *Unsheathing the Samurai Sword: Japan's Changing Security Policy*, Sydney: Lowy Institute for Strategic Policy, 2004.

American Interests and UN Reform: Report of the Task Force on the United Nations, The Endowment of the United States Institute of Peace, 2005.

Amnesty International, 'China', *Amnesty International Report 2004*, London: Amnesty International Publications, 2004.

Anderson, Perry, 'The Antinomies of Antonio Gramsci', *The New Left Review* 100, 1976, pp. 5–78.

Anghie, Antony, *Imperialism, Sovereignty and the Making of International Law*, Cambridge: Cambridge University Press, 2005.

Anthony, Ian, 'Major Trends in Arms Control and Non-Proliferation', *SIPRI Yearbook 2004*, New York: Humanities Press, 2004, pp. 575–602.

Arai, Shinichi, *Senso Sekinin* (War Responsibility), Tokyo: Iwanami Shoten, 1995.

Armacost, M.H. and Daniel I. Okimoto (eds), *The Future of America's Alliances in Northeast Asia*, Stanford: Asia-Pacific Research Centre, 2004.

Australian Department of Foreign Affairs and Trade, *Advancing the National Interest: Australia's Foreign and Trade Policy White Paper*, Canberra: Commonwealth of Australia, February 2003.

Australian Government, *Weapons of Mass Destruction, Australia's Role in Fighting Proliferation: Practical Responses to New Challenges*, Canberra: Commonwealth of Australia, 2005.

Australian Government: Department of Defence, *Our Future Defence Force*, Canberra: Australian Government Publishing Service, 2000.

Australian Government: Department of Foreign Affairs and Trade, Economic Analytical Unit, *Papua New Guinea: The Road Ahead*, Canberra: DFAT, 2004.

Australian Strategic Policy Institute, *Strengthening Our Neighbour: Australia and the Future of Papua New Guinea*, Canberra: Australian Government Publishing Service, 2004.

Axline, W. Andrew and James A. Stegenga, *The Global Community*, New York: Dodd, Mead, and Co., 1972.

Bain, William, *Between Anarchy and Society: Trusteeship and the Obligations of Power*, Oxford: Oxford University Press, 2003.

Bamyeh, Mohammed A., *The Ends of Globalization*, Minneapolis: University of Minnesota Press, 2000.

Barnaby, Frank and Shaun Burnie, *Thinking the Unthinkable: Japanese Nuclear Power and Proliferation in East Asia*, Oxford & Tokyo: Oxford Research Group & Citizen's Nuclear Information Center, August 2005.

Barnes, Samuel H., 'The Contribution of Democracy to Rebuilding Postconflict Societies', *American Journal of International Law*, 95, 2001, pp. 86–101.

Barnet, Richard J. and John Cavanagh, *Global Dreams: Imperial Corporations and the New World Order*, London: A Touchstone Book, 1994.

Barnett, Thomas P. M., *The Pentagon's New Map*, New York: Berkley Books, 2004.

Bauer, Peter, Savenaca Siwatibau and Wolfgang Kasper, *Aid and Development in the South Pacific*, Sydney: CIS, 2003.

Beck, Ulrich, 'The Terrorist Threat: World Risk Society Revisited', *Theory, Culture & Society*, 19, August 2002, pp. 39–55.

Bednar, Charles Sokol, *Transforming the Dream: Ecologism and the Shaping of an Alternative American Vision*, Albany NY: SUNY Press, 2003.

Beeson, Mark, 'Australia's Relationship with the United States: The Case for Greater Independence', *Australian Journal of Political Science*, 38 (3), 2003, pp. 387–405.

Bell, Philip and Roger Bell, *Implicated: The United States in Australia*, Melbourne: Oxford University Press, 1993.

Bhuta, Nehal, 'A Global State of Exception? The United States and World Order', *Constellations*, 10 (3), 2003, pp. 371–391.

Bijian, Zheng, 'China's "Peaceful Rise" to Great-Power Status', *Foreign Affairs*, 84 (5), 2005, pp. 18–23.

Bix, Herbert, *Hirohito and the Making of Modern Japan*, New York, NY: HarperCollins Publishers, 2000.

Blondel, J., *Political Leadership*, London: Sage, 1987.

Boeha, Beno and John McFarlane (eds), *Australia and Papua New Guinea: Crime and the Bilateral Relationship*, Canberra: Australian Defence Studies Centre, 2000.

Borden, William S., *The Pacific Alliance: United States Foreign Policy and Japanese Trade Recovery, 1947-1955*, Madison: The University of Wisconsin Press, 1984.

Boulding, Kenneth, 'The Concept of World Order,' *American Behavioural Scientist*, 34, May/June 1991, pp. 581–593.

Broadhead, Lee-Anne, *International Environmental Politics: The Limits of Green Diplomacy*, London: Lynne-Rienner, 2002.

Broinowski, Alison, *About Face: Asian Accounts of Australia*, Melbourne: Scribe Publications, 2003.

Broinowski, Alison, *The Yellow Lady: Australian Impressions of Asia*, Melbourne: Oxford University Press, 1992.

Broinowski, Richard, *Fact or Fission: The Truth About Australia's Nuclear Ambitions*, Melbourne: Scribe Publications, 2003.

Brooks, Stephen G., and William C. Wohlforth, 'American Primacy in Perspective', *Foreign Affairs*, 81, 2002, pp. 20–33.

Brown, Lester, *Eco-Economy: Building an Economy for the Earth*, London: W.W. Norton, 2001.

Brzezinski, Zbigniew, *The Choice: Global Domination or Global Leadership*, New York: Basic Books, 2004.

Cainkar, Louise, 'Arabs, Muslims and Race in America – No Longer Invisible: Arab and Muslim Exclusion After September 11', *Middle East Report*, 32 (3), 2002, pp. 22–29.

Calhoun, Craig, Paul Price and Ashley Timmer (eds), *Understanding September 11*, New York: New Press, 2002.

Callinicos, Alex, *The New Mandarins of American Power: The Bush Administration's Plans For The World*, Cambridge, UK: Polity, 2004.

Camilleri, Joseph A., 'A Leap into the Past – in the Name of the National Interest', *Australian Journal of International Affairs*, 57 (3), 2003, pp. 431–453.

Camilleri, Joseph A., *Regionalism in the New Asia-Pacific Order: The Political Economy of the Asia-Pacific Region*, Vol. II, Cheltenham: Edward Elgar, 2003.

Camilleri, Joseph A., *States, Markets and Civil Society in Asia Pacific: The Political Economy of the Asia-Pacific Region*, Volume I, Cheltenham, UK: Edward Elgar, 2000.

Camilleri, Joseph A., 'The Multilateral Dimensions of Australia's Security Policy', in Des Ball (ed.), *Maintaining the Strategic Edge: The Defence of Australia*, Canberra: The Australian National University Strategic and Defence Studies Centre, 1999, pp. 307–334.

Camilleri, Joseph A., *Australian–American Relations: The Web of Dependence*, Melbourne: Macmillan, 1980.

Campbell, Kurt M. and Tsuyoshi Sunohara, 'Japan: Thinking the Unthinkable' in Kurt M. Campbell, Robert J. Einhorn and Mitchell B. Reiss (eds), *The Nuclear Tipping Point: Why States Reconsider Their Nuclear Choices*, Washington D.C., Brookings Institution Press, 2004, pp. 218–253.

Cavanagh, John, and Jerry Mander (eds), *Alternatives to Economic Globalization: A Better World is Possible,* San Francisco: Berrett-Koehller, 2002.

Cheong, W. and H. Umebayashi et al., 'Move toward a Northeast Asia NWFZ,' presentation at NPT Review Conference, 11 May 2005, http://www.peacedepot.org/e-news/frame.html (sighted on 25 September 2005).

Chiddell, Fleetwood, *Australia: White or Yellow,* London: William Heinemann, 1926.

Chimni, B.S., 'International Institutions Today: An Imperial Global State in the Making', *European Journal of International Law*, 15 (1), 2004, pp. 1–37.

China, Republic of, State Council, *The Human Rights Record of the United States in 2004*, Beijing: State Council of the People's Republic of China, 2005.

Chomsky, Noam, *9-11*, New York: Seven Stories Press, 2001.

Cirincione, J. et. al., *Universal Compliance – A Strategy for Nuclear Security,* Carnegie Endowment for International Peace, March 2005 at http://www.carnegieendowment.org/files/UC2.FINAL3.pdf (sighted on 25 September 2005).

Coghlan, James E. and Deborah J. McNamara (eds), *Asians in Australia: Patterns of Migration and Settlement,* Melbourne: Macmillan, 1997.

Cohen, Warren I., *The Cambridge History of American Foreign Relations, Vol. IV: America in the Age of Soviet Power, 1941-1991*, Cambridge: Cambridge University Press, 1993.

Colas, Alejandro, *International Civil Society,* Cambridge: Polity Press, 2002.

Collingwood, Vivien, 'Achieving Global Economic Justice: Assistance with Fewer Strings Attached', *Ethics and International Affairs* 17 (1), 2003, pp. 55–68.

Commission on Human Security, *Human Security Now*, New York, 2003.

Connolly, William E., 'The New Cult of Civilizational Superiority,' *Theory and Event*, 2 (4), 1999, pp. 1–6.

Cooper, Andrew F. (ed.), *Niche Diplomacy: Middle Powers After the Cold War,* London: Macmillan, 1997.

Cooper, Andrew F., Richard Higgott, and Kim Nossal, *Relocating Middle Powers: Australia and Canada in a Changing World,* Melbourne: Melbourne University Press, 1993.

Cossa, Ralph A. and Brad Glosserman, *U.S.-Japan Defense Cooperation: Has Japan Become the Great Britain of Asia?*, Issues & Insights, Pacific Forum CSIS, 5 (3), March 2005.

Cox, Michael, 'American Power Before and After 11 September: Dizzy with Success?', *International Affairs*, 78 (2), 2002, pp. 261–276.

Cox, Michael, 'September 11th and U.S. Hegemony – Or Will the 21st Century be American Too?, *International Studies Perspectives*, 3 (1), 2002, pp. 53–70.

Cox, Michael, 'Whatever Happened to American Decline? International Relations and the New United States Hegemony,' *New Political Economy*, 6, 2001, pp. 311–340.

Cox, Robert W., *Production, Power, and World Order: Social Forces in the Making of History*, New York: Columbia University Press, 1987.

Cox, Robert W., 'Social Forces, States and World Order: Beyond International Relations Theory', *Millennium: Journal of International Studies*, 10 (2), Summer 1981, pp. 126–155.

Crocombe, Ron, *The South Pacific*, Suva: University of the South Pacific, 2001.

Curtis, Gerald L., *The Logic of Japanese Politics: Leaders, Institutions, and the Limits of Change*, New York: Columbia University Press, 1999.

Dallmayr, Fred R., 'Globalization and Inequality', *International Studies Review*, 4 (2), 2002, pp. 137–157.

Dalrymple, Rawdon, *Continental Drift: Australia's Search for Regional Identity*, Aldershot: Ashgate, 2003.

Daly, Herman, *Steady-State Economics: The Economics Of Biophysical Equilibrium And Moral Growth*, San Francisco: W. H. Freeman, 1977.

Daly, Herman (ed.), *Toward A Steady-State Economy*, San Francisco: W.H. Freeman, 1973.

Dauvergne, Peter (ed.), *Weak and Strong States in Asia-Pacific Societies*, Sydney: Allen and Unwin, 2003.

Democratic Party of Japan Constitution Review Committee, *Minshutou Kenpou Teigen* [Democratic Party of Japan Constitution Proposal], 31 October, 2005.

Denoon, Donald, *A Trial Separation: Australia and the Decolonisation of Papua New Guinea*, Canberra: Pandanus Press, 2005.

Der Derian, James and Michael J. Shapiro (eds), *International/Inter-textual Relations: Postmodern Readings of World Politics*, Lexington, MA: Lexington Books, 1989.

Dillon, Michael, 'Network Society, Network-Centric Warfare and the State of Emergency,' *Theory, Culture & Society*, 19 (4), 2002, pp. 71–79.

Dillon, Michael, 'Sovereignty and Governmentality: From the Problematics of the "New World Order" to the ethical Problematic of the World Order', *Alternatives*, 20, July/September 1995, pp. 323–368.

Dinnen, Sinclair, 'Lending a Fist? Australia's New Interventionism in the Southwest Pacific', *State, Society and Governance in Melanesia Project*, Discussion Paper No. 5, Canberra: Research School of Pacific and Asian Studies, Australian National University, 2004.

Dower, John W., *Embracing Defeat: Japan in the Wake of World War II*, New York: W. W. Norton & Company, 1999.

Du Boff, Richard B., 'U.S. Hegemony: Continuing Decline, Enduring Danger', *Monthly Review*, December 2003, at http://www.monthlyreview.org/1203duboff.htm (sighted on 22 November 2005).

Dupont, Alan, *Unsheathing the Samurai Sword: Japan's Changing Security Policy*, Sydney: Lowy Institute Paper 3, 2004.

Evans, Gareth and Grant, Bruce, *Australia's Foreign Relations in the World of the 1990s*, Melbourne: Melbourne University Press, 1995.

Falk, Richard A., *The Declining World Order: America's Imperial Geopolitics*, New York: Routledge, 2004.

Falk, Richard A., *Predatory Globalization: A Critique*, Cambridge: Polity Press, 1999.

Feldman, Noah, *After Jihad: America and the Struggle for Islamic Democracy*, New York: Farrar, Straus & Giroux, 2003.

Frazer, Ian, 'The Struggle for Control of Solomon Island Forests', *The Contemporary Pacific*, 9 (1), 1997, pp. 44–52.
Friedman, Jonathan and Christopher Chase-Dunn (eds), *Hegemonic Decline: Present and Past*, Boulder: Paradigm, 2005.
Friedman, Thomas L., *Lexus and the Olive Tree*, N Y: Farrar, Straus & Giroux, 2000.
Fukai, Shigeko N., 'Building the War Economy and Rebuilding Postwar Japan: A Profile of Pragmatic Nationalist Nobusuke Kishi,' in Ofer Feldman and Linda O. Valenty (eds), *Profiling Political Leaders: Cross-cultural Studies of Personality and Behaviour*, London: Praeger, 2001, pp. 167–184.
Fukase, Tadakazu, *Senso Hoki to Heiwateki Seizonken* (Renunciation of War and the Right to Live in Peace), Tokyo: Iwanami Shoten, 1987.
Garnaut, Ross, *Australia and the Northeast Asian Ascendancy*, Canberra: Australian Government Publishing Service, 1989.
George, Jim, *Discourses of Global Politics: A Critical (Re) Introduction to International Relations*, Boulder, CO: Lynne Rienner Publishers, 1994.
Germain, Randall D. and Michael Kenny, 'Engaging Gramsci: International Relations Theory and the New Gramscians', *Review of International Studies*, 24, 1998, pp. 3–21.
Gill, Stephen, 'Globalisation, Market Civilization and Disciplinary Neoliberalism', *Millennium: Journal of International Studies*, 23 (3), 1995, pp. 399–423.
Goldblat, Jozef, *Arms Control: The New Guide to Negotiations and Agreements*, London: Sage, 1994.
Goldsworthy, David, *Losing the Blanket: Australia and the End of Britain's Empire*, Melbourne: Melbourne University Press, 2002.
Goodland, Robert, Herman E. Daly, and Salah El Serafy (eds), *Population, Technology, and Lifestyle: The Transition to Sustainability*, Washington DC: Island Press, 1992.
Gramsci, Antonio, *Selections from the Prison Notebooks*, New York: International Publishers, 1971.
Grant, Bruce, *Fatal Attraction: Reflections on the Alliance with the United States*, Melbourne: Black Inc., 2004.
Gutmann, Amy (ed.), *Multiculturalism: Examining the Politics of Recognition*, Princeton, NJ: University Press, 1994.
Gyngell, Allan and Michael Wesley, *Making Australian Foreign Policy*, Cambridge: Cambridge University Press, 2003.
Hamel-Green, Michael, 'The South Pacific: The Treaty of Rarotonga', in Ramesh Thakur (ed.), *Nuclear Weapons-Free Zones*, London: Macmillan/St Martin's Press, 1998, pp. 59–80.
Hampson, Fen Osler, *Madness in the Multitude: Human Security and World Disorder*, Ontario: Oxford University Press, 2002.
Hardt, Michael, and Anthony Negri, *Empire*, Cambridge, MA: Harvard University Press, 2000.
Held, David, *Democracy and the Global Order: From the Modern State to Cosmopolitan Governance*, Cambridge: Polity Press, 1995.
Held, David, Anthony McGrew, David Goldblatt and Jonathan Perraton, *Global Transformations: Politics, Economics and Culture*, Stanford, CA: Stanford University Press, 1999.
Henderson, Gerard, 'World Order – From the Old to the New', *Australian Journal of International Affairs*, 57 (3), 2003, pp. 473–484.
Hettne, Björn, 'Karl Polanyi and the Search for World Order', available at Karl Polanyi Institute of Political Economy, Concordia University, http://artsandscience.concordia.ca/polanyi/pdfs/Hettne-2004.pdf (sighted on 11 December 2005).

Hollander, Jack M., *The Real Environmental Crisis: Why Poverty, not Affluence, is the Environment's Number One Enemy,* Berkeley: University of California Press, 2003.

Hughes, Christopher W., *Japan's Re-emergence as a 'Normal' Military Power,* Adelphi Paper No. 368-9, Oxford: Oxford University Press/IISS, 2004.

Huntington, Samuel P., *The Clash of Civilizations and the Remaking of World Order,* New York: Simon and Schuster, 1996.

Hurrell, Andrew, and Ngaire Woods, 'Globalization and Inequality', *Millennium,* 24, 1995, pp. 447–470.

Ichiro, Ozawa, *Nihon Kaizo Keikaku (Blue Print for Reform of Japan),* Tokyo: Kodansha, 1993.

Ikenberry, G. John, 'American Power and the Empire of Capitalist Democracy', *Review of International Studies,* 27, 2001, pp. 191–212.

Independent International Commission on Kosovo, *Kosovo Report: Conflict, International Response, Lessons Learned,* New York: Oxford University Press, 2000.

International Commission on Intervention and State Sovereignty (ICISS), *The Responsibility to Protect,* Ottawa: International Development Research Centre, 2001.

Ishikawa, Masumi, *Sengo Seiji-shi (Postwar Political History),* new edition, Tokyo: Iwanami Shoten, 2004.

Jackson, Robert, *Quasi-States: Sovereignty, International Relations and the Third World,* Cambridge, UK: Cambridge University Press, 1990.

Japan, House of Councillors Constitution Review Committee, *Nihonkoku Kenpou ni Kansuru Chousa Houkokusho* [Report of Review on the Japanese Constitution], April 2005.

Jisi, Wang, 'China's Search for Stability with America', in *Foreign Affairs,* 84 (5), 2005, pp. 39–48.

Johnson, Chalmers, *The Sorrows of Empire: Militarism, Secrecy, and the End of the Republic,* New York: Metropolitan, 2004.

Johnson, Chalmers, *Blowback: The Costs and Consequences of American Empire,* London: Time Warner Books, 2002.

Joll, James, *The Origins of the First World War,* London: Longman, 1992.

Josephson, Paul R., *Resources Under Regimes: Technology, Environment, and the State,* London: Harvard University Press, 2004.

Kagan, Robert, 'The Benevolent Empire', *Foreign Policy,* 111, 1998, pp. 24–35.

Kagan, Robert and William Kristol (eds), *Present Dangers: Crisis and Opportunity in American Foreign and Defense Policy,* San Francisco: Encounter Books, 2000.

Kahin, Audrey R. and George M. Kahin, *Subversion as Foreign Policy,* Seattle: University of Washington Press, 1997.

Kahler, Miles and David A. Lake (eds), *Governance in a Global Economy: Political Authority in Transition,* Princeton: Princeton University Press, 2003.

Kaldor, Mary, *Global Civil Society: An Answer to War,* Cambridge: Polity Press, 2003.

Kassiola, Joel Jay (ed.), *Explorations in Environmental Political Theory: Thinking About What We Value,* London: M. E. Sharp, 2003.

Kassiola, Joel Jay, *The Death of Industrial Civilization: The Limits to Economic Growth and the Repoliticization of Advanced Industrial Society,* Albany NY: SUNY Press, 1990.

Kato, Tetsuro, *Shocho Tennnosei no Kigen (Origin of Emperor as Symbol),* Heibonsha, 2005.

Kaul, Inge, Isabelle Grunberg, and Marc A. Stern (eds), *Global Public Goods: International Cooperation in the 21st Century*, Oxford: Oxford University Press, 1999.
Keating, Paul, *Engagement: Australia Faces the Asia-Pacific*, Sydney: Macmillan, 2000.
Kevin, Tony, 'Foreign Policy', in Robert Manne (ed.), *The Howard Years*, Melbourne: Black Inc. Agenda, 2004, pp. 291–313.
Kile, Shannon, 'Nuclear Arms Control, Non-Proliferation and Ballistic Missile Defence', *SIPRI Yearbook 2003*, New York: Humanities Press, 2003, pp. 577–609.
Kindleberger, Charles P., 'International Public Goods without International Government,' *The American Economic Review*, 76 (1), 1986, pp. 1–13.
Kobayashi, Naoki, *Heiwa Kenpo to Kyousei 60 Nen* (A Sixty Year Symbiosis with the Pacifist Constitution), Tokyo: Jigakusha Shuppan, 2006.
Koichi, Kishimoto, *Politics in Modern Japan: Development and Organization*, Tokyo: Japan Echo Inc., 1997.
Krasner, Steven D., 'Sharing Sovereignty: New Institutions for Collapsed and Failing States', *International Security*, 29(2), Fall 2004, pp. 85–120.
Krasner, Steven D., *Sovereignty: Organised Hypocrisy*, Princeton: Princeton University Press, 1999.
Krauthammer, Charles, 'The Unipolar Moment', *Foreign Affairs*, 70 (1), 1990–1991, pp. 23–33.
Krisch, Nico, 'International Law in Times of Hegemony: Unequal Power and the Shaping of the International Legal Order,' *European Journal of International Law*, 16 (3), 2005, pp. 369–408.
Krisch, Nico, 'More Equal than the Rest? Hierarchy, Equality and US Predominance in International Law', in Michael Byers and Georg Nolte (eds), *United States Hegemony and the Foundations of International Law*, Cambridge: Cambridge University Press, 2003, pp. 135–175.
Kunihiro, Masao and Charles M. Overby, *Chikyu Kenpo Dai 9 Jo* (Article 9 as a World Constitution), Tokyo: Kodansha International, 1997.
Larmour, Peter (ed.), *Governance and Reform in the South Pacific*, Canberra: National Centre for Development Studies, ANU, 1998.
Larmour, Peter, 'Corruption and Governance in the South Pacific', *Pacific Studies*, 20 (3), 1997, pp. 1–17.
Leacher, Michael, Geoffrey Stokes, and Ian Ward (eds), *The Rise and Fall of One Nation*, Brisbane: Queensland University Press, 2000.
Leaver, Richard and Dave Cox (eds), 'Introduction', *Middling, Meddling, Muddling: Issues in Australian Foreign Policy*, Sydney: Allen and Unwin, 1997.
Lorimer, James, *The Institutes of the Law of Nations: A Treatise of the Jural Relations of Separate Political Communities*, Vol. 1, Edinburgh: William Blackwood and Sons, 1883.
Ludlow, Peter, 'Wanted: A Global Partner', *Washington Quarterly*, 24 (3) 2001, pp. 163–171.
Lyon, Rod, *Alliance Unleashed: Australia and the US in a New Strategic Age*, Canberra: ASPI, 2005.
Mallaby, S., 'The Reluctant Imperialist: Terrorism, Failed States and the Case for American Empire', *Foreign Affairs*, 81, 2002, pp. 2–7.
Mamdani, Mahmood, 'Good Muslim, Bad Muslim: A Political Perspective on Culture and Terrorism', *American Anthropologist*, 104 (3), 2002, pp. 766–775.
Mann, Michael, 'Globalization and September 11', *New Left Review*, 112, November/December 2001, pp. 51–72.

Manosevitz, Jason U., 'Japan and South Korea: Security Relations Reach Adolescence', *Asian Survey*, 43 (5), 2003, pp. 801–825.

Mastanduno, Michael, 'Incomplete Hegemony: The United States and Security Order in Asia' in Muthiah Alagappa (ed.), *Asian Security Order: Instrumental and Normative Features*, Stanford, CA: Stanford University Press, 2003, pp. 141–170.

May, R. J., 'Disorderly Democracy: Political Turbulence and Institutional Reform in Papua New Guinea', *State, Society and Governance in Melanesia Project*, Discussion Paper No. 3, Canberra: Research School of Pacific and Asian Studies, Australian National University, 2003.

McCormack, Gavan, 'Remilitarizing Japan', *New Left Review*, No. 29, Second Series, September October 2004, pp. 29–45.

Meaney, Neville, *Towards a New Vision: Australia and Japan Through 100 Years*, Sydney: Kangaroo Press, 1999.

Medeiros, Evan S. and M. Taylor Fravel, 'China's New Diplomacy', *Foreign Affairs*, 82 (6), November/December 2003, pp. 22–35.

Michael, Michális S. and Larry Marshall, *Securing the Region Post-September 11*, Melbourne: Politics Program, La Trobe University, 2005.

Milner, Anthony (ed.), *Australia in Asia: Comparing Cultures*, Melbourne: Oxford University Press, 1996.

Milner, Anthony and Mary Quilty (eds), *Australia in Asia: Episodes*, Melbourne: Oxford University Press, 1998.

Milner, Anthony and Mary Quilty (eds), *Australia in Asia: Communities of Thought*, Melbourne: Oxford University Press, 1996.

Mitchell, Timothy, 'McJihad: Islam in the U.S. Global Order', *Social Text*, 73, Winter 2002, pp. 1–18.

Mizushima, Asaho, *Buryoku Naki Heiwa* (Peace Without Force), Tokyo: Iwanami Shoten, 1997.

Morrison, Roy, *Ecological Democracy*, Boston: South End Press, 1995.

Murphy, Craig N., 'Global Governance: Poorly Done and Poorly Understood', *International Affairs*, 76 (4), 2000, pp. 789–804.

Muzaffar, Chandra, 'The Interface between Southeast Asia and the US: A Contemporary Analysis', paper presented at an international conference on the theme 'Their America: The US in the Eyes of the Rest of the World' organised by the New School in New York City, 18–19 October 2004.

Muzaffar, Chandra, *Muslims Dialogue Terror*, Malaysia: International Movement for a Just World, 2003.

Nakasone, Yasuhiro and Miyazawa Kiichi, *Tairon – Kaiken/Goken* (Debate on the Constitution – Revise or Uphold?), Tokyo: Asahi Shinbunsha, 1997.

Nef, Jorge, *Human Security and Mutual Vulnerability: The Global Economy of Development and Underdevelopment*, 2nd ed., Ottawa: International Research Development Centre Press, 1999.

Nkrumah, Kwame, *Neo-Colonialism: The Last Stage of Imperialism*, New York: International Publishers, 1965.

Nye, Joseph S., 'Limits to American Power,' *Political Science Quarterly*, 117 (4), 2002/03, pp. 545–559.

Nye, Joseph S., 'The American National Interest and Global Public Goods', *International Affairs*, 78 (2), 2002, pp. 233–244.

Nye, Joseph S., *The Paradox of American Power*, New York: Oxford Uni Press, 2002.

Nye, Joseph S., 'Coping with Japan', *Foreign Policy*, 89, Winter 1992–3, pp. 96–115.

Nye, Joseph S., *Bound to Lead: The Changing Nature of American Power*, New York: Basic Books, 1990.

O'Neill, John Terrence and Nicholas Rees, *United Nations Peacekeeping in the Post-Cold War Era*, New York: Routledge, 2005.
Oakeshott, Michael, *Rationalism in Politics and Other Essays*, Indianapolis: Liberty Press, 1991.
Ohta, Masahide, *Minikui Nihonjin: Nihon no Okinawa Ishiki* (Ugly Japanese: The Japanese View of Okinawa), Tokyo: Iwanami Shoten, new edition, 2005.
Okole, Henry and David Kavanamur, 'Political Corruption in Papua New Guinea: Some Causes and Policy Lessons', *South Pacific Journal of Philosophy and Culture*, 7, 2003, pp. 7–36.
Onuma, Yasuaki (ed.), *Toa no Koso* (Vision of East Asia), Tokyo: Chikuma Shobo, 2000.
Ophuls, William and A. Stephen Boyan, *Ecology and the Politics of Scarcity Revisited: The Unravelling of the American Dream*, New York: Freeman, 1992.
Osius, Ted, *The U.S.-Japan Security Alliance: Why it Matters and How to Strengthen it*, Westport CT & London: Praeger, 2002.
Ozawa, Ichiro, *Nihon Kaizo Keikaku* (a Blueprint for Reforming Japan), Tokyo: Kodansha, 1993.
Paal, Douglas, *Nesting the Alliances in the Emerging Context of Asia-Pacific Multilateral Processes: A U.S. Perspective*, Washington: Asia/Pacific Research Center, July 1999.
Paris, Roland, 'Human Security: Paradigm Shift or Hot Air?', *International Security*, 26 (2), 2001, pp. 87–102.
Pasha, Mustapha Kamal, 'Fractured Worlds: Islam, Identity, and International Relations,' *Global Society: Journal of Interdisciplinary Studies*, 17 (2), 2003, pp. 111–120.
Pasha, Mustapha Kamal, 'Globalization, Islam, and Resistance', in Barry K. Gills (ed.), *Globalization and the Politics of Resistance*, Houndmills, Basingstoke, Hampshire: Macmillan Press, 2000, pp. 241–254.
Patience, Allan, 'The ECP and Australia's Middle Power Ambitions', *State, Society and Governance in Melanesia Project*, Discussion Paper No. 4, Canberra: Research School of Pacific and Asian Studies, Australian National University, 2005.
Pauling, Linus (ed.) *World Encyclopedia of Peace*, Vol. 1, New York: Pergamon Press, 1986.
Peffer, Nathaniel, 'Regional Security in Southeast Asia', *International Organization*, 8 (3), 1954, pp. 311–315.
Pekkanen, Robert and Elis Krauss, 'Japan's "Coalition of the Willing" on Security Policies', *Orbis*, 49 (3), Summer 2005, pp. 429–444.
Pirages, Dennis Clark (ed.), *The Sustainable Society: Implications for Limited Growth*, New York: Praeger, 1977.
Pitts, Maxine, *Crime, Corruption and Capacity in Papua New Guinea*, Canberra: Asia Pacific Press, 2002.
Pogge, Thomas W., *World Poverty and Human Rights: Cosmopolitan Responsibilities and Reforms*, Cambridge: Polity Press, 2002.
Pogge, Thomas W., 'Rawls on International Justice', *Philosophical Quarterly*, 51, Part 203, 2001, pp. 246–253.
Polanyi, Karl, *The Great Transformation*, New York: Farrar and Rinehart, 1944.
Pratt, Cranford (ed.), *Middle Power Internationalism: The North-South Dimension*, Kingston and Montreal: McGill-Queen's University Press, 1990.
Project for a New American Century (PNAC), *Rebuilding America's Defenses: Strategy, Forces and Resources for a New Century. A Report of the Project for the New American Century*, September 2000.

Rajagopal, Balakrishnan, *International Law from Below: Development, Social Movements and Third World Resistance*, Cambridge: Cambridge University Press, 2003.
Renouf, Alan, *The Frightened Country*, Melbourne: Macmillan, 1979.
Reus-Smit, Christian, *American Power and World Order*, Cambridge, UK: Polity, 2004.
Rivett, Kenneth (ed.), *Australia and the Non-White Migrant*, Melbourne: Melbourne University Press, 1975.
Roberts, Susan, Anna Secor, and Matthew Sparke, 'Neoliberal Geopolitics', *Antipode: A Radical Journal of Geography*, 35 (5), November 2003, pp. 886–897.
Roche, Douglas, *Deadly Deadlock: A Political Analysis of the Seventh Review Conference of the Non-Proliferation Treaty, New York, May 2–27, 2005*, San Francisco: Middle Powers Initiative, June 2005.
Romberg, Alan D. and Michael McDevitt (eds), *China and Missile Defense: Managing U.S.-PRC Strategic Relations*, Washington, Henry L. Stimson Center, 2003.
Rosecrance, Richard, *Australian Diplomacy and Japan*, Melbourne: Melbourne University Press, 1962.
Rosenau, James N. and Ernst-Otto Czempiel (eds), *Governance without Government: Order and Change in World Politics*, Cambridge, UK: Cambridge University Press, 1992.
Ross Gelbspan, *Boiling Point: How Politicians, Big Oil and Coal, Journalists, and Activists are Fuelling the Climate Crisis – and What We Can Do to Avert Disaster*, New York: Basic Books, 2004.
Rourke, John T., *International Politics on the World Stage*, Guilford CT: Dushkin/ McGraw-Hill, 1997.
Rowan, Joshua P., 'The U.S.-Japan Security Alliance, ASEAN, and the South China Sea Dispute', *Asian Survey*, 45 (3), 2005, pp. 414–436.
Rozman, Gilbert, *Northeast Asia's Stunted Regionalism: Bilateral Distrust in the Shadow of Globalization*, Cambridge: Cambridge University Press, 2004.
Rumley, Dennis, 'The Geopolitics of Asia-Pacific Regionalism in the 21st Century', *The Otemon Journal of Australian Studies*, 31, 2005, pp. 5–27.
Sachs, Jeffrey, *The End of Poverty: How We Can Make it Happen in Our Lifetime*, London: Penguin, 2005.
Sakamoto Yoshikazu Shu (Selected Works), Tokyo: Iwanami Shoten, 2004.
Sassen, Saskia, *Losing Control? Sovereignty in an Age of Globalization*, New York: Columbia University Press, 1996.
Sassoon, Anne Showstack (ed.), *Approaches to Gramsci*, London: Writers and Readers, 1982.
Schaller, Michael, *The American Occupation of Japan: The Origins of the Cold War in Asia*, New York: Oxford University Press, 1985.
Schmidheiny, Stephan, *Changing Course: A Global Business Perspective on Development and the Environment*, Cambridge, MA: The MIT Press, 1992.
Schmitt, Carl, *The Concept of the Political*, trans. George Schwab, New Brunswick, NJ: Rutgers University Press, 1976.
Scholte, Jan Aart, *Globalization: A Critical Introduction*, New York: St. Martin's Press, 2000.
Sen, Amartya, *Development as Freedom*, New York: Anchor Books, 2000.
Smith, Steve, 'The End of the Unipolar Moment? September 11 and the Future of the World Order', *International Relations*, 16 (2), 2002, pp. 171–183.
Smith, Steve, 'The United States and the Discipline of International Relations: "Hegemonic Country, Hegemonic Discipline"', in Mustapha Kamal Pasha and

Craig N. Murphy (eds), *International Relations and the New Inequality*, Oxford: Blackwell, 2002, pp. 67–85.
Snyder, Glenn H., *Alliance Politics*, Ithaca: Cornell University Press, 1997.
Sriram, Chandra Lekha and Karin Wermester (eds), *From Promise to Practice: Strengthening UN Capabilities for the Prevention of Violent Conflict*, Boulder, CO: Lynne Rienner Publishers, 2003.
Stuart, Douglas T. and William T. Tow, *A US Strategy for the Asia-Pacific*, Adelphi Paper 299, London: IISS, 1995.
Sudo, Sueo, *Evolution of ASEAN-Japan Relations*, Singapore, Institute of Southeast Asian Studies Publications, 2005.
Suganami, Hidemi, *The Domestic Analogy and World Order Proposals*, Cambridge, UK: Cambridge University Press, 1989.
Sung-Joo, Han (ed.), *Coping with 9-11: Asian Perspectives on Global and Regional Order*, Tokyo & New York: Japan Center for International Exchange, 2003.
Sutter, Robert G., *The United States and East Asia: Dynamics and Implications*, Boulder, CO: Lynne Rienner, 2002.
Sylvester, Christine, *Feminist Theory in a Postmodern Era*, Cambridge, UK: Cambridge University Press, 1994.
Takahashi, Tetsuya, *Sengo Sekinin Ron* (On the Postwar Responsibility), Tokyo: Kodansha, 1999.
Takemura, Masayoshi, *Chiisakutemo Kirari to Hikaru Kuni (Japan as Shining State Even if it is Small)*, Tokyo: Kobunsha, 1993.
Tamaki, Taku, 'Taking the "Taken-for-Grantedness" Seriously: Problematizing Japan's Perception of Japan-South Korea Relations', *International Relations of the Asia-Pacific*, 4, 2004, pp. 147–169.
Tanter, Richard, 'With Eyes Wide Shut: Heisei Militarisation and the Bush Doctrine' in Mel Gurtov and Pete Van Ness (eds), *Confronting the Bush Doctrine: Critical Views from the Asia-Pacific*, London: Routledge Curzon, 2005, pp. 153–180.
Thomas, Caroline, *Global Governance, Development and Human Security: The Challenge of Poverty and Inequality*, London: Pluto Press, 2000.
Thomas, Caroline and Peter Wilkin, *Globalization, Human Security and the African Experience*, Boulder, CO: Lynne Rienner Press, 1999.
Tow, William T., 'Deputy Sheriff Or Independent Ally? Evolving Australian-American Ties In An Ambiguous World Order', *Pacific Review*, 17 (2), 2004, pp. 271–290.
United Nations Development Program, *Human Development Report 2005*, New York: UNDP, 2005.
United Nations Doc. A/59/2005, *In Larger Freedom: Towards Development, Security And Human Rights For All*, 21 March 2005.
United Nations Doc. A/59/565, *A More Secure World: Our Shared Responsibility: The Report Of The High-Level Panel On Threats*, 2 December 2004.
United Nations Secretary General, Millennium Report, *'We the Peoples': The Role of the United Nations in the 21st Century*, New York: United Nations, 2000.
United States Department of Defense, *The United States Security Strategy for the East Asia-Pacific Region 1998*, Washington, DC: USGPO, 1998.
Van Ness, Peter, 'Hegemony, not Anarchy: Why China and Japan are not Balancing US Unipolar Power', *International Relations of the Asia-Pacific*, 2 (1), 2002, pp. 131–150.
Vitalis, Robert, 'Black Gold, White Crude: An Essay on American Exceptionalism, Hierarchy and Hegemony in the Gulf,' *Diplomatic History*, 26, 2002, pp. 185–213.
Wainwright, Elsina, 'Responding to State Failure – the Case of the Solomon Islands', *Australian Journal of International Affairs*, 57 (3), 2003, pp. 485–498.

Walker, David, *Anxious Nation: Australia and the Rise of Asia, 1850-1939*, Brisbane: University of Queensland Press, 1999.

Walker, R.B.J., 'After the Future: Enclosures, Connections, Politics,' in Richard Falk, Lester Edwin J. Ruiz, and R.B.J. Walker (eds), *Reframing the International: Law, Culture, Politics*, New York and London: Routledge, 2002, pp. 3–25.

Walker, R.B.J., 'International/Inequality,' in Mustapha Kamal Pasha and Craig N. Murphy (eds), *International Relations and the New Inequality*, Oxford: Blackwell Publishers, 2002, pp. 7–24.

Wallerstein, Immanuel, 'U.S. Weakness and the Struggle for Hegemony,' *Monthly Review*, 55 (3), 2003, pp. 23–50.

Wallerstein, Immanuel, *Alternatives: The US Confronts the World*, Boulder, CO: Paradigm, 2004.

Wallerstein, Immanuel, *The Decline of American Power: The U.S. in a Chaotic World*, New York: New Press, 2003.

Wander, Philip, 'The Rhetoric of American Foreign Policy', *The Quarterly Journal of Speech*, 70, November 1984, pp. 339–361.

Ward, Robert E. and Sakamoto Yoshikazu (eds), *Democratizing Japan: The Allied Occupation*, Honolulu: University of Hawaii Press, 1987 [Japanese edition, *Nihon Senryo no Kenkyu*, Tokyo: University of Tokyo Press, 1987].

Watt, Alan, *The Evolution of Australian Foreign Policy: 1938-1965*, Cambridge: Cambridge University Press, 1967.

Webb, Janeen and Andrew Enstice, *Aliens and Savages: Fiction, Politics and Prejudice in Australia*, Sydney: Harper Collins Publishers, 1998.

Windybank, Susan and Mike Manning, 'Papua New Guinea on the Brink', *Issue Analysis*, 30, 12 March 2003.

Wolfson, A., 'Conservatives and Neo-Conservatives', *The Public Interest*, Winter 2004, 32–48.

Xiang, Lanxin, 'Washington's Misguided China Policy', *Survival*, 43 (3), 2001, 7–23.

Yamaguchi, Jiro, *Sengo Seiji no Hokai (Collapse of Postwar Politics)*, Tokyo: Iwanami Shoten, 2004.

Yamaguchi, Jiro, 'Tou Kaikaku no Seijigaku (Politics of Party Reform)' in Yamaguchi and Ishikawa (ed.), *Nihon Shakaito* (Japanese Socialist Party), Tokyo: Nihon Keizai Hyoron Sha, 2003, pp. 130–139.

Yamaguchi, Jiro, 'The Gulf War and the Transformation of Japanese Constitutional Politics', *The Journal of Japanese Studies*, 18 (1), Winter 1992, pp. 155–172.

Yamamoto, Mari, *Grassroots Pacifism in Post-War Japan: The Rebirth of a Nation*, London: Routledge Curzon, 2004.

Yoichi, Funabashi, *Alliance Adrift*, New York: Council on Foreign Relations Press, 1999.

Yoichi, Funabashi, *Domei Hyoryu (Drift of Alliance)*, Tokyo: Iwanami, 1998.

Yoshihide, Soeya, 'Japan as a Regional Actor', in Japan Center for International Exchange, *ASEAN-Japan Cooperation: A Foundation for East Asian Community*, Tokyo & New York: Japan Center for International Exchange, 2003.

Index

Aborigines and Torres Strait Islanders 158
Aceh 207, 211
advanced industrial states 168
Afghanistan 28, 30, 31, 32, 46, 48, 80, 82, 84, 98, 146, 153, 200, 202, 205, 214
Africa 6, 63, 68, 71, 210
   North 23
   South 23, 80, 138, 148
Agamben, Giorgio 39
Agence France Presse 83
Agnew, John 39
AIDS see HIV/AIDS
Alliances 11, 12, 43–56, 131–2, 138, 139, 193–218
   definition 45
   system 5, 46, 49, 50, 53
Amnesty International Report 71
An Agenda for Peace 210
Anderson, Perry 18
Angola 97
Annan, Kofi 168, 203, 204
Anthony, Ian 142
anti-Communism 108
anti-nuclearism 112
anti-Semitism 30
APEC Civil Society Advisory Council 209
Applegarth, Claire 142
Arai, Shinichi 119
architecture
   global 10
   regional 10, 18
Argentina 148
Armitage, John 26
Armitage, Richard 84, 101, 154
arms control 11, 210
Article 9 (Japanese Constitution) *xiv*, 12, 13, 75, 76, 79, 83, 84, 93, 94, 95, 96, 97, 99, 101, 102, 109

Asahi Shimbun 91, 104, 118, 119
   opinion polls 110, 111, 118
asceticism 37
ASEAN Regional Forum (ARF) 10, 17, 20, 55, 205, 209, 210, 211
ASEAN+3 10, 17, 20, 205, 209, 210
Ashida, Hitoshi 88
Asia 59, 102, 112, 195
   anti-Communism 60, 61
   democratisation 115–7
Asia Cooperation Dialogue (ACD) 20
Asia Europe Meeting (ASEM) 20, 178, 205, 208, 209, 210, 211
Asian Human Rights Commission 20
Asian Treaty of Friendship and Cooperation see Treaty of Amity and Cooperation
Asia Monitor Resource Centre 20
Asia Pacific *xiii*, 3, 4, 5, 7, 8, 9, 10, 11, 12, 17, 18, 43–56, 133, 139, 193, 197, 202, 205, 206, 207, 212
   definition 3
   post-Cold War 43
   security 50
Asia-Pacific Economic Cooperation Group (APEC) 3, 4, 20, 205, 208, 209, 210, 217
   Business Advisory Council (ABAC) 20
Asia-Pacific Research Network 20
Asia-Pacific War (1931–45) 105, 111
Association of Southeast Asian Nations (ASEAN) 17, 20, 43, 50, 61, 70, 205, 206, 207, 209, 211, 215, 217, 218
atomic bomb 111
Australia *xiii*, 3, 4, 6, 8, 9, 11, 12, 13, 15, 17, 18, 44–9, 51–6, 60, 80, 145–57, 172, 173, 193–218
   Aborigines and Torres Strait Islanders 158
   ambivalence towards Asia 194

and UN disarmament efforts 123–43
as middle power 18
Breaker Morant 84
British influence 194
Cairns Group 149
culture 195, 199
demography 196, 199
Department of Defence 160
Department of Foreign Affairs and Trade (DFAT) 159, 133, 136, 142, 213, 215, 217
dependence on US 194
deputy sheriff 155
engagement with Asia 195
European influence 194
Federation 194
Gallipoli 84
geography 194, 195, 199, 212
history 194, 195, 199, 212
identity 146
Immigration Restriction Act 157
indigenous rights 195
insularity 195
Iraq War 48
Joint Strike fighter (F35) 48
M1 tanks 48
nuclear free zones 137
primary exports 194
psychology 198, 199
racism 194, 195
regional engagement 193
relations with Asia 195
relations with British Empire 146
relations with East Asia 48
relations with US 17, 44, 47, 198, 202, 203
security 54
settlement as invasion 81
Solomon Islands crisis 154
threat perception 49, 195
'war on terror' 48
White Australia 145
Australia-ASEAN Joint Declaration for Cooperation to Combat International Terrorism 217
Australian Defence Force (ADF) 48
Australian Defence White Paper 154
Australia/Japan Alliance with the US 131–2, 139, 141
Australia, New Zealand, US (ANZUS) Pact 48, 84, 146, 153

Australia Strategic Policy Institute (ASPI) 155, 160
Australia–US Alliance 47, 124, 131–2, 138, 139, 141, 145
Australia–US Free Trade Agreement (FTA) 48
Axline, W. Andrew 189
Azim Zabidi 158

Bain, William 174
Bajpaee, Chietigj 72
Bali bombings 153
Ball, Des 212
ballistic missile defence (BMD) 43, 47, 48, 51, 67
Balkans 96
Bamyeh, Mohammed A 39
Barker, Debi 189
Barnaby, Frank 217
Barnes, Samuel H. 174
Barnet, Richard J. 189
Bauer, Peter 159
Beck, Ulrich 40
Beeson, Mark 57, 213
Beijing 65, 66, 67, 70
Belgium 148
Bell, Philip 158
Bell, Roger 158
Berlin Wall 197
Bhuta, Nehal 40
bilateralism 7, 207
biological weapons 87
bird flu 216
Bird, Gillian 142
Bix, Herbert 196, 212
Blair, Tony 123
Blondel, Jean 181, 189
Bobbio, Noberto 183
Boer War 80, 84, 87
Bolton, John 133, 142
Borden, William S. 118
Bougainville 154, 211
Boulding, Kenneth 39, 189
bound to ally 51
Boutros-Ghali, Boutros 210
Bowen, James 91
Boyan, A. Stephen 190
Boznia-Herzegovina 171
Brazil 68, 138, 148, 169
British empire 194
Broad, Robin 189

Index

Broadhead, Lee-Anne 184, 190
Broinowski, Alison 158
Broinowski, Richard 213
Brooks, Stephen G. 19
Brown, Lester 185, 190
Brunei 65
Brzezinski, Zbigniew 19
Buddhism 64
Burnie, Shaun 217
Bush, George W. 7, 8, 44, 48, 65, 66, 67, 68, 84, 123, 124, 131, 132, 202
   Administration 47, 153, 165
   doctrine 54
   National Security Directive (17) 135
Business civilization 34
Business Council for Sustainable Development (BCSD) 186
Byers, Michael 174

Cainkar, Louise 40
Cairns Group 149
Callinicos, Alex 19
Calvinism 37
Cambodia 50, 60, 61, 81, 97, 112, 210, 211, 216
Campbell, Kurt M. 217
Canada 3, 9, 148, 149, 172
Canberra 55
Canberra Commission on the Elimination of Nuclear Weapons 139, 143, 204, 216
capitalism 29, 171, 181, 183
capital transnationalisation 27
Catholicism 62, 64
Cavanagh, John 188, 189
Central Asia 6, 23, 82
Central Intelligence Agency (CIA) 60, 62, 83, 201
Centre for Asia-Pacific Women in Politics 20
Chamberlain 79
Chase-Dunn, Christopher 19
chemical weapons 87
Chevron 68
Chiang Kai-shek 59, 65
Chiddell, Fleetwood 81, 90
Chile 3
Chimni, B. S. 171, 174
China *xiii*, 4, 6, 7, 15, 18, 43–4, 46–56, 59–72, 77, 102, 103, 116, 117, 123, 135, 136, 138, 148, 157, 194, 195, 200, 201, 202, 205, 207, 208, 209, 214, 215, 217
   Amnesty International Report 71
   bilateral trade with US 67
   Cultural Revolution 63
   economic growth 9, 11, 12, 49, 63, 67, 68, 201
   energy needs 68–9
   'Greater China' 206
   human rights 12, 63, 65
   Kuomintang 59
   militarisation 46, 50, 65
   military spending 65, 66
   military threat 63
   modernisation 50, 52
   National Offshore Oil Corporation (CNOOC) 68
   National People's Congress 65
   Paracel Islands 65, 66
   People's Republic of China (PRC) 43, 54
   post-Maoist 11
   regional power 50
   relations with Africa 68, 71
   relations with India 66, 70, 72
   relations with Iran 68–9
   relations with Japan 8, 77, 102, 138, 196, 201, 202, 206
   relations with Kazakhstan 68
   relations with Latin America 68
   relations with Russia 82, 90
   relations with US 47, 52, 59, 66, 70
   relations with Venezuela 68
   religion 64
   rise of 44, 52, 55
   Spratly Islands 65, 66
China National Offshore Oil Corporation 68
China–US rivalry 55
Chinese Communist Party 59, 61, 63
Chomsky, Noam 40
Christianity 8, 31
Citizen's Nuclear Information Center 217
citizenship 178–9, 183
civil conflict 207
civil society *xiv*, 9, 10, 17, 18, 36, 140, 188, 194, 206
   global 30
civilised (civiliser)-barbarian dichotomy 27, 31, 33
Clash of Civilisations 150, 171

class 36
Clinton, Bill 98, 124, 125, 130, 131
Club of Rome 17, 178
Coalition of the Willing 139
coercive arms control 139, 140, 141
Cohen, Warren I. 83, 90
Colas, Alejandro 159
Cold War 4, 6, 7, 9, 17, 31, 43, 46, 49, 54, 67, 79, 80, 87, 93, 94, 95, 96, 108, 115, 163, 172, 193, 196, 199, 205, 206, 207, 215
  alliances 12
  end of 165, 166, 168, 171
  origins 45
collective security 50, 85, 86, 87, 168
  bilateral relationships 87
  multilateral relationships 87
collective self-defence 7, 76, 78, 79, 85
Collingwood, Vivien 189
Colombo 158
colonialism 3, 45
Commission on Human Security 19
communications 27
Communism 12, 60, 63, 108
  in Australia 81
community 35
Comprehensive Action Plan on Indo-Chinese Refugees 210
comprehensive security 206, 207, 208, 210
Comprehensive Test Ban Treaty 123, 124, 125, 130, 131, 132, 134, 139, 141
Concert of Europe 166
confidence-building 133, 207, 209
conflict prevention 9, 166, 209
conflict resolution 209
Confucius 64
Congo 97
Connolly, William E. 39
constructivism 25
consumerism 35
consumption 35
containment 193
Convention on the Prohibition of the Use, Stockpiling, Production and Transfer of Anti-Personnel Mines and on their Destruction (Ottawa Convention) 138
Cook Islands 151
Cook, Malcolm 217
Cooper, Andrew F. 149, 159

Corbridge, Stuart 39
Cossa, Ralph A. 90
Costa Rica 140
Council on East Asian Community (CEAC) 20
Council for Security Cooperation in the Asia Pacific (CSCAP) 20, 209
Council on Security and Defence Capabilities 78
counter-terrorism 200
Cox, Dave 159
Cox, Michael 19, 39
Cox, Robert W. 18, 39
Crocombe, Ron 151, 159
cultural diversity 28
Cultural Revolution 63
culture 33, 36, 37, 38, 39, 40
Curtis, Gerald L. 146
Czempiel, Ernst-Otto 39

Dallmayr, Fred R. 159
Dalrymple, Rawdon 158
Dalrymple, William 30, 40
Daly, Herman 181, 182, 184, 189, 190
Dauvergne, Peter 159
decolonisation 24, 30
demilitarisation 108
democracy 33, 107, 108, 117, 188
  global 26
Democratic Party 75, 89, 93, 103
democratisation 33, 38, 108, 116, 117, 210
demography 194, 196
Deng Xiaoping 63
Denmark 148
Denoon, Donald 159
Department of Foreign Affairs and Trade (DFAT) 159, 213, 215, 217
dependency theory 25
Der Derian, James 39
détente 108, 111
deterrence 80, 134
developed countries 178
development 25, 40, 180, 208, 211
dialogue *xii*, 10
dialogue of civilisations 211, 212
Diaoyutai Islands 207
dignity 34
Dillon, Michael 39
Dinnen, Sinclair 159, 160

disarmament 11, 141
　UN Department of 141
disarmament education 139
domino theory 80, 81
double standard 107–12, 113, 114
Dower, John W. 94, 104, 119, 196, 212
Downer, Alexander 139, 143, 213, 216, 217, 218
Du Boff, Richard B. 19
Dulles, Foster 87
Duncan, Macgregor 90
Dupont, Alan 56, 157, 160, 215

East Asia 3, 4, 7, 11, 51, 63, 68, 97, 103, 112, 195, 196, 201, 202, 203, 205, 206, 207, 209, 215, 217
　arms race 15
　economies 7
　relations with Europe 210
　security 112
East Asia Analytical Unit 158
East Asian Community 214
East Asian Region 103
East Timor 4, 97, 165, 171, 198, 207, 208, 210, 211, 216
East-West rivalry 27, 163, 166
ecological problems 87
economic development 193
economic interdependence 206
economic sanctions 200
economics and sustainability 182
Egypt 138
Eisaku, Sato 110
El Serafy, Salah 190
Emperor Hirohito 196
empire 23–41
end of history 171
energy security 208
England
　and corporations 178
Enhanced Cooperation Program (ECP) 154, 155
Enstice, Andrew 81, 90
environment 9, 208, 209, 211
　obligations of industrialized countries 180
environmental degradation 178–81, 183
epistemic communities 209
Europe 30, 63, 80, 197, 199, 202, 205, 210
European Community (EC) 149

European Union (EU) 4, 172, 205, 209, 210
　embargo 51
Evans, Gareth 146, 173, 212
exceptionalism 39
exchange 35
exclusion 24, 27
failed state 171
Falk, Richard 40, 153, 160
Falun Gong 64
fascism 182
Feldman, Ofer 189
Feldman, Noah 41
Fiji 151, 211
Fissile Material Cut-off Treaty (FMCT) 124, 130, 132, 139
Focus on the Global South 20
Foramu, Kempo Saisei 104
foreign direct investment (FDI)
　localisation and 186–7
foreign policy 184
Fourth UN Special Session on Disarmament 140
France 60, 110, 112, 123, 148
　and corporations 178
　nuclear tests 123
Fravel, M. Taylor 57
Frazer, Ian 159
free market 164
free trade 177
Friedman, Jonathan 19
Friedman, Thomas L. 40, 41
Fukai, Shigeko N. 189
Fukase, Tadakazu 119
fundamentalism 35, 36

G7 Summit 188
G8 Summit 149, 188
Garnaut, Ross 158
Gelbspan, Ross 189
gender 36
gender equality 171
geography 194
George, Jim 39
German, Randall D. 18
Germany 105, 112, 116, 148, 169, 196, 199, 201
　and corporations 178
Gill, Stephen 40
Gills, Barry K. 40
global civil society 30, 179–80

global community 28
global crisis 11, 15
global democracy 26
global environment 17
global inequality 177, 180
global north 210
global parliament 183
Global Partnership for the Prevention of Armed Conflict (GPPAC) 20
global political economy 29
global processes 194
global public goods (GPG) 176–7
  and criteria 177
'global risk' society 31, 38
Global South 210
'global state of emergency' 12, 23, 24, 26, 27, 28, 29, 32–8
global sustainability 31
global totalitarianism 39
globalisation 5, 10, 16, 24, 26, 27, 28, 29, 30, 39, 40, 171, 177, 203
  and democracy 183
  hyper- 37
  neo-liberal 29, 38
  predatory 153
globalism 203, 205, 210
Glosserman, Brad 90
Golan Heights 97
Goldblat, David 39
Goldblat, Jozef 142
Goldsworthy, David 158
Goodland, Robert 190
Gordon, Philip H. 216
Gorton, John 195
governance 15, 40, 149, 151, 208, 210
  global 10, 171, 180
Gramsci, Antonio 5, 18
Grant, Bruce 146, 158, 212, 213
grass-roots democracy 182
Gross Domestic Product (GDP) 181, 185
Group of 77 (G77) 167
Grunberg, Isabelle 188
Gulf War (first) 80, 84, 97, 112, 146
Gyngell, Allan 153, 160, 217

Habermas, Jürgen 183
Haïti 152
Hamson, Fen Osler 40
Hanson, Pauline 213
Hansonism 198
Han Sung-Joo 214

Haraguchi, Koichi 216, 217
Hardt, Michael 39
Harries, Owen 57
Haruki, Wada 118, 212, 214, 218
Hashimoto, Ryutaro 13, 101
Hawke, Robert J. 153, 195
Hayato, Ikeda 94, 95, 110
health issues 87
hegemonic stability theory 177
hegemony *xiv*, 4–6, 7, 10, 11, 12, 23, 24, 25, 35
  see also US
Held, David 39, 183, 190
Helms, Jesse 176
Henderson, Gerard 153, 160
Henry L. Stimson Center 214
Hettne, Björn 18
Hidenao, Nakagawa 101
hierarchical international order 170
hierarchy 24, 27, 28
Higgott, Richard 159
High-Level Panel on Threats, Challenges and Change 168, 169
Hiroshima atom bomb survivors 111
HIV/AIDS 9, 151, 216
Ho Chi Minh 60, 81
Holbraad, Carsten 148, 158
holism 34
Hollander, Jack M. 189
Horne, Donald 146
Hosokawa, Morihiro 13, 101
host nation support 47
Howard, John 44, 47, 48, 133, 146, 153, 198, 213, 216
Hueting, Roefie 185, 190
Hughes, Christopher W. 54, 56, 213, 214, 215
human rights 7, 9, 79, 150, 171, 204, 208, 209, 211
Human Rights Watch 160
human security 5, 8–11, 16, 18, 19, 23–41, 171, 207
humane internationalism 150
humanitarian aid 9
humanitarian intervention 96, 169, 171
Huntington, Samuel 27, 40
Hurrell, Andrew 159

Ichiro, Hatoyama 109
Ichiro, Ozawa 99, 104

identity 5, 33, 39
  cultural 178
  religious 178
ideology 34, 35, 108
  of economic growth 108
Ikenberry, G. John 19
Immigration Restriction Act 157
imperialism 5, 39, 170, 171
inclusion 24, 27
Independent International Commission on Kosovo 164
India 66, 67, 70, 71, 72, 111, 123, 134, 148, 169
  relations with China 66, 71, 72
India-Pacific Conference 206
Indian Ocean 98, 200
indigenous beliefs 187
Indo-China 61
Indonesia 4, 15, 60, 61, 65, 148, 157, 208
  Communist Party (PKI) 61, 62
  Islam 62
inequality 24, 28
infectious diseases 50, 53
insecurity
  global 10
  regional 10
Institute for International and Strategic Studies (ASEAN–ISIS) 20
Institute of Southeast Asian Studies (ISEAS) 217
interconnectedness 27
interdependence 29, 31, 36
intergovernmental organisations 10
inter-imperialist rivalry 29
internally displaced persons (IDP) 164, 171
International Atomic Energy Agency (IAEA) 135, 139
International Commission on Intervention and State Sovereignty (ICISS) 149, 159
international community 175
international cooperation 78, 79, 85
International Criminal Court 204
  Rome Treaty 204
international criminal law 211
international institutions 171
International Monetary Fund (IMF) 71, 171, 210, 215
International Movement for a Just World 20

International Peace Cooperation Law 97
international public goods (IPG) 176–7
international society of states 23, 24, 28
investment 186, 187
Iran 68–9, 135, 148
Iraq 6, 14, 28, 30, 31, 32, 46, 69, 80, 84, 86, 96, 98, 99, 102, 153, 163, 164, 198, 200, 202, 205
Iraq War 6, 48, 112, 133, 135, 139, 153, 169, 173
  poll on 19
Ireland 138
Ishikawa, Masumi 104
Islam 8, 30, 31, 32, 40, 64, 198
  democracy 41
  diaspora 23
  political movements 37
Islamic cultural zones (ICZ) 12, 23, 31, 32–8
Islamic World 6
Israel 123, 134
Italy 147, 148

Jackson, Robert 39
Jacques, Michael 157
Japan *xiii*, 3, 4, 6, 7, 8, 9, 11, 12, 15, 17, 18, 43–9, 51–6, 60, 67, 68, 69, 70, 75–91, 93–104, 123, 137, 145–51, 156–7, 163, 166, 169, 170, 173, 183, 184, 188, 193–218
  in Afghanistan 84
  aggression in World War II 197
  alliance with US 13, 84, 124, 131–2, 139, 141, 172, 199
  Angola 97
  as middle power 18
  Cambodia 97
  collective self-defence 76, 78, 79, 89
  comfort women 116
  Communist Party 88
  Congo 97
  conservativism 94
  Constitution *xiv*, 11, 12, 13, 75, 77, 83, 84, 87, 88, 89, 93, 94, 95, 96, 97, 99, 100, 101, 102, 103, 105–19
  and corporations 178
  culture 194
  defence rationale 79
  Diet *xiv*, 75, 78, 88, 89, 95, 97, 99, 104, 112
  disarmament 87

disarmament education 123
East Timor 97
  economic growth 109
economy 200
Emperor 93, 105, 106, 116, 196
exclusively defensive defence 95
expansionism 81
geography 212
Golan Heights 97
Gulf War 97
history 115, 194, 196, 197, 212
history textbook revision 102
humanitarian intervention 76
human rights 79
industrialisation 194
intelligence sharing with US 47
international cooperation 78, 79
International Peace Cooperation Law 97
Liberal Democratic Party (LDP) 75, 88, 89, 93, 95, 97, 98, 99, 100, 104, 114, 119, 197, 199
LDP draft of proposed changes to Constitution 75, 76, 78, 85, 87
militarism 93, 106, 116, 196, 197
military bases 13
military budgets 83, 110, 201
military strength 83
Ministry of Foreign Affairs 101, 213, 214
Mozambique 97
national defence 76
nationalism 13, 199
National Protection Law (2004) 114
non-nuclear principles 111
normal country 115
nuclear free zones 137
pacifism 13, 78, 87, 94,
positive pacifism 79
postwar 108
peace clause 11, 75, 87
peace constitution 82, 84, 86, 93, 98, 196
peacekeeping missions 76, 145, 200
Peace Treaty 115
plutonium stockpiles 204
post-war 14, 117, 145
pre-emptive strikes 77, 78, 83
Prime Minister's Council on Security and Defence Capabilities 78, 83
psychology 199

rearmament 109
relations with Australia 138
relations with China 47, 77, 102, 196, 201, 202, 206
relations with Iraq 84, 85, 86, 99, 102
relations with Korea 102, 196
relations with North Korea 13, 47, 77, 98, 100, 200, 201, 206
relations with South Korea 13, 197, 206
relations with US 13, 44, 46, 60, 68, 77, 78, 83, 84, 94, 95, 96, 97, 99, 100, 101, 102, 103, 111, 196, 201, 202, 203
reparations 115
role post World War II 103
security dilemma 13, 82, 83
security policy 44, 46, 54, 93, 98
Security Treaty with US (1960) 95, 96, 97, 99, 108, 110, 111, 112, 113, 114, 145
Self-Defense Forces (SDF) 13, 46, 77, 85, 86, 88, 89, 95, 97, 98, 99, 102, 109, 110, 112, 113, 118, 199
  Army 76, 88
  Maritime 20
self-reliant defence 77
Social Democratic Party (SDP) 100
Socialist Party 95, 97, 98, 99, 100
traditionalists 94
and UN disarmament efforts 123–43
US military bases 108
US Occupation Policy 107, 108, 118
war crimes 102,
war crimes trials 196
World War II 79, 196
Japan Times 89
Japan Defense Agency 56
Japanese Coast Guard 201
Jiang 71
Jihad 41
Johnson, Chalmers 19, 63, 71, 199, 213
Joint Australia-Japan Workshop 20
Josephson, Paul R. 189
Judaism 30

Kagan, Robert 19, 71
Kahin, Audrey R. 71
Kahin, George M. 71
Kahler, Miles 189
Kaldor, Mary 159

Kashmir 123, 207
Kassiola, Joel Jay 190
Kato, Tetsuro 104
Kaul, Inge 188
Kavanamur, David 159, 160
Kawashima, Yutaka 213, 216
Kazakhstan 68
Keating, Paul 153, 158, 195, 204, 212
Kenny, Michael 18
Kevin, Tony 213
Kiichi, Miyazawa 100, 119
Kile, Shannon 142
Kindleberger, Charles 188
Kiribati 151
Kishi, Nobusuke 95
Kishimoto, Koichi 145
Kissinger, Henry 176, 188
Kitazume, Takashi 90
Kobayashi, Naoki 119
Koichi, Kato 100
Koichi, Kishimoto 157
Koizumi, Junichiro 13, 44, 46, 99, 100, 102, 103, 116, 200, 201, 213, 214, 215, 216
Komeito 75, 88
Korea 4, 7, 49, 61, 80, 102, 107, 116, 117, 123, 137–38, 194, 202, 207, 208
  relations with Japan 13, 116
Korean War 59, 61, 95, 109, 146
Koseki, Shoichi 118
Kosovo 16, 164, 171
  bombing of 169
Krasner, Steven 174
Krauss, Elis 56
Krauthammer, Charles 19
Krepon, Michael 214
Krisch, Nico 173, 174
Kristol, William 71
Kunihiro, Masao 119
Kurdish populations 173
Kuriles 207
Kuwait 84, 96, 163, 164

labour 183, 186, 187
labour laws 208-9
labour migration 208
Lake, David 189
Lanxin Xiang 57
Laos 50, 61, 80
Larmour, Peter 159
Latin America 6, 62, 68, 210

Law of the Sea 210
Leacher, Michael 158
League of Nations 87, 166
Leaver, Richard 159
Leblanc Claude 212
Lee Kwan Yew 43
legitimacy 36, 170, 179–80, 186, 189
Liberal Democratic Party (LDP) 75, 76, 78, 85, 86, 88, 89, 93, 95, 97, 98, 99, 100, 104, 114, 119, 197, 199
less developed countries (LDCs) 178
liberalism 5, 105
  Kantian 27
Libya 135
limits to growth 17, 184
'Limits to Growth' report 178
  updated editions ('Beyond the Limits') 178
localisation principle 187
Lorimer, James 174
Lowy Institute 216, 218
Ludlow, Peter 188
Lyon, Rod 57

MacArthur, Douglas 59, 77
Macdonald, Barrie 159
Mackie, Jaimie 158
MacKinnon, Rebecca 77, 89
McAinsh, Garrett L. 79, 89
McCormack, Gavan 212, 213, 214, 215, 218
McDevitt, Michael 214
McGrew, Anthony 39
McMahon, John 195
Maeda, Tetsuo 118
Mainichi Shinbun 104
Makiko, Tanaka 213
Malaysia 11, 15, 60, 61, 62, 65, 133, 140, 157
Mallaby, S. 19
Malthus, Thomas R. 181
Mamdani, Mahmoud 32, 40
Mander, Jerry 188, 189
Manichean logic 27, 28, 30
Mann, Michael 40
Manning, Mike 159
Manosevitz, Jason U 215
Mao Tse Dung 64
Maritime SDF 200
market civilisation 40
market fetishism 35

Marquardt, Erich 215
Marr, David 158
Marshall Islands 151
Marxism 25, 105
Masaharu, Gotoda 100
Masashi, Nishihara 218
May, R. J. 159
Meadows, Donella 178
Meaney, Neville 157, 160
Medeiros, Evan 57
Melanesia 211
Menzies, Robert 158
Mexico 3, 137, 139, 148
Micronesia 151
Middle East 6, 69, 80, 123, 139, 202
middle powers 11, 15, 123, 124, 148, 150, 156, 163, 167, 172
  and nuclear weapons 167
migration 9, 27
militarism 32
Mill, John Stuart 189
Millenium Development Goals (MDGs) 203
Millenium Report 216
Millenium Summit 216, 217
Milner, Anthony 158
Mindanao 211
Ming Dynasty 66
Ministry of Foreign Affairs of Japan 101
Mitchell, Timothy 37, 40
Mizushima, Asaho 75, 88, 119
Mochizuki, Mike 215
modernity 33, 37
Mohamed Jawhar Bin Hassan 217
Mohamed Mossadegh 69
Mongolia 137
Morgenthau, Hans 175
Mori, Yoshiro 75
Morihiro, Hosokawa 196-7
Morrison, Roy 183, 190
Mount Hagen 154
Mozambique 97
multiculturalism 33, 41
multilateral institutions 27
  legitimacy 167
multilateralism 29, 30, 35, 166, 169, 171, 198, 206, 207
  and middle powers 172-3
multipolarity 15, 17, 202
Munich 80
Munro, Ross H. 71

Murata, Kiyoaki 88
Murayama, Tomiichi 99, 114, 197
Murphy, Craig N 39, 190
Muslim world *see* Islam
Mustanduno, Michael 56
Myanmar 152

Naoto, Kan 99
Nagasaki atom bomb survivors 111
Nakasone, Yasuhiro 119
narcotics trade 209, 211
Narushige, Michishita 214
nation state 3
National Defense Program Outline 47
national interest 175, 187
nationalism 37, 45
National People's Congress 65
natural gas 69
Nauru 151
Nef, Jorge 40
Negri, Anthony 39
neo-colonialism 15, 39
neo-liberal globalisation 29
neo-liberalism 23, 25, 32, 34, 35, 36, 37, 38, 40
Network of Asian Think Tanks (NEAT) 20
New Agenda Coalition 134, 138, 141
  and Australia 138
  and Japan 138
New American Century 39
New Cold War 72
new international economic order 168
new world order 16, 39, 153, 163-4
New York 178
New Zealand 3, 9, 60, 146, 151
niche diplomacy 15, 149
Nigeria 148
Niue 151
Nkrumah, Kwame 39
Nobel Peace Prize 111
Nobusuke, Kishi 108
Nolte, Georg 174
Non-Aligned Movement (NAM) 136
non-governmental organisations (NGOs) 9, 10, 137, 140, 171
  regional 20
non-interference 208
Nordic countries 167
North 29, 32
North America 206

North Asia
  pre-emptive strikes 83
North Atlantic Treaty Organisation
    (NATO) 7, 48, 164
  bombing of Kosovo 169
  military intervention 164
Northeast Asia *xiv*, 138, 139, 207, 213, 214, 215, 217
North Korea (Democratic People's Republic of Korea) 7, 8, 43, 54, 61, 77, 98, 99, 100, 116, 123, 134, 135, 141, 152, 200, 201, 212, 214
  nuclear ambitions 50, 82
North Korean Six Party talks 135, 137, 141
Northern Territories 207, 208
North-South divide 27
North-South relations 168, 170, 178-80, 186
  and labour migration 187
Norway 148
Nossal, Kim 159
nuclear disarmament 15
nuclear non-proliferation 210
Nuclear Non Proliferation Treaty (NPT)
  consensus voting 131
  Review Conference (2000) 124, 125, 130, 136, 139, 141
  Review Conference (2005) 123, 130-1, 136, 141-3, 204
  Review Conference (2010) 131
  violation of 135
nuclear proliferation 111, 204
nuclear safeguards 132
nuclear tests 123, 136
  verification 134
nuclear threat 7, 82
nuclear umbrella 111, 112
nuclear visits 111
nuclear weapons 80, 87, 110, 123-43, 204
  Canberra Commission 139, 143, 204, 216
  reductions 134, 140
  role in security policies 124, 135
Nuclear weapon-free zone (NWFZ) 123, 124, 136-8, 140
  Australia 137
  Central Asia 124, 132, 136, 137, 140
  Japan 137
  Middle East 124, 132, 140

Northeast Asia 140
nuclear weapon state (NWS) 123, 124, 125, 130, 131
Nye, Joseph S. 19, 40, 51, 57, 145, 157, 175-6, 188, 189

Oakeshott, Michael 145, 157
Oceania 3, 206
Ogata, Sadako 173
O'Hanlon, Michael 215
Ohta, Masahide 119
Okinawa 62, 106, 111
Okole, Henry 159
O'Neill, John Terence 163, 173
Ophuls, William 182, 190
Organisation for Economic Cooperation and Development (OECD) 184
organised crime 53
orientalism 34
Oshima, Kenzo 216, 217
Osius, Ted 215
Ottawa Convention 138
Oxford Research Group 217
Ozawa, Ichiro 119

Paal, Douglas 19
Pacific America 3
Pacific Asia 3, 206, 212
  definition 3
Pacific Economic Cooperation Council (PECC) 20
Pacific Islands 194
Pacific Islands Forum (PIF) 151, 153, 211
Pacific Ocean 6, 123
Pacific War 94
Pakistan 11, 60, 111, 123, 134
Palau 151
Papua 207, 208, 211
Papua New Guinea 3, 11, 15, 151-7, 211
  failing state 152
  governance 153
  independence 151
  relations with Australia 152
Paracel Islands 65, 66
Paramore, Kiri 213
Paris, Roland 40
Pax Americana 18
peace-building 171, 210
Peace depot 142
peace dividend 16

peacekeeping 9, 96, 112, 211,
Peffer, Nathaniel 3, 18
Pekkanen, Robert 56
Peru 3
Pew Research Centre 19
Philippines, the 15, 60, 61, 62, 65, 157, 211
   Clark Base 62
   Subic Base 62
piracy 209
Pirages, Dennis Clark 189
Pitts, Maxine 159
pluralism 33
Pogge, Thomas W. 180, 189
Poland 148
Polanyi, Karl 18, 40
political economy 25, 31
   global 29
political space 3
Pol Pot 210
Pons, Philippe 212
Port Moresby 154
Portugal 148
post-Cold War period 5, 11, 15, 16, 17, 171, 193, 194, 197, 199, 210, 216
postmodernism 25, 39
postwar 114, 119
Potts, Michael 160
Powell, Colin 84, 90
Pratt, Cranford 150, 159
precautionary principle 184
pre-emption 7, 23, 28, 30, 31, 32, 33
pre-emptive strikes 7, 77, 78, 83
prevention principle 184
primary commodities 194
proliferation (missile) 134, 138, 139, 141
Proliferation Security Initiative (PSI) 14, 133, 139, 200
Protestantism 37, 64
public goods 176

Quilty, Mary 158

race wars 81
radioactive fallout 123
Rajagopal, Balakrishnan 174
rationalism 27
Reagan, Ronald 6, 68
realism 31
   classical 27
Realpolitik 175

Rees, Nicholas 163, 173
refugees 87, 164, 171
regimes 166
regional architecture 207
Regional Assistance Mission to the Solomon Islands (RAMSI) 154, 156
Regional Centre for Dialogue and Cooperation 211
regional conflicts 123
regional economic communities 182
regional governance 193
regional stability 10, 12
regionalisation 206
regionalism 3, 10, 193-218
   cooperative 194
religion 34, 35, 37
Renouf, Alan 90
Reus-Smit, Christian 19
Ricardo, David 181
Rice, Condoleeza 16, 175
Rio de Janeiro 68, 178
'risk society' 40
Rivett, Kenneth 157
Roberts, Susan 36, 40
Roche, Douglas 141
Roh Moo-Hyun 117, 212
Romberg, Alan D. 214
Rosecrance, Richard 145, 157
Rosenau, James N. 39
Rourke, John T. 188
Rowan, Joshua P. 215
Rozman, Gilbert 213, 214, 215, 217
Ruiz, Lester Edwin J. 40
Rumley Dennis 18
Russia 3, 90, 123, 125, 136, 138, 197
   relations with China 82, 90
Russo-Japanese War 82
Rwanda 16, 164
Ryutaro, Hashimoto 97

Sachs, Jeffrey 159
sacred 33
Sadakazu, Tanigaki 103
Saddam Hussein 84, 173
Samoa 151
San Francisco Peace Treaty 109, 111
Sapporo 137
Sassen, Saskia 39
Saudi Arabia 69
Schaller, Michael 119

Schmidheiny, Stephan 186, 190
Schmitt, Carl 40
Scholte, Jan Aart 39
Seattle 188
second track diplomacy 209
Secor, Anna 36, 40
secularism 31, 33
securitisation 30
security *xiv*, 7, 8, 10, 25, 26, 31, 34, 38, 193
  assurances 131, 133, 135, 136, 140
  dilemma 54, 82, 83, 87
  global 11, 16, 184
  regional 12, 49
  spheres 49
Seiji, Maehara 101
Selden, Mark 214-5
Self-Defense Forces (SDF) 13, 46, 85, 86, 88, 95, 97, 98, 99, 109, 110, 112, 113, 118, 199
  Army 76, 88
  Maritime SDF 20
self-determination 114
  individual 105–7, 115
  of peoples 118, 170
Sen, Amartya 159
Senkaku Islands 207
September 11 (2001) 4, 7, 9, 11, 23, 24, 25, 26, 29–32, 39, 40, 43, 87, 150, 153, 164–5, 173
  post-September 11 (2001) 5, 6, 11, 15, 18, 25, 28, 36, 38
severe acute respiratory syndrome (SARS) 216
Shalom, Stephen R. 214
Shapiro, Michael J. 39
Shidehara, Kijuro 77
Shigeru, Yoshida 108
Shinzo, Abe 98
Shiratori, Toshio 77
Showstack Sassoon, Anne 18
Sihanouk, Norodom 60, 61
Singapore 53, 60, 61, 62
Singer, Hans 180, 189
Sino-Japanese War 197
Sino-Soviet threat 49
Smith, Adam 181
Smith, Steve 39
Snyder, Glenn H. 57
social capital 187
social inequity 16

Sokol Bednar, Charles 189
solar energy 182
Solomon Islands 151, 211
  crisis 154
  independence 154
Somalia 16, 164
South 35
South Africa 23, 80, 138, 148
South Asia 23, 139
South China Sea 65, 208, 215, 215
Southeast Asia 3, 10, 23, 46, 66, 71, 115, 198, 202, 207
Southeast Asia Treaty Organisation (SEATO) 60, 61, 62
  relations with China 61
South Korea 9, 10, 43, 53, 60, 61, 62, 68, 70, 115, 117, 201, 205, 212, 215
  nuclear ambitions 82
South Pacific 15, 123, 136, 145–57, 204
  failed states 15
  identity 151
South Pacific Nuclear Free Zone 1985 (SPNFZ) 136
sovereignty 9, 23–9, 30, 33, 37, 38, 39, 40, 168, 171, 172, 179, 183, 207, 208
Soviet Union 4, 60, 95, 96, 97, 193, 195, 197
Spain 148
Sparke, Matthew 36, 40
Special Air Service Regiment (SAS) 48
Spratly Islands 55, 65, 66, 207
Sriram, Chandra Lekha 166, 173
state of nature (Hobbesian) 28
state security 9
state sovereignty 5
state transnationalisation 27
steady state economy 181, 184, 186
Stegenga James A. 189
Stern, Marc A. 188
Stockholm International Peace Research Institute (SIPRI) 83
Stokes, Geoffrey 158
strategic triangle 4
Street, Tony 158
Stuart, Douglas T. 56
subsidiarity 182
Sudan 80
Sudo, Sueo 217, 218
Suez Canal 6
Suganami, Hidemi 173

Suharto 198
Sukarno, 'Bung' 60, 61
Sunohara, Tsuyoshi 217
superpower 71, 87
sustainability 175–89
   global 31
sustainable peace 17
Sutter, Robert G. 56
Sylvester, Christine 39
Syria 32, 135

Taiwan 4, 50, 51, 53, 54, 59, 62, 65, 66, 68, 123, 148, 201, 207, 208
Taiwan Straits 49, 51, 65
Takahashi, Kosuke 214, 215
Takahashi, Tetsuya 119
Takako, Doi 100
Takemura, Masayoshi 104
Takeo, Hiranuma 100
Takeshima islets 117
Tamaki, Taku 215
Tanaka, Makiko 200
Taniguchi, Tomohiko 214
Tanter, Richard 56
Taoism 64
Taylor, Charles 41
Tehran 68
terrorism 7, 8, 40, 54, 153, 165, 178, 208
Tetsuo, Maeda 119
Thailand 60, 61, 62
Thawley, Michael 48
Theatre Missile Defense 200
Third World 150, 167, 182, 195
   poverty 87
Third World Network 20
Thomas, Caroline 40
threat perception 80
thought suspension 107–112
Tiananmen 117, 201
Tibet 207
time–space compression 30
Timmer, Ashley 40
Tinbergen, Jan 185, 190
Tokyo 55, 106
Tokyo International Military Tribunal 115
Tonga 151
totalitarianism 26
Tow, William T. 56, 57
track three diplomacy 10
track two diplomacy 10, 20

trade 186
trade liberalisation 208
tradition 33
transnational crime 209
Treaty of Amity and Cooperation 146, 207, 217
tri-polarity 49
Truman, Harry 59
Tsunami disaster 210
Tuvalu 151
Tyson, Rhianna 142

underdeveloped countries 168
underdevelopment 25
unilateralism 6, 23, 25, 26, 30, 31, 35, 164–5, 169
unipolarity 39
United Kingdom 30, 60, 84, 110, 123, 136, 148, 173, 199, 201
United Nations (UN) 10, 11, 16, 17, 66, 86, 88, 111, 113, 118, 194, 198, 200, 203, 204, 207, 209, 211, 216, 217
   Angola 97
   authority 169
   budget 167, 172, 176
   Cambodia 97
   conflict prevention 166
   Congo 97
   Commission on Human Rights 169
   corruption 166
   Council on Human Rights 169
   decolonisation 167–8
   disarmament 123, 170
   division of membership 168, 169
   East Timor 97
   Fourth Special Session on Disarmament 140
   General Assembly 14, 168, 169, 172
   global strategy 47
   Golan Heights 97
   High-Level Panel on Threats, Challenges and Change 168, 169
   humanitarian intervention 96, 169, 171
   human security 5, 8–11, 16, 18, 19, 171, 207
   In Larger Freedom 203
   international community 86
   isolationism 43
   military intervention 164

Index

Millennium Declaration 133
Millennium Report 203
Mozambique 97
multilateralism 167
norm setting 164, 173
peace and security 163
peace-building 171, 210
Peace-Building Commission 169
peacekeeping 86, 97
　bill 112
peace operations 85, 112, 113, 114, 204
　post-Cold War 163
　reform 163, 168–72, 173
Secretariat 166, 172
Secretary-General 16, 203, 210, 216, 217
use of force 205
World Summit (2005) 16, 170, 213, 217
UN Conference on Trade and Development (UNCTAD) 168
United Nations Charter 118, 163, 165, 166, 168, 169, 173
UN Department of Disarmament Affairs 141
United Nations Development Program (UNDP) 9, 159, 177
　Human Development Report 203
United Nations Educational, Scientific and Cultural Organization (UNESCO) 173
United Nations General Assembly (UNGA) 123, 125, 131, 137, 139, 143
United Nations Security Council 6, 112, 123, 133, 135, 164, 169, 171, 204, 210
　and Cold War 166
　and Group of Four 169
　reform 169, 170, 172
UN Security Council Resolution 984 (1995) 135 *see also* security assurances
unilateralism 11, 29, 133, 207
universalism 33
United States (US) 3, 4, 5, 6, 7, 8, 16, 23–41, 43–56, 60, 61, 62, 63, 66, 71, 77, 80, 81, 93, 94, 95, 96, 97, 98, 100, 101, 108, 110, 111, 112, 118, 123, 166–7, 168, 172, 173, 193, 194, 196, 198, 199, 200, 201, 202, 203, 204, 205, 206, 209, 213, 214, 215, 216, 217
alliance system 12, 13, 44, 140, 141
allies 6
ballistic missile defence (BMD) 43, 47, 48, 51, 67
bases 60, 112
capitalism 62
Congress 124, 176
Constitution 81
containment 49, 52, 193
containment of the Soviet Union 193
conventional forces 132–3
corporations 63, 178
Democratic Party 94
Department of Defense 19, 56, 101
Department of State 56, 101
dependence on 194
failed state 171
foreign policy 59, 175–6
global strategy 50, 84
hegemony 5, 12, 46, 55
host nation support 47
House of Representatives 68
imperial decline 202
in Asia Pacific 11, 45
invasion of Iraq 169
Japan Alliance 46, 138, 145, 172
Japan/Australia Alliance 131–2, 141
Japan Commission on Arms Control, Disarmament, Proliferation and Verification 134
Japan Intelligence sharing 47
Japan Security Consultative Committee 44
Japan Security Treaty 95, 96, 97, 99, 145
leadership 51
legitimacy 6
military 11, 67, 103
missile defence programs (MD) 15, 125, 134, 139, 213, 214
National Security Strategy 70
neoconservatives (neocons) 50, 97, 166
new imperium 11
new world order 16, 153, 163–4
nuclear umbrella 111
regional image 43
regional policy 45
relations with Asia Pacific 45

relations with Australia 44, 47, 48, 85, 138
relations with China 47, 52, 55, 65, 68, 70
relations with India 71
relations with Indonesia 60
relations with Iraq 85, 86
relations with Japan 44, 46, 60, 68, 77, 78, 83, 84, 94, 95, 96, 97, 99, 100, 101, 102, 103, 118, 196, 201, 202, 203
relations with Middle East 69
relations with Philippines 60
relations with Saudi Arabia 69
relations with South Korea 44, 60, 68
relations with Taiwan 68
relations with Thailand 60
relations with UN 123–43, 166–7, 169
relations with Vietnam 59, 86
Republican Party 94, 124
Secretary of Defense Donald Rumsfeld 67, 214
Senate 68
Sixth Fleet 53
soft power 45
status of forces 47
two-war policy 44
unilateralism 11, 164–5, 167, 207
UNOCAL 68, 71
world order 83
Uzebekistan 82

Vaile, Mark 217
Valenty, Lina O. 189
Van Ness, Peter 56
Vanuatu 151
Venezuela 68
verification 139
Vietnam 50, 59, 60, 61, 65, 66, 80, 81, 86
Vietnam War 146
violence 23
Vitalis, Robert 39

Wainwright, Elsina 154, 159
Walker, David 146, 158
Walker, R. B. J. 40
Wall Street 200
Wallerstein, Immanuel 19, 40
Wallich H. 184
Wander, Philip 40

Wang, Jisi 215
Ward, Robert E. 119
'war on terror' *xiii*, 6, 8, 10, 11, 16, 26, 27, 28, 31, 36, 37, 46, 48, 165, 198, 202, 205
Washington 55, 60, 61, 64, 65, 67, 68, 69, 70
Watanabe, Osamu 196
Watt, Alan 158
weapons of mass destruction (WMDs) 8, 9, 133, 140, 173
Webb, Janeen 81, 90
welfare retrenchment 35
Wermester, Karin 173
Wesley, Michael 153, 160
Western civilisation 12, 37
Western consciousness 36
Western nuclear powers 135
Western Pacific 145, 148
Westphalian international system 179, 181
White Australia 145
Whitlam, Gough 195
Wilkin, Peter 40
Windybank, Susan 159
Wohlforth, William C. 19
Woods, Ngaire 159
Woolcott, Richard 213
World Bank 171, 210
world government 166
world order 23, 39, 83, 114
World Trade Organisation (WTO) 171, 210
World War I 80, 82, 83, 90
World War II 5, 9, 30, 67, 69, 79, 80, 83, 93, 196, 197, 200, 213
post World War II 24, 26, 105

Yamada 204
Yamaguchi, Jiro 104, 118
Yamamoto, Mari 119
Yasakuni war memorial shrine 102, 103, 215
Yasuo, Fukuda 103
yellow peril 81
Yoichi, Funabashi 56, 104
Yoshida, Yutaka 196
Yoshihide, Soeya 214
Yuan 68
Yugoslavia 164
Yunnan 66

Zheng Bijian 215
Zhibn Gu, George 215

Zifcak, Spencer 217